I0040651

Risk Management
Safety
and
Control of Loss

Willem Top

Protecting Your Organization
- An Introduction-

© 2014, Author: Willem N. Top
Self publishing

First edition; revision 0

Contact Information:
Email: topves@ziggo.nl

ISBN 9789082041132

TO SET THE TONE

Peter Drucker

The first duty of management is to survive and the guiding principle of
business economics is not the maximization of profit, it
is the avoidance of loss

Peter F. Drucker (1909 –2005) - management consultant, educator, and author

Vincent T. Lombardi

Winning is not a sometime thing; it's an all time thing. You don't win once
in a while, you don't do things right once in a while ...

You do them right all the time.

Winning is a habit.

Unfortunately, so is losing

Vincent Thomas Lombardi (1913 – 1970) was an American football coach

The essence of the management function is to control loss

To close the gap between "practice" and "theory"

Between "how it is (done)" and "how it should be (done)"

Mishaps, errors, accidents etc. occur in the gap
between "what is" and "what should be"

They drain away your profits

CONTENTS

Appendices

FOR WHOM THIS BOOK IS

This book is about safety, risk management and control of loss. This book is about management and organizational success. About reaching objectives and controlling unwanted events that may keep you from getting where you want to be. It is for you if:

- You are interested to start a career in (safety) management
- You are working as a consultant – internal or external - with the task to help your management or client to improve their organization and its results
- You want to communicate the importance of safety and risk management to your management to help them understand what safety really is
- You want to make your organization better
- You are interested for any other reason

Controlling problems, unwanted events and their consequences is the theme throughout this book. Controlling losses may be the only way for many people to contribute to the success of their organization and to make sure that they will still have a job tomorrow. Continuous improvement is THE way to survive and probably the ONLY way.

Peter Drucker

In case of keen competition and low profit margins, learning from accidents can contribute more to profits than an organization's best salesperson

---

Peter F. Drucker (1909 –2005) - management consultant, educator, and author

TIP. If you cannot get your management's interest for safety, tell them that you know how to increase business results. Tell them that safety is more than dealing with injury type accidents. Tell them that safety may help them to sleep better at night and may also protect them against liability claims and even criminal charges. How? By eliminating and reducing unwanted events, risks and losses and having a system to do this. Does your management know how much the company is losing due to things that happen but which should not? In the construction chain in The Netherlands the average failure costs have been estimated to be between 10 and 15 percent of total turnover – every year!

Louis A. Allen

Minimizing loss is as much improvement as maximization of profit

---

Louis A. Allen, management consultant and writer. Founder of Louis Allen Worldwide

Peter Drucker was not a safety person. Neither was Louis Allen.

ABOUT OF THIS BOOK / DISCLAIMER

The main purpose of this book is to put safety, risk management and loss control in the proper business perspective: controlling problems, unwanted events and losses that downgrade the efficiency of our organizations and companies.

One of the main reasons why I am writing this book is that I feel that these important business areas are undervalued. This is in particular true for "safety" which was often seen as being limited to injury type events only and I feel this is still the thinking of many people. "Risk management" used to be seen mainly as an insurance function but really should be incorporated into each job or function within the organization. "Loss control" is more generic and less colored by history. All three areas overlap extensively and basically have the same objectives: to control (future) loss or, rather, to control (unwanted) events preceding loss.

I hope that this book will contribute to a better understanding of how the three areas: safety, risk management and loss control can contribute to making our organizations and societies better and keep them better – all the time!

I am not writing this book for the "expert". I am writing it for people who want to make their career in safety and risk management, for the professional and for the layman in the hope that they will find something in it to better explain to others what safety and risk management really are. Having said that, this book may also help the expert to get a broad view of the areas of his/her expertise and I realize that expert and professional can very well be combined into one person. After all, they both deal with the same business areas, only at a different level.

Other than information that is also available from other sources, this book contains some ideas, models and tools that I developed during my career in risk management and safety that started in 1968. Where I refer to the work of others, I try to give credit to those who deserve it. If I refer to the work of others without giving credit or when possibly infringing on copyrights, I do so unintentionally.

English is not my native language. I am from The Netherlands also known as Holland and I am sure that you will find that my control over grammar is not always correct, for which I apologize. But as long as it is not "double Dutch" and I am not insulting anybody or using improper language, please consider it as added charm.

Do I write this text in a logical order of subjects? To some extent I hope, but I like to add things here and there. I also repeat things at several places where I find it useful also knowing that you do not have to go back to the page where the subject was mentioned before.

I like to think that I am writing this book as if I am sitting here talking with you. And, just as in a normal conversation, once in a while my mind may wander off a bit. Anyway, I am not writing a scientific book but hope that it will give you a better understanding as to what comes under the umbrella of risk management, safety and control of loss. I will be happy if my book contributes to the understanding that these areas of management are vital to the functioning of an organization. In fact you may come to the conclusion that these areas form the essence of the management function: to continually reach objectives with minimal efforts, unwanted events and loss.

NOTE: I titled this book "Risk Management, Safety and Control of Loss" without the intention to present them as different subjects. I know that these terms are frequently being used separately, safety dealing with injury, loss control looking at material damage and risk management concerning insurable business risks. I consider these three areas the same or so similar that they are practically the same. So when I mention "safety", I also mean risk management and loss control and environmental management. These areas all deal with risks, losses, accidents and unwanted events. They also (have to) deal with the consequences of those events - financial or otherwise - with finances being the common denominator. I may refer to risk management to also include safety and loss control or to loss control to also include risk management and safety.

This book contains a mix of what I learned from others and my 45 years of experience and then some ideas I developed which I have not been able to test much in practice due to circumstances. The content of this book is certainly not scientific or 100 % correct so do not expect that. Look at the big picture to see the scope of "safety" as well as the contribution that it can make to organizations and society. I hope this book will stimulate your own ideas and thinking.

Willem Top

The Netherlands, 2014

www.topves.nl

**The quality of (a) management (team)
is determined by:**

1. Knowing in advance what problems may occur in their organization or unit
2. Knowing the number and size of problems that may occur
3. Knowing what the causes of those problems could be
4. Knowing what to do to remedy the causes at the earliest stages
5. Knowing which actions to take to minimize the negative effects

(A) quality management (team) should only have known problems with limited consequences

I think the above came from Phil Crosby (1926 – 2001), businessman and author who contributed to management theory and quality management practices.

FOREWORD

In 1988 I wrote a small book "Risk/Loss Control Management" which, at that time was the first book of a safety related series published in the Dutch language. I also wrote the second book which was on "Safety Auditing". After the fourth book was issued early 1990's the publisher found that sales did not meet the expectations and the series was terminated.

When I wrote the 1988 book I also did not have the experts in mind. Rather, I intended to reach the people who are not working in the areas of safety and risk management. The reason why I did that was that I felt that safety was much more important to the continuation, cost control and profitability of an organization than just considering injury type accidents or insurance. I think this had to do with my background as I came to the safety world from the world of property insurance. When I say that "safety" is more than just considering injury accidents I do not mean to downgrade that part of controlling unwanted events; on the contrary, I think that extending the scope of "safety" to include other types of "accidents" would make it more important to business and to (top) management. This is why the sub-title of this book is "Protecting Your Organization".

In 1988 my hope was that my little book would help people to recognize the importance of controlling unwanted events within an organization, any organization whatever its purpose. Controlling unwanted events is the shared objective of safety, risk management and loss control. My objective was to show people what risk and safety management intend to accomplish and how it can contribute to the better functioning and efficiency of organizations; by controlling risks and unwanted events that could, and do, lead to loss. My objective with this book is still the same.

Writing this book, I found it interesting to read what I wrote in 1988 and to find that the principles and ideas of 25 years ago are as valid today as they were then. I am convinced that these ideas and principles will still be valid 25 or 50 years from now as they are based on the work of those people who shared their thoughts allowing me to write this book. The differences with the 1988 situation are the names of accidents that are making the headlines now.

As it was 25 years ago, society today is confronted with waste. Waste of human lives, of materials, environment, money, time, etc. as the consequences of malfunctioning systems and organizations. Names that made the headlines past and present are: Bhopal, Mexico City, Chernobyl, Challenger, Herald of Free Enterprise, Ocean Ranger, Three Mile Island, Soveso, Sandoz, Kinross Mine, Piper Alpha, Exxon Valdez, Texas City refinery, Deepwater Horizon oil spill, Fukushima, Costa Concordia.

While I am still writing this text:

April 17, 2013 - the small town of West, Texas makes the news after the explosion of the fertilizer plant killed 14 people and injuring over 200. Property damage estimated around $ 100 million and liability insurance coverage said to be limited to $ 1 million only.

24 April, 2013 - Savar, suburb of Dhaka, capital of Bangladesh, collapse of industrial building with over 1000 death and expected to further increase as reported on May 10.

May 4, 2013 a chemicals transportation train carrying acrylonitrile derailed in Belgium at the village of Schellebelle near Wetteren. Explosions caused fire over a 500 meter distance releasing cyanide vapors killing one person and his dog 1.600 meters away from the disaster and wounding over 100. Imagine what could have been.

May 7, 2013 an explosion on a freight train carrying chemicals and oil products hurled part of a railcar into a residential block in southern Russia, injuring 27 people of whom 13 were taken to hospital, officials said.

July 6, 2013 an explosion of an oil train in the small town of Lac-Mégantic, Quebec, Canada. Estimated one third of the total population (6000) forced from their homes. Possibly 50 people died in the accident.

July 24, 2013. Again a train derailment, this time at Santiago de Compostela, Spain killing at least 78 people. The accident happened in a bend which is the first curve after an 80-kilometre stretch of a new high-speed track where speed is limited to 200 km/h. This track has ERTMS-compliant security system which is designed to slow or stop a train when the driver ignores signals or speed limits. However, this new high-speed line joins an older conventional track, shared with low-speed trains, at the curve where the accident happened. This conventional track only had the older ASFA system, which will warn drivers if they are exceeding speed limits, but will not automatically slow or stop a speeding train. The train driver told the investigating magistrate that he suffered a "lapse of concentration" as he approached the curve when the train should have been slowed to 80 km per hour.

March 22, 2014 Oso, Washington, USA landslide reported 41 dead and 4 still missing on April 21.

April 16, 2014, Sewol ferry capsized and sank of the coast of South Korea. On April 21 news mentioned 64 deaths and 250 missing with change of survival considered nil.

I stop here or I never get this book done.

Willem N. Top
The Netherlands
2014

INTRODUCING MYSELF and how I came to "safety".

This may be of interest to you if you are considering "safety", or rather "safety management" as a career. I did not come to safety through a well-thought process - it happened more or less "by accident".

I was born in The Netherlands in 1940 where I still live with my wife Marry and our three children: Frank, Marieke and Willemijn.

After secondary school in Voorburg, The Netherlands, the military and working with Shell as a chemical analyst, I managed to get two BSc degrees: in Chemical Engineering (1965) and Industrial Engineering (1966). My first job was doing market research with a Dutch chemical company. In 1968 I got a job with INA (Insurance Company of North America) in their European head office in Brussels, Belgium. My job as a technical representative was to visit industrial companies to provide the underwriters with underwriting reports based on which they would make their decisions concerning fire and allied perils property damage and business interruption insurance.

Important to my further life – business as well as personal - was meeting Mr. Frank E. Bird, Jr. who, in 1969, was the Director of Engineering Services of INA in Philadelphia. I had the honor to know Mr. Bird and his family for more than half of my present life.

During my time with INA, I followed a fire protection training course (for insurance inspectors) provided by FIA (Factory Insurance Association) in Hartford, Connecticut in 1970 and later got my registration as a Fire Protection Engineer.

It was through Frank Bird that I came in contact with the "safety" world and I would never have guessed that I would make my career in that area of business or rather safety "management". When I went to college learning about chemical engineering, safety was a low level interest area and not really an important subject of my study. Safety taught in college was about ladders and legislation and not very interesting. In addition, "management" was no subject at all. Looking back at that, I find it "strange" that "managing safety" that is so important in the chemical process industry was hardly given any attention. To be true I should say that it was given "no attention". I hope it is different today, not only in chemical engineering but in any education intended to produce the next generation of managers. That would do a lot of good to "safety" which is still very much driven by legislation.

Coming from the insurance industry and after meeting Mr. Bird, I had this broad view on safety, risk management and control of loss, not limited to lost time injury accidents only. When I became a member of a working group of the Dutch association of safety professionals, talking about property damage accidents and financial implications when referring to "safety" was not done. Safety was considered to serve a "higher" purpose: preventing human suffering. After meeting Frank Bird and reading his first book "Damage Control" (Bird and Germain, 1966) I always considered that a too limited view; if you want to get management attention and appreciation for safety, you need to embrace the total scope of what could and does go wrong and put that in actual and potential loss figures – financial figures. Talk "unwanted events" rather than "accidents". Talk about loss in monetary terms and not just in terms of Lost Time Incident Frequency Rates (LTIFR).

Anyway, that is how I came to safety.

But what is "safety"?

Good question. I wish you would tell me and then we could have a discussion about that. But that is a bit difficult, me sitting here and you reading this, possibly years later. But I give you one description of what safety is: the "control of accidents" and that will have us to answer the questions: "What is control" and: "What is an accident". Well, not to make it too complex: "control of accidents" is keeping the number of unwanted events and their loss consequences at an accepted (low) level. It includes reducing the occurrence of the accident – or rather the unwanted event – and the limitation of the consequences, the loss be it human loss, property loss or any other type of loss. So put that together and we may agree that safety is keeping losses at an acceptable level. Any type of loss!

Safety, in my opinion, is undervalued from a business point of view and I could see some reasons for that:

- History – safety has an extensive legislative background. It is mandatory by law and this may be a reason why it was rejected originally as it was interfering with "getting things done". To some extent this still may be the case.
- Legislation – separate legislative requirements for safety and environment creating separate governmental departments, separate regulations.
- The safety profession – to some extent this ties in with the points above as it was the "safety officer" telling people that it could not be done that way and that he would stop the whole thing unless … So safety did interfere with getting the job done and this may have led to a situation "safety function versus the line function".

- Conflict with the line function. "Safety" became the area of the "safety person" who may have been very happy to claim this as his or her territory. Quality became the territory of the quality person, environment became ..... etcetera. So what was left to the line? Right: getting things done!
- An "accident" traditionally was – and in many cases still is – considered an unwanted event resulting in human suffering. These events are relatively rare compared with the total number of events that result in loss of any kind.
- Safety losses are normally expressed in frequency rates meaning number of events resulting in workdays lost per number of hours worked. Frequency rates such as LTIFR's have little meaning to people – (top) management - who think in monetary terms.
- Other professions - quality, environment and occupational health - each with their own "expert" claiming their own territory separating each area from the others and separating them for their common cause: controlling unwanted or undesired events.
- Parallel to this separation of areas, we saw the development of a safety management system, a quality management system, one for environment etc., Each with their own sponsors and identity underlining the separation of these business areas that all deal with the control of unwanted events and things that go wrong.
- And of course (?) each of these areas having its own certification system. ISO 9000 for quality, ISO 14000 for environment and OHSAS 18000 for safety.

Do you really need different systems to control unwanted events that share the same basic causes? Does separation of these areas help to get the attention of top management?

Separating safety, quality, environment, risk management and other areas such as cost control, may not be a desired situation. Each of those areas relate to work done by people and separation may lead to sub-optimization ending with different sets of procedures to do the job, one procedure for safety, one set of guidelines for quality, one for the environment, and so on.

I think that history put safety in a certain corner: first came safety, then health became an issue; quality came on stage later and after that the environment. Did safety miss the boat and was this why these other areas were added and got more attention?

Maybe it is more mundane. Maybe we just care less about people safety if it does not directly affect us? Quality is an issue because we do not want bad products - but don't we accept quality products even if they are made in unsafe companies? Environment is an issue and we do not want companies to pollute our backyard - but if they do not do that would we be concerned about the safety there as long as we, our friends or family members do not work there?

So, am I saying that safety is not important? No, I do not and I do not intend to. But maybe, we should be looking at safety in a broader sense and make it part of a more holistic approach directed at the control of unwanted events including risk and loss, any type.

If we would have been smart enough from the beginning we could have considered all these aspects together being related to the same source: the work that is being done, (management) decision making and operational work. It is often the outcome of something going wrong that determines whether we see it as a safety issue, a quality aspect, an environmental incident or something else. If we would have been smart enough we should have been talking "unwanted events". There is still hope; we see more and more the combination of these seemingly different business aspects into functions and into management systems. Functions such as HSE managers, QESH managers and talk about "integrated management systems". There is now a PAS (Publicly Available Specification) document on "Specification of common management system requirements as a framework for integration" (PAS 99:2012).

Should it not be better to approach the safety issue from a more holistic point of view? The same for quality, the same for environment, the same for …….. Should it not be better to focus on "unwanted events" rather than naming the event after the consequences which often depend on the circumstances that exist when the event takes place?

Just a little side step as I am presently reading the book "The UltraMind Solution" by Mark Hyman. This book is about brain health and well-being and offers an approach different from the traditional medical system that is influenced by different specialists each with their own territory and, of course, by the pharmaceutical industry and related lobby groups. Talking about the traditional medical approach, Hyman says:"These people are stuck in the one-disease, one-drug model of thinking. It is an example or reductionistic thinking that misses the whole point of how systems work – of how the body works. …. Many symptoms are caused by a multitude of irritants and a variety of irritants cause a multiple of symptoms."

Basically, Hyman relates brain health – actually he talks about "broken brain" meaning mental disorders like depression, ADHD, learning capabilities, dementia etc. - to what we eat and drink and what the body does with this. That relates to the old saying "Mens sana in corpore sano" (a sound mind in a sound body) that came from Decimus Iunius Iuvenalis - known in English as Juvenal, a Roman poet active in the late 1st and early 2nd century AD. And of course it is true, think about what alcohol does to mind and behavior. Think about what drugs do. Some materials will kill you right away when swallowed or inhaled. Many materials will not do that but still may affect health and behavior when taken over a longer period of time. So what Hyman really points at is that, if you want to heal the (broken) brain, you need to heal the body first. Treat the causes, not the symptoms. I have friends in Australia – actually he has been a friend ever since we met early sixties when we both started in college. He and his wife had a son in the seventies who was "hyperactive" (today he would probably be labeled ADD or ADHD). To find out more about this, I bought a book called "Why your child is hyperactive" by Benjamin Feingold, MD (1899 – 1982). In his 1975 book Dr. Feingold related the mental disorder to artificial food additives, colors and flavors. Feingold's message was the same as that of Hyman: what you put in will determine what comes out.

Organizations are organic structures, like our bodies. If you want to improve the organization, start thinking "unwanted events" rather than the lost time accidents of the traditional safety world. That approach may lead to healing the organization's "brain" by going from the event or "symptom" to the (integrated) management system via direct and basic causes, limiting sub-optimization and possibly receiving more attention from top management on the way. Think about what you put into the organization to heal the organization. Treat the causes, not the symptoms.

1.   INTRODUCTION

Risk-, safety- and loss control management are hardly new concepts and have been around for a great number of years. Definitions and approaches to the control of unwanted events have changed somewhat over time; "safety" is no longer limited to "injuries" alone and "accident" has become more than just the event leading to injury. An accident is no longer considered a work floor issue only.

From the quality world:

80 % of the underlying causes of quality are due to the improper functioning of the "management system" with the remaining 20% attributable to the people performing the job.

Quality work is work without errors, mistakes, interruptions, failures, losses, waste, pollution, breakdowns, rework and without …. "accidents" which is …. safety?

It is important to realize that "theory" tells us how things should be and should be done whereas practice shows us how things are and are done. Possibly because people are not be able to do their work as it should be done or do not know how to do it properly. Or maybe they do not do their work as it should be done because they feel it is too much effort. This is not just operational work; it is management work and decision-making in the first place.

It is in the gap between "theory" and "practice" that the adverse, unwanted or undesired events take place which, looking backwards, we probably wanted to avoid in the first place. It is one of the main responsibilities of all involved in the organization to see that this gap is closed or at least as narrow as possible under the circumstances. It should be one of the main objectives of the management function: to close the gap - the MANAGEMENT GAP.

THE MANAGEMENT GAP

One of the main objectives of the management function is
to control loss

To know problems in advance

To control unwanted events and their consequences

To close the gap between "practice" and "theory"

Between "what is (done)" and "what should be (done) "

Please note that I refer to the management <u>function</u>. That function is present at all levels in the organization and part of each job. It is not, and shall not be, just part of the job of a "manager" but is also part of operational work. The degree of freedom in decision-making varies and is normally more limited at the operational level, at the "point of control".

The principle of point of control
The greatest potential for control tends to exist at the point where the action takes place

Louis A. Allen, management consultant and writer. Founder of Louis Allen Worldwide

Control of unwanted events – the objective of risk-, safety and loss control management – is, in principle, not difficult. Bottom line is to apply universal principles and methods/techniques used for (proactive) problem solving. Central to the control of unwanted events is a management system involving everyone in the organization to contribute to this objective. A management system to be initiated by top management and build with the help of all in the organization allowing emotional ownership making "their" system" into "our system".

The principle of emotional ownership
People tend to be more willing to participate in planned change when they have an opportunity to participate and influence <u>the process</u> leading to change

The control of unwanted events requires no miracle cure that some of us may be looking for when trying to solve problems. There are no miracle cures! The book "Beyond the Quick Fix" (Ralph H. Kilmann, 1984) says it all in its title: there is no quick fix to solving problems and managing an organization. No quick fix to safety. No quick fix to control losses/risks. Basic is the ongoing application of methods of problem solving to ensure consistently high quality of work and as such risk-, safety- and loss control management will combine with other aspects of management and quality control. The saying goes: "If you can't manage safety, you can't manage" and you can say the same things about other aspects of business - methods of problem solving, of "problem management" are generic.

I do not aim to cover all aspects of risk- and safety management which would be an underestimation of the extensive area involved: to control (all) risks, losses and unwanted events that (may) occur at all levels in an organization in decision making and in operational work. Included are technical issues as well as organizational, behavioral and cultural aspects. But I hope to give you an overview of some aspects that are relevant within the context of risk and loss control management and hope that this will give you a good idea of how "safety" may fit into your organization contributing to organizational efficiency and success.

Please consider that the management of risk forms an important part of the management function: achieving the goals of the organization with minimal errors, mistakes, failures, problems, damage, accidents, losses, and so on.

I will not attempt to answer the question "What risks are (still) acceptable?" This question, consciously or unconsciously, is in everything we do. A simple answer to such question is not possible and will depend on things such as:

- Is the risk taken voluntarily or is it imposed?
- What are the potential benefits of accepting the risk?
- What are the possible adverse effects?
- What is the probability that benefits or adverse effects may occur?

My own experience plays a role in determining the subjects and their depth of treatment in this book. My experience in risk- and loss control management covers a period of about 45 years now and extends from the assessment of risks (for an American insurance company) at the beginning of my "safety" career to running my own consulting firm in the field of safety management (related to the Frank E. Bird, Jr., world renowned safety leader, founder of ILCI and spiritual father of the ISRS – International Safety Rating System). Should you be interested to learn more about my background, please visit my website www.topves.nl and click "About me" at the top of the screen.

I will mention some safety management techniques in this book but, please, do not expect any in-depth discussion. I am, however, providing some appendices including examples that may help you to visualize what I am referring to. If you are looking for more of those, you may want to look at:

- Practical Loss Control Leadership (Bird, Germain – 1986, ISBN 0880610549)
- Safety Health, Environment and Quality (Germain, Bird, Labuschagne – 2011, ISBN 9780615447124)

And, of course, you can search the Internet for topics of interest to you.

NOTE: In this book I mention so-called "management principles". While these can be found on the Internet and in a number of books, including those written by Frank E. Bird Jr., at least a number of these principles, maybe even most, were first used by Louis A. Allen. Books written by Mr. Allen such as "Professional Management" (1973) were of great help to me when trying to understand the management process.

2. TERMINOLOGY USED

Below I will give descriptions of some terms that I use in this book. These "definitions" may not be those that you are using. Please consider that for many concepts there are no clear-cut definitions. In some cases, searching for definitions may reveal ten to twenty different descriptions for the same term. All I try to do here is to use some workable descriptions while trying to avoid the limitations that are often attached to "scientific" definitions. In your company or organization situation you will have to agree with your colleagues about the meaning of the terms that you are going to use. If you are using a description of an "accident" as an injury related event then your focus will be limited and the results of your efforts may be limited. If you broaden the scope of your definitions, your focus, efforts and results will broaden as well. Having said that, I realize that for several reasons you may need to start with limited descriptions so as to focus attention and then broaden your approach later on.

Management

There are various definitions of the term "management". One of those is "to obtain results through and with others". I think this should be subject to certain conditions; obtaining results alone is not sufficient. This must be done with "minimal" losses in terms of human suffering, property damage, damage to the environment, loss of resources, etc.

In combination with "risk" and "loss" the word "management" has at least two meanings:

- It is about managing or controlling risks and losses. This can be achieved by applying the same methods of problem solving that are used in other areas of management. Management of risk is pro-active problem solving to determine what can go wrong and taking adequate measures to prevent related unwanted events and limit their (potential) consequences.
- Managing risks and losses is a management function and a first task of managers, joining forces with staff functions and operational personnel

Since "management" is one of the main themes throughout this book, I extend a little here.

When describing "management", Louis A. Allen recognized the following main functions:

- Planning
- Organizing
- Leading
- Controlling

While these functions are really inseparable, the "controlling" function is of particular importance within the context of this book and includes:

- Establishing performance standards
- Comparing actual performance against standards
- Taking corrective action when necessary

I think it was Frank Bird, Jr. who added "identification of management activities" which gave us the acronym ISMEC:

- Identification of areas of management activity (the content or "elements" of the "standing plan" or "management system")
- Standards or criteria for activities in those elements
- Measuring performance
- Evaluating or assessing performance against standards set
- Correcting in case of deviations, commending if none

When looking at "performance", consider input and output. This also comes back in the structure that I recommend for management system elements. So add two things to the above:

- When setting standards, also set objectives to be obtained by the (element) activities
- When evaluating performance, also look at results versus objectives set

Please note that "management" and "managers" are not synonymous. The function of management, as described above can, and normally will, be carried out by many in an organization, including operational personnel. Combination of Top-down AND Bottom-up is the key to obtain lasting success.

Manager

A manager is a person responsible for planning and directing the work of others, coaching them, monitoring their work, taking corrective action when necessary and commending for a job well done as the case may be.

A manager per se is not an entrepreneur, not a leader, not a risk taker. A manager is first of all an "administrator". It is the manager's job to "keep the show on the road". Entrepreneurs are, first and foremost, ideas people, people who take (commercial) risks and leading others towards commercial success. If a manager is a risk taker, he or she may be the source of an accident or other unwanted event waiting to happen.

> **Peter Drucker**
>
> Management is doing things right; leadership is doing the right things.

Peter Drucker (1909 – 2005) – management consultant, educator and author

There is a risk: if the person at the top of the organization is primarily an entrepreneur dealing with the external world, he or she may forget to pay sufficient attention to the "world within", to the "administration", to the "control" of what takes place in the organization and how.

In relation to the above, allow me a brief sidestep following the article "Leaders are often self-destructive" that was published in Elsevier magazine on January 4, 2014 providing an interesting view on leaders and leadership. The article was based on an interview with Mr. Manfred Kets de Vries, Professor of Leadership Development at INSEAD, one of the world's leading graduate business schools.

From the article (free translation):

Mr. Kets de Vries has given courses on leadership for top managers including intensive group sessions based on socio-psychoanalysis. He dissects his students psychologically, and then confronts them with shortcomings, pitfalls and challenges. Being a certified psychoanalyst he cannot reveal who have been on the couch, but: "The count is well over a thousand. Many former students are top CEO's and ministers. "

His impression after all these meetings? Not so good. "They - the leaders - are above average often neurotic, and especially narcissistic. They often surround themselves with the wrong people and are very susceptible to group thinking. Furthermore, they are often driven by greed and they have no contact with the reality."

Mr. Kets de Vries continues: "I regularly come across leaders who are self-destructive. After seven years in the same place they get bored. Then they can do weird things that do not serve the interests of the company. They want, for example, all kinds of takeovers, while all the statistics show that the majority of them failed. Or they keep themselves occupied with external affairs, such as their image. Not that that's necessarily unimportant, but there must also be someone running the business."

"After about seven years a leader has to go. This applies to many organizations, perhaps only except family businesses. It is really dangerous if someone is proclaimed for example Businessman of the year. That is often a sign that he is too busy with other things than the core of his business and often this is the beginning of hubris." (hubris = arrogance, haughtiness).

"Of course there are many good, inspiring leaders", he says."Leaders like that almost always have the four H's: hope, humility, humanity and humor. They are able to give people hope of improvement, and to this end turn to humility, humanity and humor. They allow themselves to be less influenced by greed."

So does that say anything about people who are leading our organizations?

Besides the entrepreneur, do we need another type of leader? An "organizational leader" to lead the "organization within"? To make sure that the commercial success will not be eroded by unwanted events that lead to loss?

The principle below applies to most managers and supervisors; many of them are selected based on their technical qualifications and experience. Their functioning as a manager may be helped quite a bit when management systems are set up with their cooperation and consent to provide the margins in which they are expected to function. The management system will indicate what they should be doing, why, when and how.

> **The principle of technical priority**
>
> When called upon to perform both management work and technical work during the same time period, managers tend to give priority to technical work

Louis A. Allen, management consultant and writer. Founder of Louis Allen Worldwide

Today, the principle may no longer apply in all cases and to all (top) managers as many come into their functions from schools of business administration. Thus they may be lacking the technical knowledge required to understand and manage the processes that exists in the organizations they are supposed to lead. Which, of course, may create another risk.

Management System

There are various descriptions of what a management system is and some are really trying to be scientific. To me, a management system is a plan through which the organization indicates: "This is where we want to be and the way we will get there."

To be effective, a management system needs:

- To be build via a <u>process</u> to include all in the organization through a top-down/bottom-up approach.
- To have a relevant and adequate minimum <u>content</u>, a combination of management activity areas or "elements" which together are expected to bring the results of the management system. These elements include specific activities to reach the specific element objectives: what shall be done, why, by whom, when and how.
- To have a <u>structure</u> in each of the elements that will stimulate activity implementation, periodical assessment of that implementation and of the results obtained in comparison with the specific element objective set.

The process, by the way, will include both content and structure.

The principle of emotional ownership

People tend to be more willing to participate in planned change when they have an opportunity to participate and influence <u>the process</u> leading to change

---

The three aspects underlined above are not depending on the objective of the management system but are generic. At least that is the way I see it. The actual content may vary within certain margins as determined by the objectives of the management system. So a safety management system may have "elements" that are somewhat different from a quality management system but they will also share a number of the same elements, such as design, training, purchasing, hiring of personnel, etc.

A management system is normally initiated by (top) management. The main reason for this is that to build, execute, maintain and improve an effective management system requires resources and the involvement of all in the organization. This requires a well-identified and agreed upon process which, once started will never end which is a reason why I consider a management system equal to a "standing plan"; they both will be there for a long time, if not forever. This journey to improve the organization may take considerable time, depending on what the baseline situation is when starting the process.

What a Management System is

In essence, a management system is a PLAN: "this is where we want to be and the way we will get there".

That can be done orally, by example or in written form on paper or electronically.

To make it effective in reaching the desired objective you need three things: (i) process, (ii) content and (iii) structure

Basically, the boxed text says what a management system is: a management plan indicating the objective to be reached and how to get there. The process will involve people needed to make it a success and the structure will stimulate implementation as well as periodic assessment and evaluation to make sure that the right things are being done and results obtained.

Of course there several definitions to be found of what a management system is, one being more "scientific" than the other and the more scientific, the more complex and the more difficult to understand and communicate.

A contact of mine in Australia recently said: "When I first started to work in this industry I asked the question "what is a management system" to so many people, from auditors to my operations manager and everyone had different ideas and definitions, so at the end I only had a vague idea of the concept. I think from now on, when I get asked the question by my friends or family, I'll simply use your definition, it is much simpler and it makes sense! Thanks for that."

The term "management system" is often used in relation to certification. In that case the simple definition in the box above would still apply; at least in part. The objective then is to get the certificate but the process may be quite different. There is a difference between getting a certificate and getting better. For a certificate you may call in an external consultant who will help your company to obtain a certificate meeting requirements put on the company by the legislator or customers; with legislation or the certification standard serving as a reference. For certification purposes, the process to involve all in the organization, as mentioned above, may not be needed. In fact it may not be wanted as that may slow down the process to get the certificate that may be required within 3 to 6 months - or "yesterday", depending on the dominating commercial or operational needs.

A management system consists of "management activity areas" or "elements". These are more or less independent, but interacting, areas of management that are considered necessary to reach the objective of the management system be it safety, quality, cost control, risk management or anything else. To be effective, each element shall have its own specific objective which shall not be the same as the objective of the overall management system. Picture 2.1 shows this schematically.

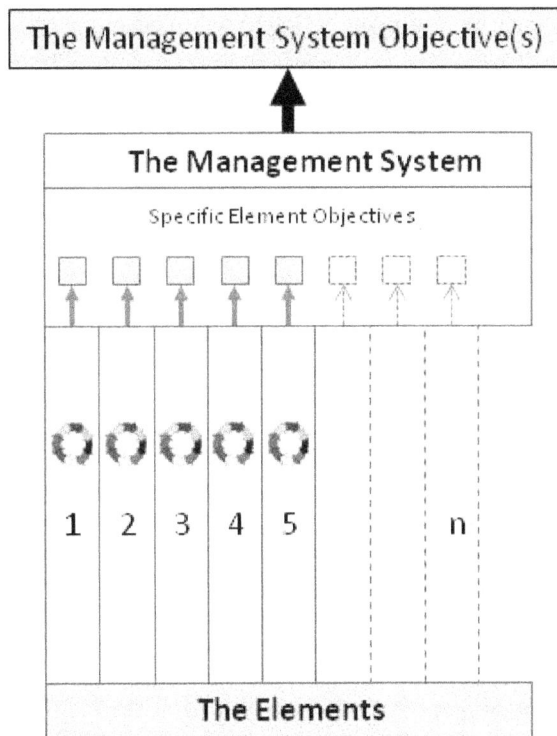

Picture 2.1 - The management system with its composing elements

A management system could be set up to obtain a desired objective, to get a certain certificate such as ISO 9000 or OHSAS 18000, or for any other purpose. Or a management system could simply be set up to control unwanted events that undermine a company's performance. In that case, you would have to define "unwanted event" and that could be the start of a broad scope integrated management system, depending on your definition.

Reaching a desired objective or controlling unwanted events are actually two sides of the same coin as reaching a certain objective would include the elimination and/or reduction of undesired events that undermine the effort to reach the objective.

In principle, a management system should have the following types of elements:

- Content elements containing activities to meet element objectives required to reach overall system objectives.
- One or more elements to early detect management system deviations prior to developing into unwanted events; detection of deviations is also included in the structure that I suggest for each element.
- One or more elements including activities to act in case of emergency situations – what to do if things go wrong.
- An element to learn from unwanted events – how to learn from what goes wrong.

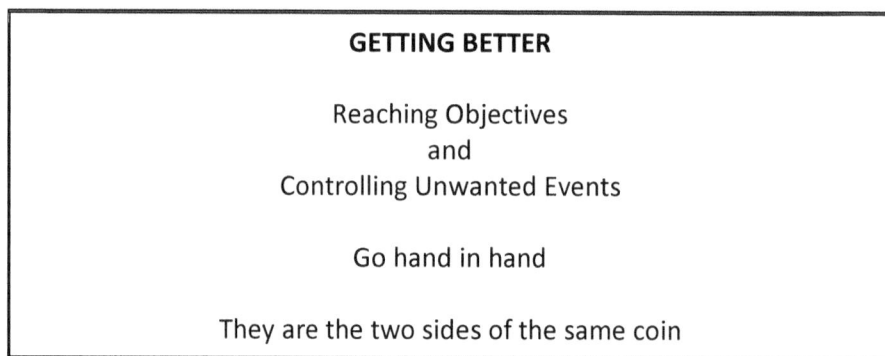

GETTING BETTER

Reaching Objectives
and
Controlling Unwanted Events

Go hand in hand

They are the two sides of the same coin

A management system is actually more than just a plan. It includes ways to carry it out. It indicates what is important to reach goals/objectives. The management system "feeds" the organization and receives information back. It provides two-way communication channels allowing top-down and bottom-up communication and feedback providing further input towards success. If you are looking for employee empowerment, you need a well developed management system.

When on the subject of "management system", I want to make some comments of two related topics:

- Integrated management systems
- Certification

Integrated management systems

What we mean by "integrated management systems" is nothing more than putting things together that belong together. A job well done is a job done without unwanted events, be it safety, or quality or environmental or anything else. That is true for (management) decision-making as well as operational work.

We call it "integrated" because we are putting together management systems that may have been set up separately - covering seemingly different business aspects such as safety, quality and environment - due to:

- Historic reasons – the focus on these aspects did not develop at the same time
- Legislative reasons – separate regulations for safety, health and environment
- Different certification schemes – OHSAS 18000 for safety, ISO 9000 for Quality, ISO 14000 for the environment, ISO 31000 for risk management and you may be able to add a couple more ISO or other schemes
- Requirements from customers – different focus at different times, depending for example on societal pressure and opinions
- Territorial claims; "my area", "my responsibility" - the safety manager, the quality manager, the environmental manager, the risk manager etc.

Separation of safety, quality, environment etc. may lead to territorial claims and sub-optimization. A good example of sub-optimization is the risk identification which is a mandatory issue of the contractor safety certificate scheme that I helped set up in The Netherlands between 1989 and 1994. The core of the certification scheme is "control of tasks with increased risks". But when you look at the risk identification process, which is the foundation on which to base the certificate, you will find that is mainly directed at personal injury type of events. This is at least regrettable as the process could be used to also find other potential problems that may originate from the same tasks or jobs. This "job safety analysis" (JSA) has been around for decennia so this sub-optimization has been with us for a long time. By extending the scope of the risk identification process to include quality risks, property damage risks and others, the efforts to obtain the certificate could go way beyond traditional safety and gain much more attention by management of the organization.

Certification

Certification means meeting certain minimum requirements to obtain a certificate. Management systems are often setup in relation to getting a certificate. But when talking about management systems as the road to getting better, I am inclined to say that certification is often a roadblock to improvement. Why do I say that?

Here are my arguments:

- Management systems are normally set up to obtain a certificate – OHSAS 18000, ISO 14000, ISO 9000, ISO 31000 or other.
- A certificate normally represents an indication for a minimum level of performance. Once a company has reached that level, the certificate will be issued.
- However, the minimum level may be less than intended by the certification scheme because there may be quite a bit of interpretation as to what is acceptable to get the

certificate. The margin for interpretation has to be there to allow a needed amount of freedom to organizations to implement the requirements such that it suits their needs and specific circumstances. The margin is also there as it is virtually impossible nor desirable to write requirements in such detail that interpretation is not possible. Due to this, it may depend on the qualifications of the auditor and the policy of the certification institute to determine what is "minimally acceptable". The level of the certificate may therefore vary quite a bit.

- Certification institutes are normally competing for business in a commercial market so price is always an issue and the lower price may mean less auditing time; possibly resulting in lower certificate quality and a certificate not really meeting the intended minimum level.

- Combination of potentially conflicting roles in one (certification) company or person: consulting, training and auditing/certification. While, formally, consulting will be separated from auditing/certification, the people involved may still be working for the same company and be colleagues answering to the same boss.

- Relations between auditors/consultants who often operate as independents. "You scratch my back and I scratch yours". One person doing the consulting for company A while the other does the certification audit. Next time, for company B, it may be the other way around.

- Relations between consultants and auditors/certification institutes. Often certification is required by a third party so the thinking of people in the company needing the certificate may be: it has to be quick, easy and should not cost much. So if those are the margins for the consultant needing the income, the consultant will know what is minimally acceptable to get the certificate from the certification institute that is also eager to get the business.

- Use of an external consultant may provide a "management system" that is certifiable but that system may not have been set up with much or any involvement of company personnel who will have to do the work "dictated" by the management system. So there is no "emotional ownership" needed at all levels within the company, it is not "our system because "we have not been involved in making it". The "principle of participation" applies here as well as the "principle of emotional ownership" (page 19) but both in a negative way; no participation = no ownership.

The principle of participation

Motivation to accomplish results tends to increase as people are given opportunity to participate in matters affecting those results.

Louis A. Allen, management consultant and writer. Founder of Louis Allen Worldwide

- Getting the certificate may be understood by company management as "we are doing a good job". That may provide a false feeling of self-satisfaction and complacency.

Does it have to be that way? No, definitely not. There are certification institutes and auditors that are different. The good consultant would ask the question: do you want a certificate or do you want to get better in what you are doing? And there are people who can see beyond certification and will use that what is required to get the certificate to make their company better, to get better control over unwanted events allowing them to survive in a competitive market.

See appendix P, page 291, where you may find my answers to some questions concerning management systems. Of course, these are my questions and my answers; yours may be different.

Risk

A simple definition is: "possibility of loss".

In this definition, there are two variables:

- The frequency with which an unwanted event will occur - failure rate (F)
- The (potential) extent of loss, the consequences (C) following the occurrence of the unwanted or undesired event

The risk (R) is calculated as: R = F x C and this combination of failure rate and (potential) consequence will often be shown in a risk matrix. The matrix combines the two aspects (F and C) and is 2-dimensional.

In the commonly used Fine/Kinney method the failure rate F is divided into two factors:

- The degree of exposure to the hazard concerned (E) which, for example, may vary from once per year or less to twice daily or continuous
- The likelihood or probability (P) that the adverse event will occur during the exposure

The Risk is then calculated as R = E x P x C making this method 3-dimensional.

Picture 2.2 indicates the range of risks to be considered within safety-, risk- and loss control management. This goes from the relatively frequent events with minimal consequences to the rare events with catastrophic results. It should be realized that these terms are subjective, and their meaning will depend on the person or company considering the risk. The events with (potentially) larger and sometimes catastrophic consequences will normally be insured or transferred to other parties. The more common events with (potentially) minimal effect will usually come under "operating expenses", losses that we consider "normal". The combination of high frequency and extensive consequences would not normally exist and the combination of (very) low-frequency and (very) limited consequences will have little significance and may indicate an "acceptable risk".

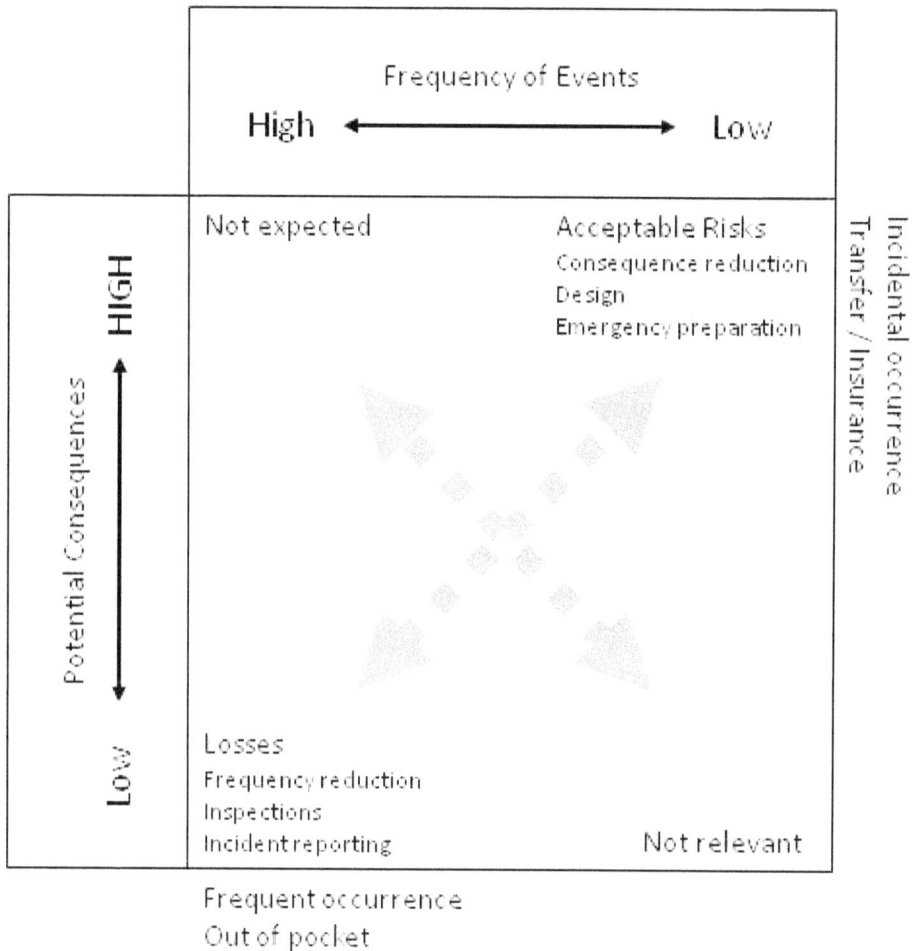

Frequency of Events
High ←——————→ Low

Not expected

Acceptable Risks
Consequence reduction
Design
Emergency preparation

Losses
Frequency reduction
Inspections
Incident reporting

Not relevant

Potential Consequences
HIGH
Low

Incidental occurrence
Transfer / Insurance

Frequent occurrence
Out of pocket

Picture 2.2 - Frequency – Consequence Matrix

From a practical point of view, it is important to recognize that "safety" management considers the broad spectrum of risks and losses, from frequent smaller losses (which may have a deteriorating effect on business results and the survival of the company) to the rare event that may at once put an end to the undertaking, organization or activity. Some people may look at risk management as related to larger risks and regard safety management as dealing with smaller (injury related) losses. I do not consider that a correct point of view. As said, all smaller losses may have an important effect on the organization and what appears to be a small loss at one time could be a catastrophe under different circumstances. There is no "on-off" situation but rather a continuous spectrum of risks and losses, as shown in picture 2.2.

The idea that risk management would focus on the larger risks may have come from the fact that risk management used to be "promoted" from within the insurance industry in which the larger (potential) loss simply gets more attention than the smaller loss. This placed risk management in the company's insurance department instead of being part of decision-making and implementation of activities in every function and at every level in the organization. Risk handled within the limits of the office of the insurance manager is not a risk management but rather an attempt to achieve better risk financing conditions. Risk management only becomes risk MANAGEMENT when it is included in the (daily) decision-making and execution of work. This means that the management of risk should also be visible where the work takes place – at the shop floor; at the point of control!

The principle of point of control

The greatest potential for control tends to exist at the point where the action takes place

---

Louis A. Allen, management consultant and writer. Founder of Louis Allen Worldwide

As said before, I consider safety-, loss control and risk management to cover the same management area: control of risk/loss, directly related to the success of an undertaking. If you see this different, you may want to look again at the definitions used in your organization.

I realize that there is also a positive connection to risk-taking in situations where there is an opportunity for profit. But remember that there is no gain without the potential of loss. Within the framework of safety-, risk- and loss control management, however, the emphasis is on the negative meaning: "possibility of loss". In addition, please recognize that there is a relationship between these two extremes. When looking to reduce the probability of loss, the opportunity for profit may also become less due to the costs associated with reducing the loss. On the other hand, without proper control of risk/loss, long term profitability may not be there. In practice it will come down to creating a balance between costs to reduce (potential) loss and the benefits that may be obtained from activities concerned.

Loss

Loss could be anything that you consider a loss. A description could be "any use or consumption of resources (money, time, effort, equipment, raw materials, energy, environment, etc.) that is not necessary to achieve the goal of the organization"

Examples of loss include:

- Damage to property, plant, equipment
- Damage to the environment
- Injury to persons

- Production interruption, delays
- Loss of information
- Loss of reputation
- Loss of key personnel
- Liability claims
- Quality problems
- Delivery problems
- Loss or disappearance of goods
- Loss of customers
- Loss of market or market share
- Absenteeism
- Staff turnover

Losses may occur during the execution of work and decision-making at every level in the organization and within each discipline. Not properly performing work could mean that someone loses his thumb, somebody else takes unnecessary risks by closing an unfavorable contract, another person takes unacceptable risks by bringing an insufficiently tested product on the market while the next one designs an unsafe product or work environment and another purchases unnecessary risks by using lowest price as the key issue.

Losses are yesterday's risks that are to be managed through risk- and loss control management and safety. Safety-, risk- and loss control management includes a very extensive area and should form a major part of the management function. Now that may look unmanageable but it is not. As we will see later on, many of the root causes of seemingly different losses are really very similar or the same. To control those needs effort, the cooperation of practically everyone in the organization, persistence and endurance.

Risk Management

Simply put risk management is the "management of risk" and could be described as "achieving results related to the control of risk/loss by applying proven management principles, concepts and methodologies". Risk management can be defined as the deliberate and structured application of management principles and activities aimed at controlling risks. Keywords here are "deliberate" and "structured".

Risk management has two main areas of activity:

- Loss Control Management (controlling unwanted events and their consequences)
- Risk financing (financing consequences of unwanted events)

```
┌─────────────────────────────┐
│      RISK MANAGEMENT         │
│   Identification and Evaluation  │
│          of Risk            │
└─────────────────────────────┘
          │
   ┌──────┴──────────────────────┐
   ▼                             ▼
┌───────────────────┐    ┌───────────────────┐
│   Control of Risk │───▶│   Risk Financing  │
└───────────────────┘    └───────────────────┘
   │
┌──┴──────────────────────┐
▼                         ▼
┌───────────────────┐    ┌───────────────────┐
│   Organizational  │───▶│    Technical      │
└───────────────────┘    └───────────────────┘
```

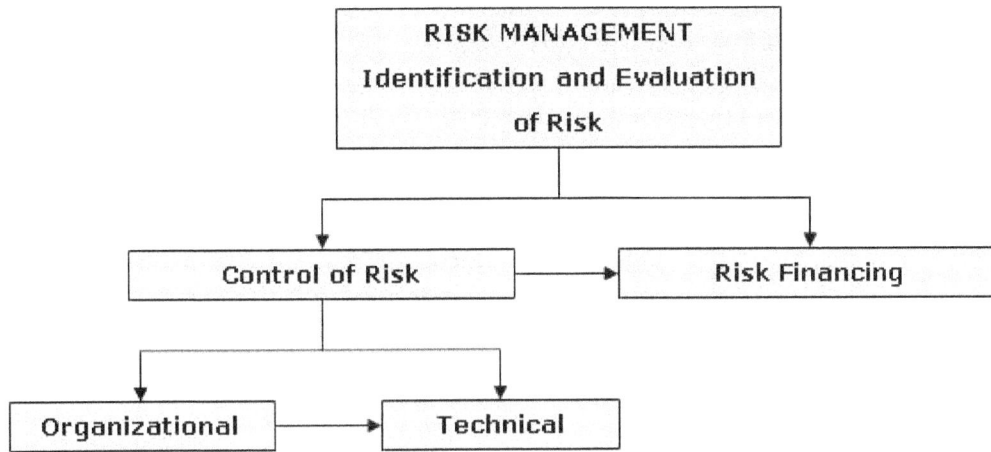

Picture 2.3 - Risk Management, combination of risk control and risk financing

Further discussion of the concept of risk management will be under the description of the risk management process later on in this book. For now, just remember that the risk financing possibilities depend on the risk control efforts and that the technical measures depend very much on the organizational issues such as the way materials and products are acquired, design of installations and management of change. And organizational measures really originate from the safety or risk "management system", the organized, structured and conscious way to control risk and the unwanted events that lead to loss.

Loss control management

Basically, loss control is the "control of loss". Similar to risk management it can be described as "controlling losses by applying proven management principles, concepts and methodologies".

Loss control management is the deliberate and structured application of management activities aimed at controlling losses. Comparing the essence of loss control management and risk management shows that these areas are very similar. In the daily practice of most managers, staff and operational personnel control of risk is, or should be, equal to control of loss; equal to management, equal to doing a job properly, equal to "as it should be (done)".

Keywords are: "conscious", "structured", "right". Remember Mr. Lombardi - winning is getting better, all the time; by eliminating and preventing "what should not be (done)", unwanted events and their consequences. You need a systems approach for that.

Safety

There are many definitions of "safety". I would suggest keeping it simple: "safety is the control of loss" which has a broad application and puts it on the right management level. Some, maybe even many, people may consider safety to be solely related to events that result in human suffering, injuries and (work related) illnesses. Some may use the description: "freedom from harm" which I think cannot be as life cannot be free of harm. Remember the saying: "A little risk is a joy in life." At the same time think also about this: "Don't risk a lot for a little."

I would suggest not to look at safety based on a limited definition of "accident" as you would most likely gain more than just a bit if you broaden the definition. I have been involved in the setting up of a safety certification scheme for contractors in The Netherlands. The scheme became accredited in 1994 and has meanwhile spread to some other European countries. Today (2014) there are close to 15.000 valid certificates in The Netherlands alone. If you take a close look at the system, you will readily come to the conclusion that the scheme is mainly focused on lost time, injury related, accidents. Which is a pity because the things a company has to do to get the certificate can also be used for much more than just control of injury related events. There may be a reason why this limitation is there: the system originated in the process industry and that industry measured safety by ... lost time accidents. And they still measure the safety efforts of their contractors by .... lost time accidents.

An interesting thing is the following and you may have heard of Mr. Frank E. Bird, Jr., one of the great safety leaders of the last century. Mr. Bird used to be working as the director of safety and security of the Lukens Steel Company in Pennsylvania when he wrote the book "Damage Control" in 1966. Basically, his message was this: "Hey guys, there are a lot of events that cause property damage. We ought to look at these too, they could cause injuries". Did the message come across? Thirty years later, in 1997, he wrote the book "The Property Damage Accident – the Neglected Part of Safety". So .....?

"SAFETY"

If you want to improve your safety performance with less effort: LIMIT the definition of what an accident is – you may even get away with it.

BUT

If you want your safety efforts to be more effective and learn from what goes wrong: EXTEND the definition and broaden the scope of your safety efforts. It just might get you the attention of top management that you may have been looking for.

Which one shall it be?

Anyway, use the definition of safety that fits you and your organization but remember that if you limit the scope at the same time you also limit the chance that this will receive top management's attention. And that attention is much needed if you want a safety management system that will do the job.

Safety includes the control of:

- Causes (preventive) – the reasons why unwanted events occur
- Consequences (repressive) – the results of unwanted events

It is good to realize that the consequences of an unwanted event often cannot be predicted as they depend on the conditions that prevail at the time of the event. For example, it will be difficult to determine in advance what the consequences will be of losing control of a forklift as aspects that play a role may include:

- Where could the event happen?
- How fast could the forklift be going? Rush job?
- Could the forklift hit a building or construction and if so, which one?
- What could the damage to the building or construction be?
- Could there be a secondary accident (e.g. fire)?
- If so, what could be the consequences?
- What materials or product could be transported?
- What could the damage to materials or product be?
- For which job could the materials or product be needed?
- Could the material or product be easily replaced?
- Could the driver be hurt?
- What could be the injury?
- Could there be other victims?
- What could the nature of injuries be?
- What could be the possible consequential loss?
- Could there be liability claims?
- Could there be a risk of losing an order?
- Could there be a chance of losing a contract or customer?

Absolute safety is not possible. Absolute in the sense that there can never be a single accident. The only possibility for that to happen is to completely stop the related activity. So if you do not want to break a leg while skiing, just do not go skiing! If you do not want to fall of a horse, do not sit on it! If you do not want any traffic accidents, no traffic! Really zero accidents in industry? Then do not start that industry! And so on.

Absolute safety is not possible. Life without risks is not possible. But we can eliminate certain risks, we can reduce the frequency of specific unwanted events and we can try to limit particular consequences in case unwanted events happen.

Safety Management

Following the definition of "safety", safety management can be described as: "controlling losses by applying proven management principles, concepts and methodologies". Or should I limit this to "lost time injury accidents" only?

This definition of safety management is virtually the same as the definition of loss control management and that of risk management. After more than 40 years working in the areas of risk management, loss control and safety, I cannot really make a difference between these areas unless I have to. You may want or need to make this difference for practical purposes; if you are working in the safety area, try to not offend your colleagues in the risk management office by claiming their area but get their cooperation as your are both working to achieve the same objectives.

As you may have noticed, my own career moved from risk management to safety and my first contacts with safety management and safety management systems were when working for INA (Insurance Company of North America) and meeting Mr. Frank Bird there. These first contacts included the INA TLC (Total Loss Control) service that was developed under the guidance of Mr. Bird and which later – in 1978 – developed into the ISRS (International Safety Rating System) via an intermediate"Loss Control Service Guide" that was developed by ILCI (International Loss Control Institute which was founded by Mr. Bird after he left INA/ISA in 1973). ISRS used to be one of the leading safety management references/audit systems between mid seventies and mid nineties and is still available as a proprietary product/service owned by DNV (Det Norske Veritas, now DNV-GL) which company acquired ILCI in 1991 following a letter of intent signed between the two parties in 1989.

Accident

While there are several definitions, my favorite would be: "an unwanted event that results in damage to persons, property or the environment". Or it could be even simpler: "an unwanted event that results in loss."

Originally, an accident was limited to injury events and often only to those that resulted in a certain number of workdays lost. While this definition may still be used by many, its application has its limitations; broadening of scope may result in added attention by management due to the larger impact on organizational effectiveness and profitability.

Incident

"An unwanted event that does, or could, cause damage to persons, property or the environment". This would include any type of loss, related to operational and non-operational work and decision-making. As needed and depending on your situation you could limit this definition to injuries only. But remember: a limited definition may mean limited attention!

Near-miss event

Near-miss or close call: "an unwanted event which, under slightly different circumstances could lead to harm to persons, property, the environment".

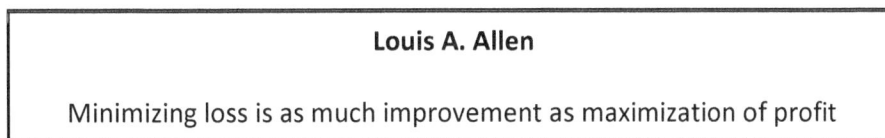

> **Louis A. Allen**
>
> Minimizing loss is as much improvement as maximization of profit

Louis A. Allen, management consultant and writer. Founder of Louis Allen Worldwide

Although not mentioned in the three definitions above, it is logical to also include consequential loss (sometimes called "indirect" loss) which may result from damage to people (including injuries), property or the environment. The consequential damages may include liability, loss of production, loss of customers, market, reputation, etcetera.

Accidents, incidents and near-miss events are all "unwanted events" and the circumstances often determine whether we call an event an accident or something else.

The three definitions given above are interrelated. I consider the incident as the undesirable event while the outcome determines whether we call it an accident (actual damage, injury or loss) or a near-miss or close call (no visible damage or loss). See picture 2.4.

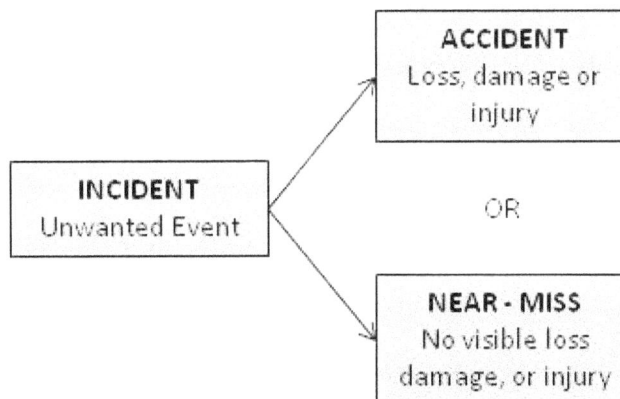

Picture 2.4 - Relation between incident, accident and near-miss event

From a risk/loss control point of view, would it be logical to make a difference between the three? My vote would be "no". What about you? All should get the attention they deserve depending on their risk classification and it does not matter whether you call them accident, incident or near-miss; just refer to things you do not want as unwanted events and treat them to prevent (future, possibly more extensive) loss. Not doing this right may just be like playing Russian roulette.

Risk financing

Simply put "financing the consequences of (possible) unwanted events."

If not a near-miss, an unwanted event will cause financial loss. Risk financing includes all activities aimed at making losses bearable for the organization so that the continuity of the organization is not endangered. Risk financing varies from out-of-pocket expense to insurance. The financing of risk though insurance is part of what is called "risk transfer" in the risk management world. A misleading term as the risk is not really transferred; the consequences are and often only partly. When insured, you may get money back for your warehouse that burned down but what about your possible loss of customers and market?

3.   THE IMPORTANCE TO THE ORGANIZATION

To recognize the role of risk management, safety and loss control we need to consider the purpose of an organization. This role depends on the contribution that these areas can make to the organizational goals and this may already be evident by the control of unwanted events; let's be honest, who really wants things to go wrong? Do you?

The precise purpose of an organization, of course, will depend on its nature and the reason why the organization has been founded. However, in general it is safe to say that organizations are there to deliver output, a product or service. Some organizations have been created for a specific duration but many or most organizations are established for an indefinite period; in practice: "forever". The anticipated lifetime of an organization certainly has an effect on the risks that an organization can afford to take; it makes a difference whether it is established for a period of one year or forever.

Risk management, safety and loss control principles still apply no matter the lifetime of the organization or activity. However, if an organization is there for only a short time it might, for example, be possible to pay less attention to maintenance of equipment as the unwanted events and their effects may not become manifest before the lifetime of the organization ends. Obviously this is "taking chances" and should only really be done if the possible consequences can be properly calculated and are acceptable. If, however, the organization is there for an unlimited period of time, like many or most companies or organizations, then such an attitude is normally not acceptable.

Simply put: you can get away with some risk taking for a short period, but not forever. And if the risk is not acceptable, you should not even try to get away with it - "Don't risk a lot for a little!"

In order to reach its objectives, an organization needs to survive during the period that the organization is expected to remain in business and if an organization is supposed to be there forever, the organization has to take many measures to make sure that this will happen. In other words, to be there forever means that you cannot gamble taking unnecessary risks. It is necessary to avoid unnecessary "cost" (unnecessary in relation to producing the final output) as much as possible. A company needs continuous attention from all in the organization to achieve its goals with minimal undue loss from unwanted events. Unnecessary costs can be continuous (e.g., absenteeism, minor damage, repairs) or incidental (such as fire, building collapse).

As is true for all models, picture 3.1 is a simplification of real life. It shows that the goal of an organization is to produce a desired output with the highest possible efficiency, subject to the restrictions that exists within the organization and influenced by the external conditions under which the organization has to operate. It is a primary task of "management" and operational personnel alike at all levels in the organization to contribute to this goal. It is the task and responsibility of top management to provide the leadership to make this possible and guide, support and motivate the organizational activities towards objectives.

Remember: when referring to "management", I generally refer to the function and not so much to the people we usually call managers. All people in the organization contribute to the function of management: managers, supervision, specialist staff and operating personnel. You ought to keep this in mind: "management" is not the prerogative or exclusive right of managers. The "shop floor" should not be excluded from the process to efficiently reaching the objectives of the organization. People at that level can provide a valuable contribution to optimize work methods and are most likely among the first to experience undesirable consequences of "upstream" processes (such as procurement, design, etc.). Remember the "Point of Control" principle.

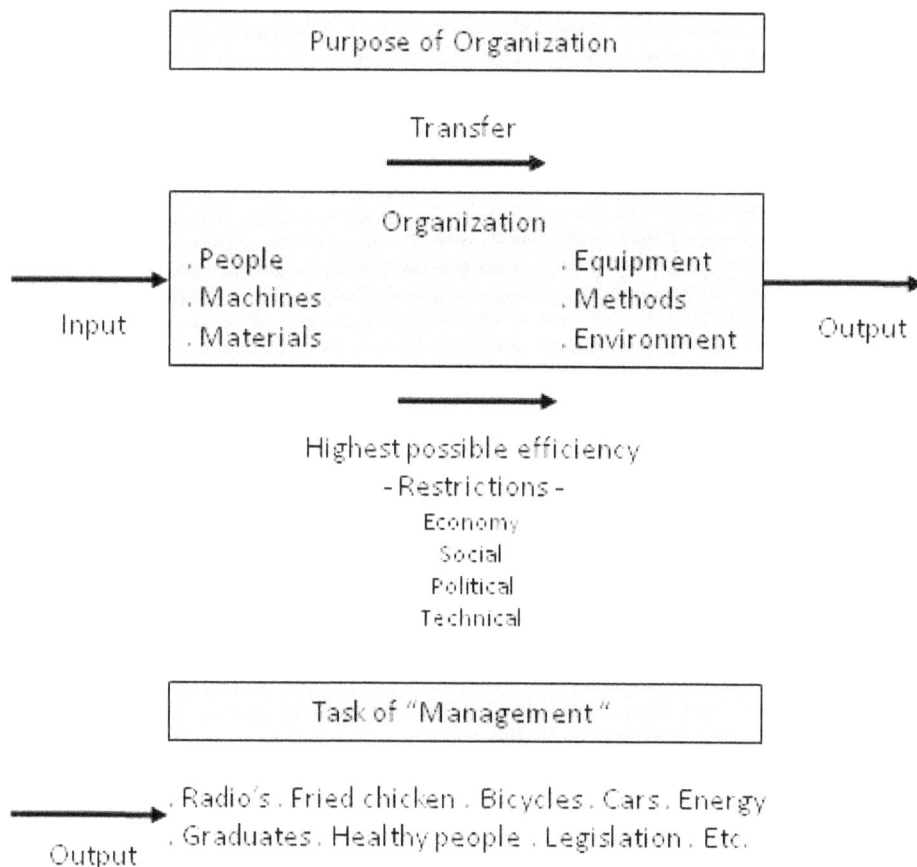

Picture 3.1 - Purpose of the organization

The efficiency of an organization is affected by unwanted costs, some of which are summarized in picture 3.2. It is a first task of managerial personnel, staff and operational personnel to maintain these costs at an acceptable (low) level. For many managers and operational personnel, this may be the only practical way through which they can contribute to the continued profitability and success of their organization. They can, in their own department, ensure that unnecessary costs are limited; within the guidelines given by their management system. And by doing this, they may just help to make sure that they still will have a job tomorrow.

Efficiency reduction due to loss/waste:	
Source of loss	Estimated or actual cost per year
• Malfunction of equipment	
• Material damage	
• Production delays	
• Quality problems	
• Delivery problems	
• Accidents	
• Absenteeism	
• Occupational disease	
• Legal liability	
• Waste	
• Theft, mysterious disappearance	
• Fraud	
• Burglary	
• Fire (internal, external)	
• Natural phenomena, flooding, earthquake, etc.	
• Mistakes, errors, mishaps	
• Inefficiency	
• Improper decision making	
• Loss of (key) personnel	
• Loss of information	
• Product liability	
• Loss of customers / market	
• Inability to obtain market position	
• Industrial espionage	
• Vandalism, rioting	
Etcetera	

Picture 3.2 - List of undesired cost influencing the efficiency of the organization

Not only should they be looking at the "normal" loss (repair, waste, absenteeism, etc.) which almost constantly occur, but also at the incidental events which may occur and could cause the company to get into trouble from one day to the next.

The frequently occurring unnecessary costs can have an important influence on business results. Although precise figures are normally missing (many companies do not register these – often unnecessary – costs which may be accepted as "normal" operating expenses) there are indications that these costs could be as high as 5 percent or more of gross national product, or 10% or more of gross turnover of individual companies. In the construction chain in the Netherlands, these "failure costs" have increased from 6% of gross turnover in 2001 to 12% in 2012 and may even be as high as between 15 to 20%. In monetary terms: 10 billion (10×10^9) Euro on a total annual building volume of around 50 billion (50×10^9).

Experiences in North America have led to the assumption that the costs resulting from accidents can be up to 50 times higher than the costs associated with injury accidents (medical and compensation costs) alone. See picture 3.3. It should be realized that the costs resulting from fire, liability, quality defects and the like are not included.

Underestimation of the true costs of accidents was caused by the fact that accidents were often defined as injury related events only and this still may be the case today. This may be one of the reasons why safety is not receiving the recognition it deserves when it comes to controlling unwanted events and their (financial) consequences as part of organizational (in)effectiveness.

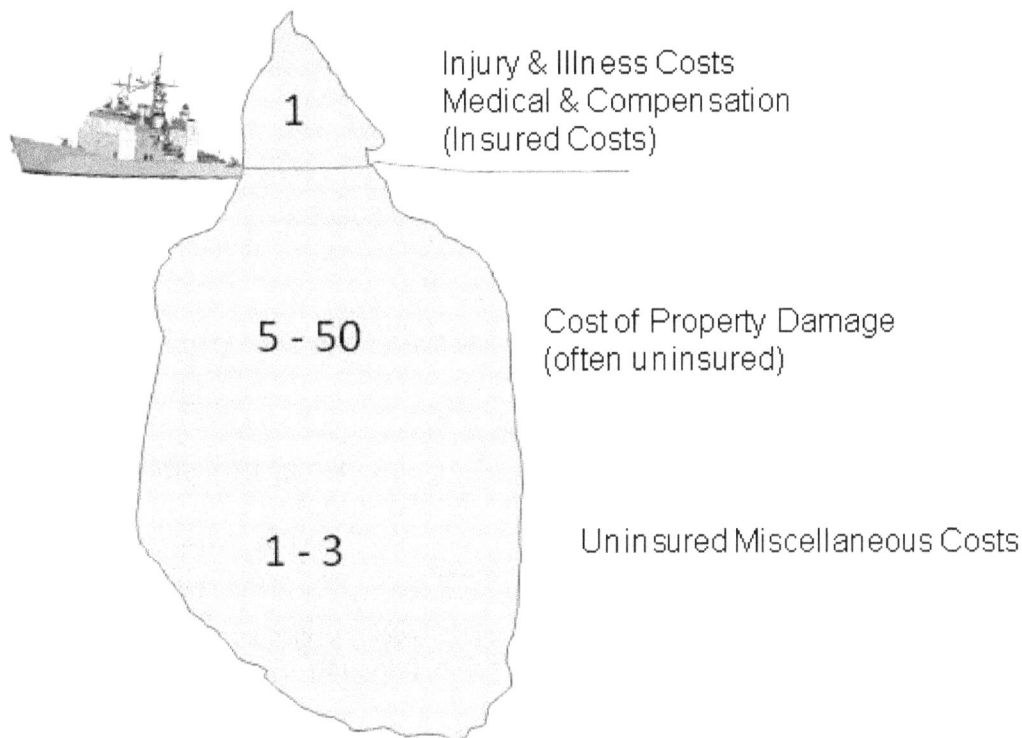

Injury & Illness Costs
Medical & Compensation
(Insured Costs)

1

5 - 50

Cost of Property Damage
(often uninsured)

1 - 3

Uninsured Miscellaneous Costs

Picture 3.3 - The real costs of accidents

Various studies have shown that the number of accidents involving property damage alone is many times greater than the number of lost time injury type accidents. This is shown in picture 3.4 in which the results are presented from the most comprehensive study ever carried out for this purpose. In this study, carried out under supervision of Frank E. Bird, Jr., at that time Technical Director of INA (Insurance Company of North America headquartered in Philadelphia), approximately 1 ¾ million incidents were investigated showing that for every serious accident (injury with lost time; actually the study referred to serious or disabling injuries according to ANSI-Z 16-1, 1967 revised) there were 30 accidents with material damage only. Although the study was conducted as far back as in 1969, the trend since then has not changed. This INA study also produced the results that are shown in the cost iceberg shown in picture 3.3. Other similar studies are mentioned in the book "Safety and the Bottom Line" (Bird, Davies, 1996, pages 277 – 287).

Please consider that numbers mentioned in both pictures 3.3 and 3.4 are indications only. You should not use these as such in your organization. But remember the message that these pictures contain: there are more unwanted events than lost time accidents alone and the total costs can be far greater than the costs associated with traditional safety (= lost time) accidents.

1 — Lost workday cases

10 — Minor injury cases

30 — Material damage cases

600 — Incidents - no visible Injury or Damage (Near-Accidents or close calls)

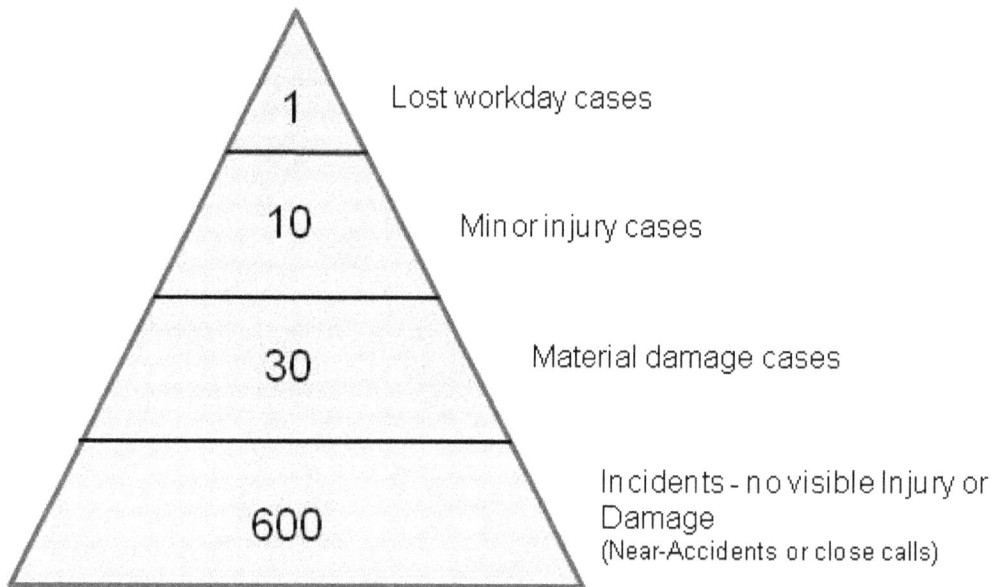

Picture 3.4 - The "Frank Bird" accident triangle: frequency relationships between several types of unwanted events. (INA study 1969)

Practically it will not be possible to eliminate all unwanted events and their financial consequences. But it should be possible to control the unnecessary costs at an acceptable level through a properly structured management system or -approach including relevant activities. Achieving the greatest possible continuity in controlling unwanted operating expenses creates the best conditions for survival year in, year out.

Yearly Incident Costs	Profit Margin				
	1%	2%	3%	4%	5%
1.000	100.000	50.000	33.000	25.000	20.000
5.000	500.000	250.000	167.000	125.000	100.000
10.000	1.000.000	500.000	333.000	250.000	200.000
25.000	2.500.000	1.250.000	833.000	625.000	500.000
50.000	5.000.000	2.500.000	1667.000	1.250.000	1.000.000
100.000	10.000.000	5.000.000	3.333.000	2.500.000	2.000.000
150.000	15.000.000	7.500.000	5.000.000	3.750.000	3.000.000
200.000	20.000.000	10.000.000	6.666.000	5.000.000	4.000.000

Picture 3.5 – Sales required to make up for incident costs.

Do you know the annual losses caused by accidents, incidents and other unwanted events in your organization?

The above table indicates the additional sales required to make up for the costs of unwanted events. For example, if losses are 10.000, the additional sales required at a profit level of 2% is 500.000. At a profit margin of 5% it would still mean an additional 200.000 in sales.

Risk management, safety and loss control activities are directed at the control of all losses at all levels in the organization and are of great importance to the survival of any organization. Certainly also true for the small businesses that often lack the financial resources to survive significant loss, even though they may have proper insurance coverage; loss of market due to being out of business following a major mishap is one example that may not be adequately covered by insurance. Control of loss should be part of all functions in an organization and it does not matter whether you call it safety, risk management, quality or anything else.

One of the main tasks of managers and operational personnel is to control loss

To close the gap between "practice" and "theory"

Between "how it is" and "how it should be"

Mishaps, errors, accidents etc. occur in the gap
between "what is (done)" and "what should be (done)"

They drain away your profits

---

4. RISK MANAGEMENT

4.1. Place in the organization

Risk/loss control management and safety are not new; they have been around for many years. Risk and loss control activities were and are practiced by every organization but not necessarily as a structured and comprehensive effort. The current situation (economic, competitive, legal, public pressure groups, etc.) requires dedicated attention to the control of unwanted events and their actual and potential consequences. This would include the coordination from a central point.

Which organizational structure is selected and how and by whom that coordination will be done depends largely on the specific situation of the organization. Nature of the business, size, risk level of operation, geographical spread, and organizational complexity play a role.

In picture 4.1 an example is provided of how the risk/loss control management functions could be structured within an organization. To what extent functions are combined in one or more individuals or departments will depend on the specific situation. What is important is that the risk management function should be situated at a high level in the organization such that adequate decision-making can be exercised to prevent unnecessary exposure to risk.

Also important is to realize that, while the coordination should be centralized, the implementation of risk management activities should be done throughout the organization and at all levels to adequately control (potential) loss. This should be evident from the fact that the management of risk covers a wide range of (potential) losses. The risk "manager" has a coordinating role which may be a subtask in a small organization and should preferably be separate from any line function to prevent possible conflict of interest.

Control of loss is important to maintain ongoing satisfactory return on investment - money, time, knowledge, effort, etc. It should be part of every function and activity in the organization, in (management) decision-making, planning, operational work etc. This is the main reason why the risk management coordinator should report directly to the CEO and will show in the organizational chart on the same level as production, finance and personnel. Depending on the situation this may also mean that a member of the board accepts to act as the high level "sponsor" with responsibility for the control of risks/loss activities.

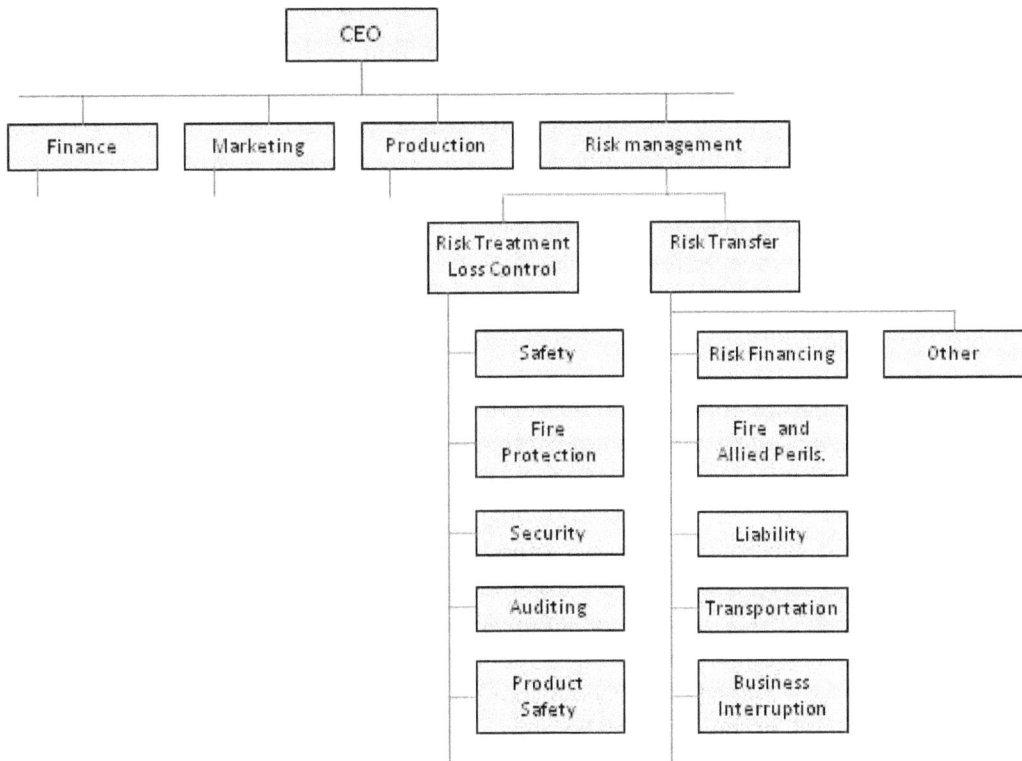

Picture 4.1 - Example Risk Management organization

The background of the risk management coordinator will depend on the specific needs of the organization. A coordinator with experience in "safety" would probably be a better choice for that position than someone with experience in "insurance". As we will see later, the control of unwanted events is at the heart of the risk/loss control or safety management activities. Control of unwanted events relate to what people do or don't do. For that reason alone, someone coming from a people related background may be preferred for the position of risk manager. "Safety" would be closer to people issues and this may help to get people's involvement when setting up a risk management system; insurance may be rather distant when it comes to people related concerns. Having said that, I certainly do not mean to say that every safety "expert" would qualify for the position of "risk manager". In larger organizations, the preference may be to have a financially qualified person to head the risk management function with support of safety, insurance, etc.

4.2. Risk management is management

Risk management used to be primarily promoted from within the insurance industry and became part of the organization's insurance office and was often considered as "a more sophisticated way to handle insurance". For this reason, the important relation between risk management and the day-to-day operation was often not there.

So we had risk management dealing with insurable risks – property damage, business interruption and liability – and "safety" dealing with people related risks such as injuries and illnesses. Not a desirable situation as risks are created by people; losses originate from work being done, directly or indirectly, operational or otherwise.

Management is sometimes defined as "to obtain results (through and with others)". Although this, in itself, is a nice description, this is not complete. In practical all organizations this should include ' .... with the least interruption and waste of resources (time, money, energy, materials, effort, etc.)." The function of management not only needs to consider people but also: machinery, equipment, environment, work methods, and so on. Management requires an approach in which all these elements come together and play a role. People are the main link as people purchase, design, place, operate, maintain, etc. machines, installations, tools and materials in a particular (occupational) environment. As said before, "management" as a function is not limited to "managers" only but should include all people from top management to operational personnel; each within the margins of their organizational position or job.

The management function can be divided into a limited number of key tasks such as planning, organizing, leading and controlling. Looking from a risk management, loss control and safety point of view, the last task is of special interest. Risk management is control of (future) losses and in practice very similar to, if not the same as, loss control management and safety. This control function of management can, in turn, be divided into a number of steps that are relevant to achieve a desired degree of control of risks, unwanted events and their losses. Basically, these steps are part of the ISMEC acronym:

- Identification of (management) activity areas or "elements" aimed at controlling losses
- Standards or criteria established for specific element activities

These two steps are really the outline of a management system containing activity areas or "elements" with their specific activities as the basis for achieving results. Together these two steps include what should be done, why, by whom, when and how.

Once these steps are taken, other main steps of the management function are:

- Measurement of activities carried out – what are we doing to control loss?
- Evaluation of what is done in comparison with criteria set - are we doing what we should be doing? Are we meeting objectives set?
- Correction/adjustment if we are not doing what we should be doing and results are not obtained.

The "C" also stands for commendation if work is being done as intended.

It is only logical that ISMEC should include setting objectives to determine what results are to be achieved. This should be done for the overall management system and for the activity areas or "elements" that form part of the overall system. If results are not achieved – for the specific elements and the overall system - then the efforts should be increased, adding elements and/or element activities or adapting them as needed. Thus, a control loop is obtained as shown in picture 4.2 (page 52).

The task of management and operational personnel at every level is to narrow the gap between "theory" and "practice", the difference between 'the way it should be (done) "and "the way it is (done)". In that gap is often the ignorance, impotence, unwillingness, lack of skill and other limitations of people making decisions and carrying the work. In that gap are also the errors, mishaps, accidents, damages, disasters, injuries, losses, etc. that we experience - because things are not done as they should have been done. The narrower the gap, the better the quality of the organization – from top to bottom.

4.3. Risk management, a matter of problem solving – before and after the unwanted event!

The process of risk management - and also of loss control as well as safety management – basically follows the generic sequence of problem solving.

Lasting results can only be obtained through a thorough set of activities aimed at reaching objectives while, at the same time, controlling undesired events that may keep us from getting where we want to be. Miracle cures do not exist. The so-called Japanese "miracle" (second half of the eighties and early nineties) was no miracle but came through consistent and continuous problem solving involving quality circles and "Kaizen": every day a little bit better. I think those concepts are also true today and boil down to the question: "can we do better what we are doing now?" Related activities have to be part of a system approach, a management system. Problem solving techniques, such as quality circles alone may not be enough. Bottom-up activities alone will not do it. Top-down activities alone will not do it either. It has to be the combination of those two, within a system – a management system – initiated by the top and build and accepted by people at all levels.

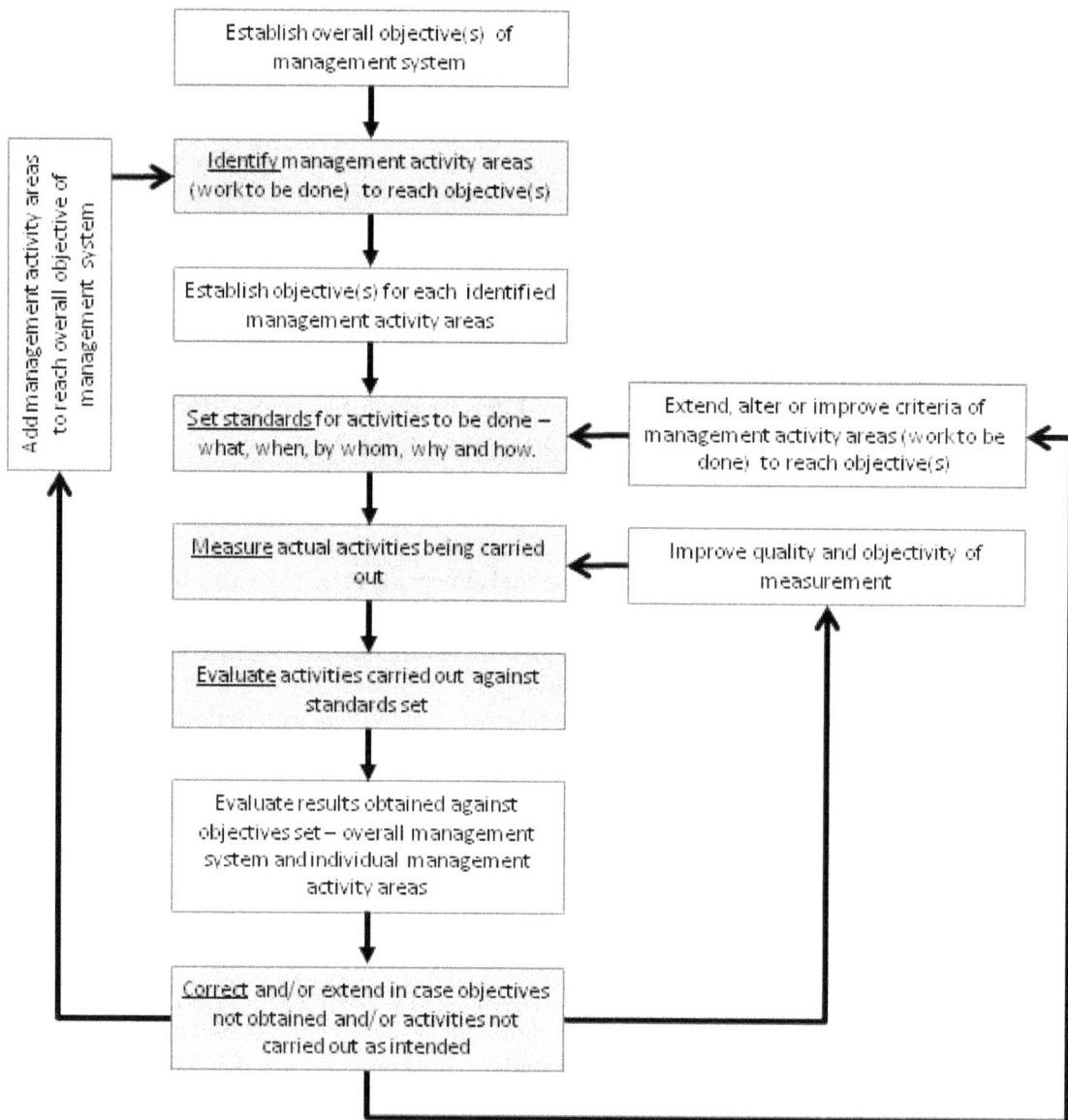

Establish overall objective(s) of management system

↓

Identify management activity areas (work to be done) to reach objective(s)

↓

Establish objective(s) for each identified management activity areas

↓

Set standards for activities to be done – what, when, by whom, why and how. ← Extend, alter or improve criteria of management activity areas (work to be done) to reach objective(s)

↓

Measure actual activities being carried out ← Improve quality and objectivity of measurement

↓

Evaluate activities carried out against standards set

↓

Evaluate results obtained against objectives set – overall management system and individual management activity areas

↓

Correct and/or extend in case objectives not obtained and/or activities not carried out as intended

Add management activity areas to reach overall objective of management system

Picture 4.2 - ISMEC PLUS, the making and implementation of an improvement plan

When discussing "problems", please consider this: is the problem the outcome of an unwanted event or is the event the problem? Or are the causes leading to the event the problem? Or is what caused the causes the problem? Is the management system the problem? Or is the problem with those who should have initiated the management system?

It is important to realize the above because people may have the tendency to seek for panaceas or "quick fixes" - actions directed at short-term results. The governing spirit in business is success oriented and potential problems may often be ignored. People may tend to wait too long finding solutions for tomorrow's problems. Only when yesterday's problems become visible today, actions may be taken to do something about it. If there is still time, resources, and motivation to make right what was wrong. Then the "problem solvers" come out of their offices with their sleeves rolled-up to "to fix it", to solve yesterday's problems. Where were these people when there was time to solve tomorrow's problems? Once they "solved" the problem do they go back into their offices again to wait for the next one?

The same is true when looking at "culture" and "behavior". Why wait, possibly during many years, to find out that behavior and culture are not what they should be? Undesired behavior and culture are often seen as causes of unwanted events and losses but I think it is better to consider them as the results of failing management and management systems. Solving behavior and culture related problems may be very difficult as they may originate from the behavior and culture at the top of the organization. Those problems can be avoided by making, execution, maintaining and improving management systems involving virtually everyone in the organization; at least that is my opinion. So why not determine desired behavior and culture in advance and work to get it? You do not need to wait until culture has gone so far down that it may be impossible to correct. The level of unwanted events – all kinds combined – may be an indicator towards culture going down the drain; they indicate deviations from "what should be (done)".

Permanent, structural, solutions cannot be found in short-term answers but are the result of quite a bit of work requiring continuous attention - work that will never end as the environment in which we live will always change. Short term solutions, whenever necessary because of the situation, should be applied against a background of a clear structure. If that structure is not there, the (possibly) initial success of the quick fix may rapidly be lost. This does not create a culture of success, but rather one of "failed again" and a continuous search for the next management "gimmick". Through my more than 45 years experience in risk and safety management I found and find the basic principles of management are still very much the same but if you look at all the management books that have come out during the past decennia, you must get the idea that management today is very, very different from what it used to be, right? But if you look closer, you may come to the conclusion that the terminology changed; the packaging became different but the contents is still very much the same: knowing in advance what can go wrong and take action.

Pro-active problem solving is the common theme when it comes to risk management: looking ahead at what can go wrong and taking action <u>before</u> undesired events result in unacceptable consequences. Management: looking ahead to prevent tomorrow's losses that are founded on what has been and is being done yesterday and today.

Not anticipating tomorrow's losses may lead to not solving today's problems and potential problem indicators may be ignored until they become so evident that the solution shall be now! When that happens, quick fixes are just around the corner.

Abnormal Situation Management (ASM) can be a very involved process but the message is simple: look for and be aware of deviations from the normal – safety-to-operate – status as early as possible and take measures to prevent the situation getting worse and out of hand. Get it back to "safe" again. ASM activities should be included in any management system and embedded in the culture of the organization. ASM and accident imaging share the same question: "What can happen if ......?"

Risk management – as well as loss control management and safety - are ideally to serve as the backbone of better management. Risk management is concerned with (potential) problems, unwanted events and their (potential) consequences. It can be said that the quality of a management team (and thus the quality of the undertaking) is determined by the problems that arise (number, type, severity). Pro-active – beforehand – problem solving is preferred far above the after the event reactions, the "firefighting" or "locking up the barn after the horses are gone."

The quality of (the) management (team)is determined by:

1. Knowing in advance what problems may occur in their organization or unit
2. Knowing the number and size of problems that may occur
3. Knowing what the causes of those problems could be
4. Knowing what to do to remedy the causes at the earliest stages
5. Knowing which actions to take to minimize the negative effects

(A) quality management (team) should only have known problems with limited consequences

---

Management without the management of risk and loss is not MANAGEMENT. That is my opinion. Would you agree?

The problem solving process includes the following steps:

1. Identify the (potential) problem: What is or could be the problem? What went wrong? What can go wrong?"
2. Evaluate the (potential) problem by estimating the consequences: How big is it? Depending on circumstances: how big could it be?
3. Analyze the (potential) problem: Why does or could this problem exist? What are the reasons? What are or could be the events causing the problem? What are the causes leading to the event? What are the causes of the causes?
4. Establish alternatives for the coping with the problem. What should be done to eliminate the problem? What can be done to prevent the unwanted event and what criteria should be set for these control activities? What can be done to mitigate the consequences once the event occurs? What are the alternatives?
5. Select the best alternatives: Which actions or combination of actions provide the best results for the least effort and cost?
6. Implement the selected actions.
7. Evaluate how the selected actions are carried out and, as necessary, take measures if not done properly.
8. Assess results of actions taken and, as necessary, take additional or other actions if desired results are not obtained.
9. Continuously investigate and analyze causes of "failures" that occur: losses, damages, accidents, breakdowns, etc. to learn if improvement of the "control system" is desired or required.

The steps above contain all aspects of the ISMEC acronym which, to me, underlines the relation between "management" and "problem solving". Management = problem solving, in advance, pro-active, being aware of deviations from "what should be (done)" and taking appropriate action.

The principle of definition

A logical and proper decision can be made only when the basic or real problems are first defined

---

Louis A. Allen, management consultant and writer. Founder of Louis Allen Worldwide

This problem-solving sequence is shown in picture 4.3 in which the word "problem" is replaced by "risk". The main steps of the risk management process are further discussed below.

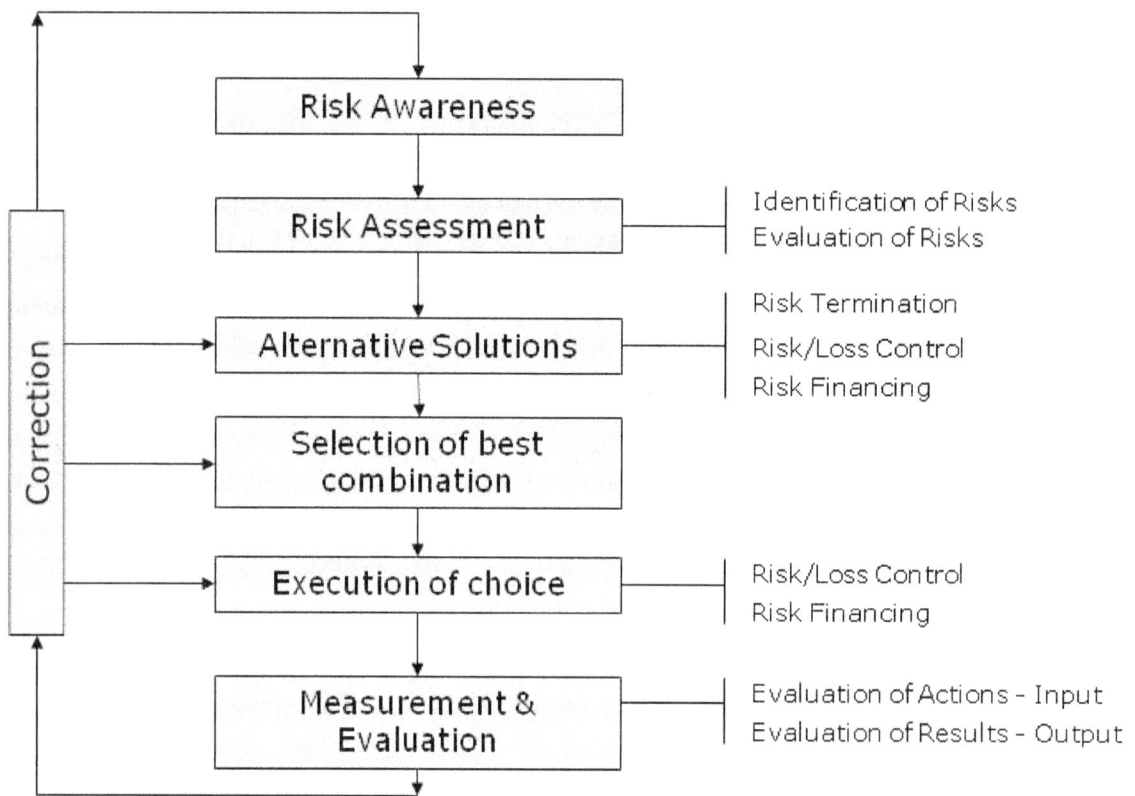

Picture 4.3 - The risk management process

4.3.1. Risk Awareness

While risk assessment is really the first step of the risk management process, risk awareness precedes that; awareness defined as: "the state or ability to perceive, to feel, or to be conscious of events, objects, or sensory patterns." If people are not aware that risks exist then the first step – assessment - may not be taken.

Aptitude is another important word in this context and described as: "a component of a competency to do a certain kind of work at a certain level, which can also be considered "talent". Aptitudes may be physical or mental."

When it comes to risk management both awareness and aptitude are important and related tests are relevant when considering hiring people for jobs that have inherent risks. Such as hiring truck drivers for transporting hazardous goods. Or hiring managers, in particular when responsible for managing hazardous operations where decision-making may put others at risk. When referring to "top managers", consider this: these people may be more entrepreneurial by nature, risk takers. As such they may not be the proper people to head the part of the organization that needs to make sure that risks – at all levels in the organization – are properly controlled. Entrepreneurial or commercial people may be inclined to take more than acceptable risks. Be aware of that as there may be a potential conflict situation. When the boss is an entrepreneur, should the risk manager or safety person report to him? Should the person with the responsibility to look after the risks of the organization report to a commercially oriented person? Maybe not, but that might just be the situation in a lot of companies.

4.3.2. Risk Identification

Risk identification is the qualitative determination of potential problems.

The potential problems here are risks, possibilities of loss. Losses in principle are not limited to a particular category; they could be anything that is not absolutely necessary to achieve the desired end product or service of the company or organization. This amounts to asking the questions like: "What can happen? Which losses can we expect to occur following decision making? Entering a new market? Execution of work? Participating into a contract? What hazards exists or may develop?" And so on.

It is good to realize that there is no essential difference between a risk and a loss. Time is the only difference. A risk is tomorrow's loss; a loss is yesterday's risk. Murphy's Law: "What can happen, will happen". If it is possible, it will happen even though it may take a while.

Risk identification is a dynamic process. It's certainly not something that is done only once and then to be forgotten.

Risk identification processes are (almost) never 100% and unidentified risks may escape the process. Picture 4.4 indicates this. It is also quite possible that risks arise tomorrow while they are not here today; tomorrow's world will not be the same as todays. Changes in legislation, increasing knowledge regarding the behavior of chemicals in the human body, changes in the behavior of customers and consumers, changes in production processes and increased understanding of local and global environmental and climate issues are just some examples of aspects that will not remain the same.

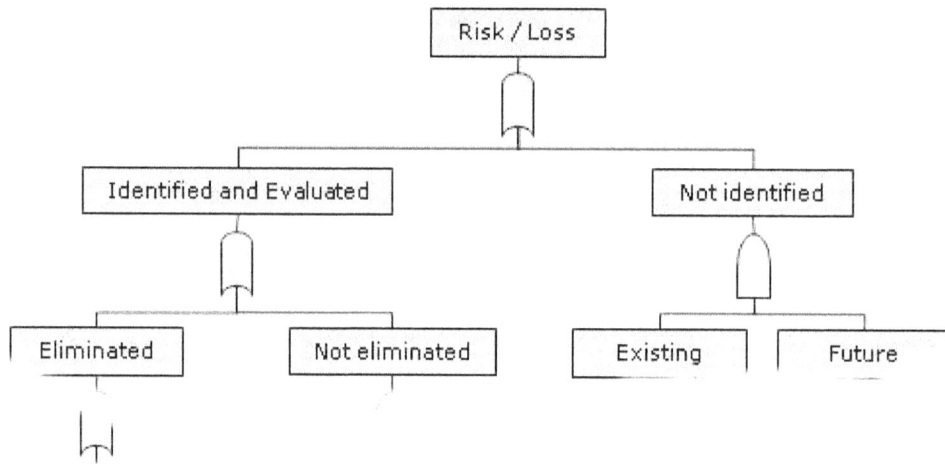

Picture 4.4 - Risks – normally not 100% identified

Risk identification should be repeated periodically, including reviews of work instructions, design criteria, procurement guidelines, guidelines for the selection of personnel and investigation of unwanted events such as accidents, damage, malfunctions. On the operational level, risk identification should be continuous through such activities as inspections, accident imaging and last minute risk assessments (LMRA) prior to execution of work.

A simple list of potentially critical operational tasks may help to identify risks as shown in picture 4.5. Part of a more extensive risk identification checklist is shown in appendix C (page 245).

Task Risk Analysis or Task Risk Assessment (TRA) – in the past limited to safety as Job Safety Analysis (JSA) - is a general good method to identify risk as it focuses on the work that needs to be done and, by doing so, main risk related aspects can be considered, such as: products involved, tools and installations, human capabilities/limitations and conditions under which tasks are to be carried out, normally as well as in abnormal and emergency situations.

Working on/in/under/over/above/with:
Height
Moving equipment
Chemicals
Enclosed space
Open flame
Water of other liquids
Extreme temperatures
High value equipment
High voltage installations
Heavy equipment
Explosives
Transportation equipment
Hoisting/lifting equipment
Production critical equipment
Flammable materials, liquids, gases
Quality critical processes
Equipment under vacuum
Equipment under high pressure
Environmentally unfriendly conditions
- Add to list as appropriate -

Picture 4.5 - A simple list of potentially critical operational tasks

TRA is more than analysis alone; it is a process involving the following steps:

- Listing of all functions in the organization
- Determination of tasks per function
- Identification of risks involved when executing tasks – use risk classification
- Control of identified risks including:
  - Possible elimination of risk
  - (Technical) risk reduction measures
  - Measures leading to task or work procedures, instructions or rules to properly handle risks remaining after elimination and reduction
- Training of people using work procedures etc. including performance observation to check training efficiency
- Periodic observation or discussion of the execution of critical tasks
- Feedback from accidents, incidents and other unwanted events

The last two points are important to improve work procedures including adaptation necessary because of introduction of new tools, changes in the working environment etc. or to add tasks that were not earlier identified as such to the "critical task list" for further processing. These last two points are also a good means to find out whether up stream activities such as design, purchasing and training are being carried out as they should.

The process above should not be limited to operational work but should include management work such as decision-making related to entering a new market, developing a new product or selecting a production process or location. The risk identification process should also include work done by staff members who carry out work such as design of installations, work environment and procedures; purchasing of tools, equipment and materials and the selection, hiring and training of personnel.

Work procedures, like any other procedure, are guidelines or requirements for the work to be carried out. Procedures also reflect desired behavior. To maximize compliance, procedures should be made, maintained and improved by including the people who are to use these procedures in the execution of their work.

The principle of deviation from normal behavior

The more a rule or procedure deviates from normal behavior, the more effort is required to reach compliance

---

In principle, procedures should have the generic structure to include:

- Management statement to underline importance and reasons – why is the procedure there
- Objective(s) – what is the expected result
- Procedure owner – coordinator
- Work/activities to be carried, when, by whom, how
- Training/instruction of relevant people
- Approval, signatures
- Publication date and definition (ID)
- Periodic review – including relevant people
- Periodic assessment to verify compliance
- Feedback from unwanted events

Up-to-date procedures should be readily available at the place where they are supposed to be used, at the "point of control".

4.3.3. Risk Evaluation /-Classification

This is about determining the extent of risk, of the potential loss and the frequency with which the unwanted event preceding the loss is expected to occur. The loss part of this evaluation normally concentrates on assessing the maximum (financial) loss that could happen following the event by which the risk materializes from the hazard that exists. For example, the hazard may be the presence of a storage tank containing volatile flammable toxic material. The risk is the release of the hazardous material to the environment. The maximum – worst case - loss would be the release of all content at once forming a vapor cloud engulfing the nearby housing development. The maximum potential loss would include the destruction of the entire development including inhabitants.

Estimating loss resulting from an unwanted event can be rather complex as it may depend on many factors including protection, containment of spills, fire protection and such. When I worked for INA, I used to inspect industrial locations to provide the underwriters with a report about the fire property and business interruption risks including two related loss amount estimations: PML (Probable Maximum Loss) and Amount Subject (AS). Within INA and at that time, the PML was the estimated monetary loss – or percentage of insured value – assuming proper operation of available protection. The Amount Subject or maximum possible loss was the maximum amount subject to loss – or percentage of insured value – assuming that available protection would fail to operate. (The meaning of PML and AS may vary per insurer by the way.)

Because of the difficulty to estimate actual loss from an unwanted event, risk evaluation normally only considers the maximum possible loss that could occur assuming failure of protective equipment that – by design – may be prone to malfunctioning. But, obviously, the actual consequence of an unwanted event – such as fire – could be anything between and virtually nothing and a total loss.

The size of the potential loss - the maximum possible consequence - is usually relatively easy to estimate compared to the problems that may arise when estimating the probability that such loss will occur. In order to establish that probability, an analysis is required of the entire sequence of steps that would lead to the loss event. Each step should be assigned a probability value and all those values will produce the chance that the maximum loss will materialize.

Let us stay with the example of the storage tank and assume the event will be a vehicle hitting the tank by moving off the road. Knowing the exact location of the tank is important. If the vehicle misses the tank within a certain distance, we may have a "near-miss". If the vehicle hits the tank, the damage will depend on such things as: collision protection, construction of the tank, angle under which the vehicle hits the tank, the speed of it and energy exchange during the impact. Depending on these factors the actual damage may range from very little to catastrophic.

To establish the probability, questions would include:

- Where is the storage tank located?
- Is the nearby road straight or curved?
- How far is the tank from the road?
- Are there any obstructions between the tank and the road?
- What is in the tank and how much of it?
- What is the construction of the tank?
- What is the probability of the vehicle moving from the road? At what speed?
- What is the change that the vehicle moves towards the tank?
- What is the change that the vehicle hits the tank?
- What is the angle under which the vehicle hits the tank?
- What is the force of the impact?
- How large will the hole in the tank be?
- What is the wind direction at the time of the incident? Wind force?
- What are other weather conditions such as rain, temperature?
- Etcetera.

To evaluate a risk the basic questions are:

1. How often can the unwanted event occur to trigger the sequence from hazard to consequences?
2. What and how large could the consequences be?

Risk evaluation/classification is not only a pre-event tool. It is also an important post-event tool to assess the potential risk as part of the investigation of accidents and other unwanted events.

The principle of dimensional value

The degree of management attention is directly related to the size of the problem

---

Louis A. Allen, management consultant and writer. Founder of Louis Allen Worldwide

Determining the risk is the goal of risk classification. The outcome of the classification process helps to determine such issues as:

- Setting priorities to deal with identified risks
- Whether a team approach should be used (highly recommended) to contribute to risk control and unwanted event investigation (in case of an accident)
- Which persons should be on the team - operational, management, staff
- The management level of the chairperson of the team

- Selecting risk control alternatives and making resources available
- Assigning responsibilities to make sure that measures will be done correctly and in time

Two important methods to classify risks are:
- Risk matrix
- Fine/Kinney

In principle, these methods are the same, both combining frequency of occurrence (of the unwanted event preceding the loss) with the potential loss. The main difference is that the Fine/Kinney method combines an exposure factor with a likelihood factor to arrive at the frequency. If you want, the matrix is 2-dimensional while Fine/Kenney has 3 dimensions.

Risk Matrix

Risk Classification using a matrix combines two factors:

- Failure rate - the chance that the event, leading to loss, will occur
- Potential (probable/possible) consequences of the event

A risk matrix could be a simple 3 x 3 matrix (using frequency values such as: low, average, high and potential loss values such as: minor, serious, catastrophic) or be more complex such as the 5 x 5 matrix shown below.

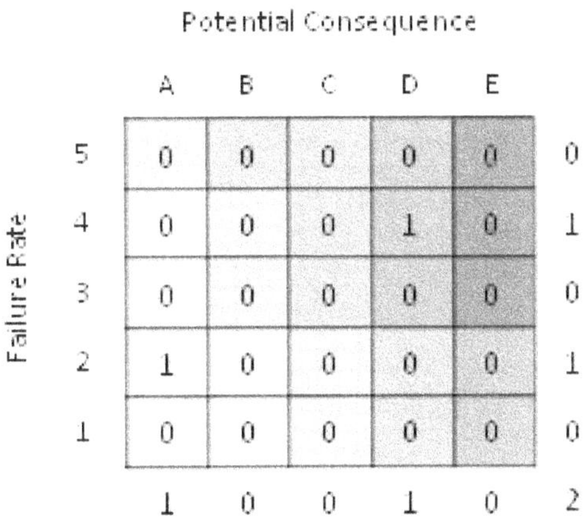

Potential Consequence

	A	B	C	D	E	
5	0	0	0	0	0	0
4	0	0	0	1	0	1
3	0	0	0	0	0	0
2	1	0	0	0	0	1
1	0	0	0	0	0	0
	1	0	0	1	0	2

(Failure Rate on vertical axis)

Picture 4.6 – Example of a 5 x 5 risk matrix

The matrix above shows failure rate levels 1 – 5 (with 1 representing the lowest frequency) and potential consequence levels going from A to E (with A representing the lowest). The numbers within the matrix, to the right and at the bottom show the number of events representing one 2A classified risk and one risk with a 4D classification; total in the matrix is 2. See appendix B (page 241) for more details.

Fine / Kinney

While the matrix example in the picture above shows a 2-dimensional approach, the method originally published in 1971 by W. Fine (later publication in 1976 by G.H.F. Kinney) is 3-dimensional dividing the failure rate into two components:

- Failure rate
    - Exposure (E) - the frequency of the activity from which the unwanted event may result (e.g. the number of times per period with which vehicles will drive by the tank)
    - Likelihood or probability (P) - the probability that the unwanted event will happen when the activity exposure occurs (e.g. chance that a vehicle hits the tank by getting off the road)
- Consequences (C) - the possible consequences of the unwanted event

The three aspects E, P and C are provided with value descriptions and value factors allowing a numeric Risk score (R) calculation (R = E x P x C). The Fine/Kinney method also allows calculation of a cost justification factor that may help to determine whether an investment for risk treatment may be acceptable.

See Appendix B (page 241) providing some more details about the risk classification aspects of the Fine/Kinney method.

4.3.4. Cause Analysis

Before taking any action, it is necessary to find out what the reasons are, or could be, for the event leading to loss. In other words what caused - or could cause - the unwanted event to take place?

As a rule, there will never be a single cause; often there will be several, or many, causes leading to the undesirable event. These causes will often be separated in time and one may lead to the other. There are causes and causes of causes and causes of causes of causes, direct causes, basic causes and management system related causes.

The principle of multiple causes

Accidents and other loss producing events are seldom, if ever, the result of a single cause

---

For example, improper personnel selection and inadequate training may lead to people who are not suitable and/or not properly trained for the work they have to do. These are just two causes that could very well lead to unwanted events. Reasons of those two causes, i.e. why there is no proper selection or training program, just add additional causal aspects.

Lack of design criteria may lead to improper design of workplace or installations thus creating an environment that is prone to accidents waiting to happen. Improper purchasing of equipment or tools may result in unsafe conditions creating a situation in which the occurrence of possibly major losses is just a matter of time.

Not having proper management (control) criteria may lead to "substandard" situations and acts of people causing unwanted events with consequences that depend on the conditions that exist at the time the event occurs. One example is the accident which is known under the name "Herald of Free Enterprise", a roll-on roll-off ferry that capsized moments after leaving the Belgian port of Zeebrugge on the night of 6 March 1987, killing 193 people. Inadequate policies, inadequate policy implementation, inadequate (safety) criteria in the design, inadequate procedures, inadequate supervision, and so on. The result was disastrous but still could have been much worse if the event had happened further from shore in deeper water, or with more people on board.

4.3.5. Alternatives to control risks

Although there are quite a number of possible alternatives, these can be reduced to a limited number of categories. After identifying and evaluating the risks, there are basically only two things you can do with a risk: (i) eliminate it or (ii) live with it.

Elimination of risk is relevant when it is considered too large or not fitting within a particular organization or company. One of the most effective solutions, when possible, is to eliminate the risk in completely. For example, not using a particular process to produce the product or not produce the product at all. Not using certain dangerous substances, not exporting to a particular country or not building in a flood- or earthquake prone area.

Another possibility may be to transfer risk to other parties that may be better equipped to handle them. Examples are to have third parties perform hazardous operations such as: paint spraying, demolition, working on high voltage or high pressure systems, etc. When transferring risks this way, keep in mind that this may introduce other risks, including possible loss of the supplier of the service. Or you can (try to) contractually transfer possible liabilities arising from certain risks to third parties via a so-called "hold harmless" (waiver of liability) agreement.

Often, risks cannot be eliminated or you do not want them eliminated as the acceptance of risks also has positive sides. You cannot go skiing without the risk of breaking a leg. You cannot ride a horse without the risk of falling off it. You cannot drive a car without the risk of collision. Most cars cannot run without (flammable) fuel produced by refineries that also create jobs. And so on.

There are many risks we need to accept because we cannot live without them. We can, however, reduce the frequency of unwanted events by taking measures that (may) prevent some or most of them from occurring. We can provide efficient first aid and emergency services to reduce the consequences of unwanted events when they occur despite the preventive measures taken. Normally, we do both: reduce the occurrence of the event and limit its consequences; sometimes consciously and well planned and sometimes not so consciously and structured and then we may suffer from more losses than really necessary.

If risks cannot be eliminated or transferred, the remaining possibilities should be directed at bringing the risk down to an acceptable level. One can attempt to minimize the risk by, for example, the replacement of a flammable liquid for cleaning metal parts by an agent which is non-flammable, or at least less flammable.

If elimination is not our choice, the possible alternatives available are:

- Reducing the frequency of the unwanted event with the focus on prevention
- Reducing the possible consequences of the event – with the focus on loss mitigation

Event prevention

The reduction of the frequency of the unwanted event directs attention to the causes of unwanted events.

In the cause – consequence sequence picture below we see three levels of causes: (i) direct causes, (ii) basic causes and (iii) the management system.

Limiting the frequency of the event may include taking measures such as: choice of production method, selection and placement of personnel, criteria for procurement of services and goods; criteria for design of installations, work environment and machinery; management of change; training of managers, staff and other personnel; work procedures; inspections/maintenance; and so on.

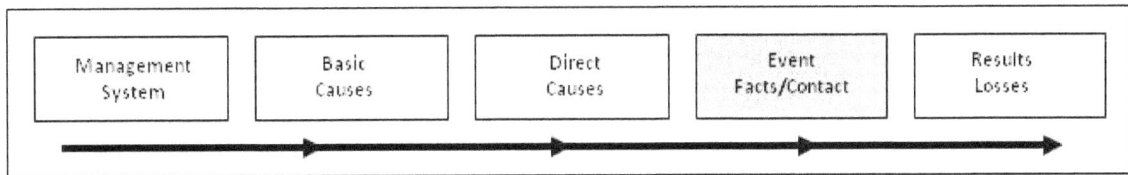

Management System	Basic Causes	Direct Causes	Event Facts/Contact	Results Losses

Loss reduction

Unfortunately even with the best possible prevention, the unwanted event may still occur as related risks have not been eliminated.

Reduction of consequences includes all measures taken to limit the results of the event when it takes place: emergency organization providing first aid to possible victims as well as fire fighting facilities, installation of smoke detection and sprinklers. But also a post event or post emergency plan (PEP) to bring the situation back to normal as quickly as possible and limit the possible loss of customers and market share.

Also included in this category are those measures taken to reduce liability claims, for example those which could arise from malfunctioning products. Measures would include knowing what to do to inform the market about possible product defects, including recall of the product.

Following the measures taken in these two categories – prevention and reduction - the one thing left to do is to take care of proper loss funding. So that the losses that occur can be compensated to make sure that the financial consequences will not force the company or organization out of business. There are a few basic possibilities for loss funding that will briefly be explained later.

4.3.6. Selection of best measures

Normally, there will not be one best measure and a combination of measures will be selected that is assumed to bring the best results for the resources invested.

For example, with regard to the possible loss of a production unit by fire:

- Choice of non-combustible, or less combustible materials for building structures, furnishings, packaging materials etc. through design and procurement
- Installation of fire/smoke detection and/or other alarm systems
- Installation of adequate fire protection means, including sprinklers
- Selection of qualified personnel
- Internal training of personnel to properly carry out "critical" jobs
- An inspection program to early detect and correct undesirable situations that could cause a fire

- Emergency plan including:
  - Procedures to alarm public emergency services
  - Private emergency services
- Agreement with business colleagues to allow continuation of market supply
- Insurance, with or without deductible, to finance property damage and business interruption losses caused by the fire

Or with regard to the prevention or reduction of product related losses:

- Research concerning product application by customers and end users
- Development of appropriate product specifications
- Establish corresponding purchasing criteria
- Selection of qualified personnel
- Preparation of proper work procedures
- Selection of appropriate quality controls and purchase of test equipment
- Design and installation of appropriate production equipment/processes
- Training of production, maintenance, quality control personnel
- Packaging and instructions for use of product
- Adequate storage facilities on- and off location and proper transport
- Preparation of marketing and sales materials
- Proper training of sales people
- Training of service personnel
- System for handling complaints, incidents, etc.
- Customer registration for possible product recall
- Product identification for possible recall of product
- Product safety committee to coordinate product life cycle events
- Insurance to cover cost of possible recall of the product
- Insurance, with or without deductible, to cover liability

Obviously, the lists of possible measures for these two cases are examples and not exhaustive.

4.3.7. Implementation of selected measures

Once selected from the range of possible alternatives, the measures should be implemented to obtain desired results. Implementation shall include periodical assessment to see if measures are done as intended and if expected results are being obtained. In the beginning these assessments should be more frequently, say every one to three months. Once the results have been obtained, the frequency could be reduced to once per 6 months or once per year to maintain the level of performance and to make sure that the implemented risk management activities remain up-to-date in relation with technical, commercial and social developments. Of course, the assessment frequency depends also on the criticality of the measures and the possible risk of deviations from "safe-to-operate".

Assessing measures taken

Purpose of this assessment is to see if the selected measures are executed as intended. To answer questions such as:

- Are inspection programs properly implemented?
- Has training been done as planned?
- Are criteria for personnel selection properly used?
- Are work procedures prepared and followed?
- Is the emergency response organization at the level required?
- Are sprinklers properly maintained?
- Are product complaints properly investigated?
- Is adequate insurance coverage in force?

This assessment, and any corrective actions that may follow, is very important. This is at the heart of good (risk) management. Without proper execution of planned measures the desired results cannot be expected. Assuming of course that the measures selected were the right ones.

Evaluation of results

The objective of the risk management plan or "system", including the selected alternatives for control risks/losses, is to make sure that damage, malfunctions, accidents, complaints etc. remain at an acceptable level. If that is not the case, it may be necessary to alter or adjust actions already taken or to look for other alternatives to reach desired objectives. This could, for example, mean that the inspection frequency should be increased, or work procedures be adjusted.

But be aware: a low accident frequency is not necessarily an indication that everything is under control. In industries with high capital investment and a high degree of automation, such as the process industry, a low accident frequency (possibly based on lost time injury accidents only) may not be a good indicator for the "safety" or "control of risk" level of the organization.

For example: someone not wearing fall protection when working at heights may not fall from the scaffold for many years, if ever. If that person will get some sort of reward for not having accidents, undesired behavior is not only allowed, it is also stimulated. This example is one indication that the traditional way of measuring safety may not be sufficient.

The above example reminds me of a presentation I gave on April 9, 1990 to the Public Relation Group of a process industry association in The Netherlands. The title of my presentation was "PRG or PRC". PRG meaning for "Public Relation Gratis", the free attention that the industry would get whenever there is a major accident, fatalities or environmental pollution. Free but negative, not really what the industry should be looking for, but often practice by lack of PRC meaning: "Positive Risk Communication" to let society know what is being done to prevent and control the occurrence of unwanted events. The ISRS – International Safety Rating System – which I was using at that time could have been the instrument to show the level of control. I don't think that my presentation changed much or anything; the industry just kept on measuring their safety level by communicating the number of lost time injuries per million hours worked. Is a low injury level – possibly representing slip, trip and fall accidents – really a good indicator of the safety level in high hazardous industry?

> If everything appears to be going well, you obviously overlooked something.

If you do use the evaluation of management system efforts and results, do not only look at those of the entire system, also look at the individual efforts and results of the system elements. That would provide you with a lot more information and which may be important in case the total system results are less than expected.

4.3.8. Learning from what goes wrong

Unfortunately we are usually not able to build systems, organizations in such way that they will function without errors, mishaps, accidents, damages and such. "Failures" therefore will occur and continue to occur. It is important that unwanted events, of which we often become aware through their visual consequences or losses, are reported and analyzed to take measures to prevent recurrence of the same, or similar, events and to avoid further loss. Important is the way reporting and analysis of losses is structured and known in the organization. More about that later.

Better than waiting for the visible losses is to implement an Abnormal Situation Management system. Such system is focused on determining precursors of unwanted events, deviations from normal (= safe-to-operate). So that actions can be taken to bring the situation back to normal before resulting in unwanted events and their consequences. ASM systems or activities can be technically complex depending on the type of industry but in its most simple form, a slippery floor is also a sign of an accident waiting to happen. Inspections and observations are part of ASM; basically anything that is directed at preventing the unwanted event from occurring. More sophisticated ASM activities may be required in those cases where unwanted events really must be prevented because of their possible consequences.

4.3.9. Some further remarks

A basic ingredient of risk management is the risk awareness of people. Of everyone in the organization but in the first place the risk awareness and -attitude of top management. It should not be expressed in slogans like "safety first" but through the structure of the risk management system, it's composing elements and activities. Activities that are measurable and therefore: manageable.

The risk management process as described in this chapter can be also displayed as in picture 4.7 using a tree-like structure. Starting point in picture 4.7 is risk, the potential for unwanted events that may result in injury, property damage or other type of loss. Risks may or may not be identified and evaluated. If they are not, this may be due to identification and evaluation methodologies not being 100%. Or because the risk did not exist at the time we carried out the identification/evaluation. Both aspects are reasons to include risk identification and evaluation on a more permanent basis as part of activities such as purchasing, design, inspections, work procedure evaluation, hazard reporting, reporting and processing of unwanted events, etcetera.

Once the risk is known, qualitatively and quantitatively, we can basically do two things: (1) eliminate it or (ii) live with it. Elimination can be done in an absolute sense or the risk can somehow be transferred to third parties.

As said before: if we are not able or willing to eliminate or transfer the risk we will generally: (i) seek to reduce the frequency of unwanted events by removing (some of the) underlying causes and/or (ii) limit their consequences should the event occur anyway. Apart from that, we should ensure adequate funding/insurance to compensate for the (financial) loss.

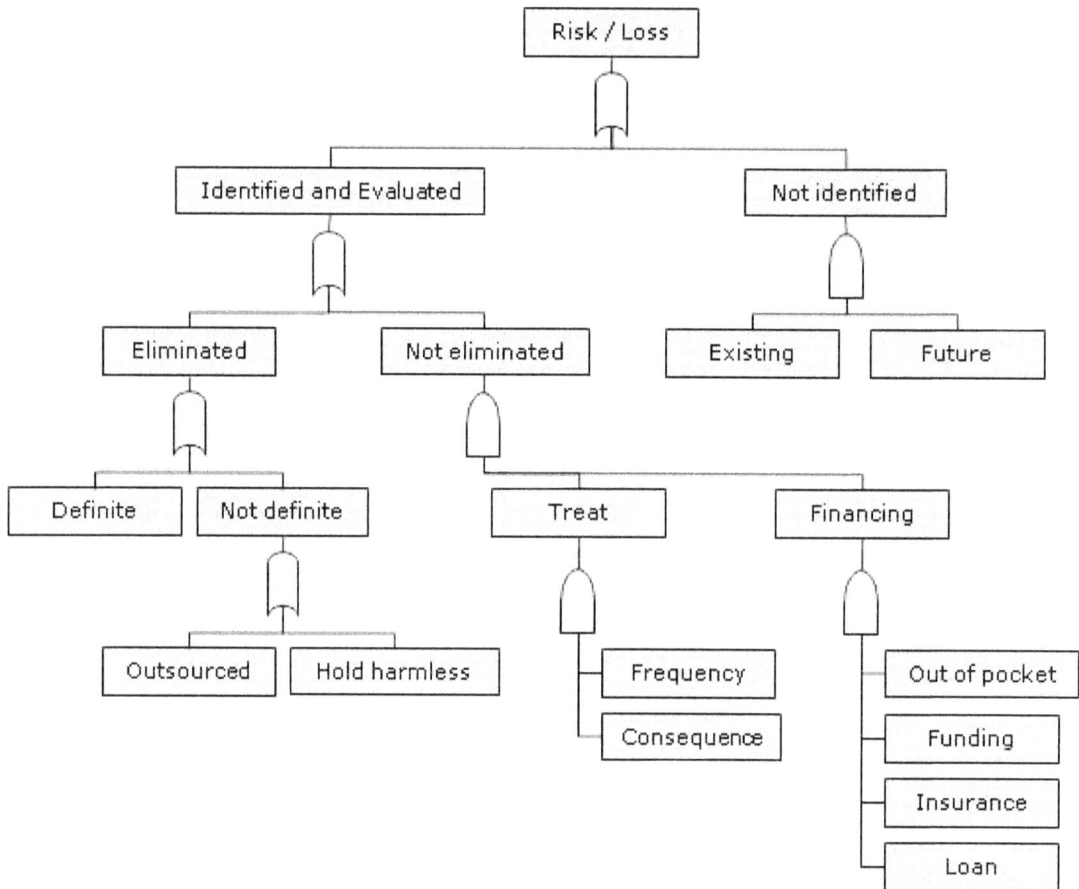

Picture 4.7 - Schematic presentation of the risk management process

Please note that others may use terminology that differs a bit from what I use above. In Risk Management/insurance land, it is not uncommon to use the following terms in relation to risks, after risks have been identified:

- Treat – take action to reduce the risk, reducing the frequency of events and limiting possible consequences
- Tolerate – accept the risk and its consequences, self insure (captive insurance or funding); decide to cover any losses "out of pocket". Risks that have not been identified also come into this category as being tolerated without knowing of them.
- Transfer - decide to pass on the risk to a party outside the organization, contract out the risk or take out insurance to cover the costs of event consequences.
- Terminate - decide to eliminate the risk by not starting an activity or discontinuing an existing one; not producing a certain product or not entering a particular market.

Since we will normally have many risks that we cannot or will not eliminate, the practice of risk management will often include (i) treating the risk (including reduction of event frequency and limitation of extent of loss) and (ii) ensuring proper financing.

Picture 4.8 shows that risk management basically consists of two main areas:

- Control of risks/losses
- Risk financing

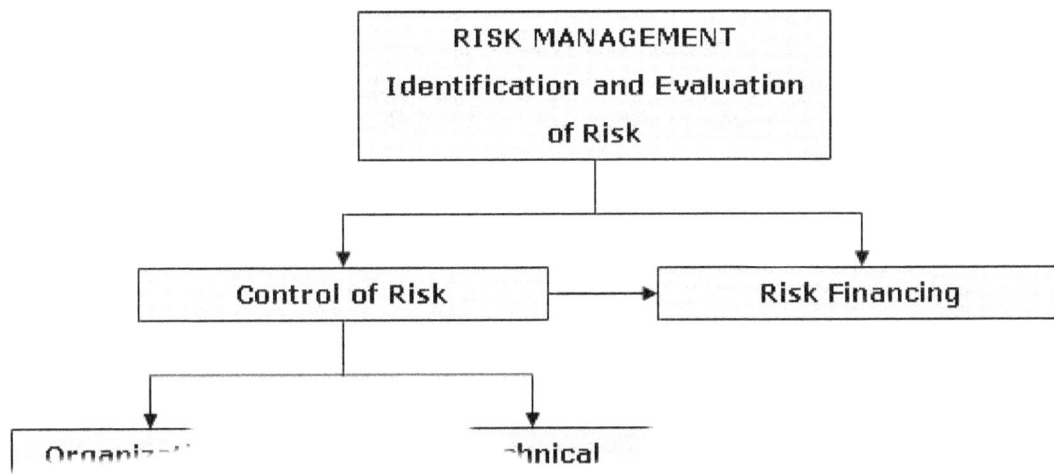

```
            ┌─────────────────────────────┐
            │      RISK MANAGEMENT         │
            │  Identification and Evaluation│
            │           of Risk            │
            └─────────────────────────────┘
                         │
          ┌──────────────┴──────────────┐
          ▼                             ▼
   ┌──────────────┐            ┌──────────────┐
   │ Control of Risk │────────▶│ Risk Financing │
   └──────────────┘            └──────────────┘
          │
   ┌──────┴──────┐
   ▼             ▼
 Organiz...     ...hnical
```

Picture 4.8 - Risk Management practice, a combination of loss control and risk financing

The method of risk financing will generally – and often to a large extent - depend on the measures taken to control the risks. Sometimes adequate (i.e. economically acceptable) risk financing cannot be obtained without a certain minimum level of control (e.g. fire insurance necessitating in-rack sprinklers in case of high rack storage or product liability insurance requiring proper recall procedures).

Control of risk/loss is central to the risk management process and will receive most attention in this book. In the not so distant past, however, much of the literature on risk management was directed at risk financing and in particularly at insurance as one of the main risk financing methods. This brought much of the risk management attention within the walls of the company insurance office. This view is not correct: risk management should be practiced at every all level of the organization and be part of every function; in decision-making and execution of work.

ISO 31000 (2009) "Risk management — Principles and guidelines" confirms my thoughts when stating:

- Risk management creates and protects value.
  - Risk management contributes to the demonstrable achievement of objectives and improvement of performance in, for example, human health and safety, security, legal and regulatory compliance, public acceptance, environmental protection, product quality, project management, efficiency in operations, governance and reputation.
- Risk management is an integral part of all organizational processes.
  - Risk management is not a stand-alone activity that is separate from the main activities and processes of the organization. Risk management is part of the responsibilities of management and an integral part of all organizational processes, including strategic planning and all project and change management processes.
- Risk management is part of decision making.
  - Risk management helps decision makers make informed choices, prioritize actions and distinguish among alternative courses of action.

In its introduction ISO 31000 (2009) provides a broader base when stating:

When implemented and maintained in accordance with this International Standard, the management of risk enables an organization to, for example:

- Increase the likelihood of achieving objectives
- Encourage proactive management
- Be aware of the need to identify and treat risk throughout the organization
- Improve the identification of opportunities and threats
- Comply with relevant legal and regulatory requirements and international norms
- Improve mandatory and voluntary reporting
- Improve governance
- Improve stakeholder confidence and trust
- Establish a reliable basis for decision making and planning
- Improve controls
- Effectively allocate and use resources for risk treatment
- Improve operational effectiveness and efficiency
- Enhance health and safety performance, as well as environmental protection
- Improve loss prevention and incident management
- Minimize losses
- Improve organizational learning, and
- Improve organizational resilience

If we have not eliminated the risk then we accept the probability that it will materialize in the future, even when chances are very small. The only thing we do not know is when the event will occur and under which conditions. This may be "favorable" like when the warehouse is almost empty but also unfavorable, e.g. a fire in a storage of skates, shortly before winter. We may, in addition to loss prevention and reduction, ensure adequate risk financing so that the financial consequences are covered, at least to some extent. To some extent, because not all consequences may be covered, such as market loss due to temporary shutdown of production units possibly due to fire or loss of a crucial supplier. It is also possible that the total loss is (much) greater than the amount paid by the insurer. In particular, this may happen in case of negative publicity following product defects, - accidents or -recall. In those cases, the damage may be enormous while the compensation under the product liability insurance policy may be relatively small.

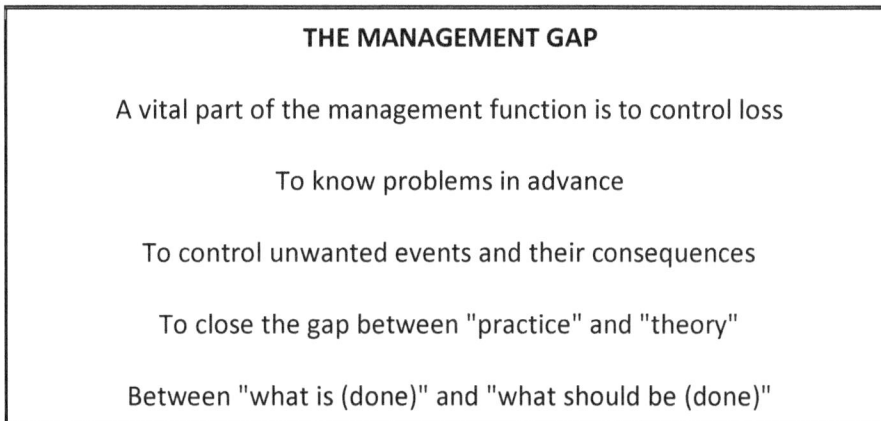

THE MANAGEMENT GAP

A vital part of the management function is to control loss

To know problems in advance

To control unwanted events and their consequences

To close the gap between "practice" and "theory"

Between "what is (done)" and "what should be (done)"

4.4. Risk financing

Within the framework of risk financing there are many alternatives. These, however, can be divided into a limited number of main categories which will be briefly mentioned below. Combination of two or more of those categories will provide a wider range of risk financing alternatives. Keep in mind that when I mention financing of risks, I mean: financing future and present losses - risk equals future loss, today's losses are the risks of the past.

4.4.1. Out of pocket

This means that losses will be paid from current resources, the money that is readily available when losses occur. Many losses are financed this way, including the losses considered "accepted" under headings such as maintenance/repair. Losses up to the deductible level of insurance coverage are also paid out of pocket. The total upper limit of the losses financed from liquid resources will depend on the financial position of the organization and the (annual) total amount of loss that management is prepared to accept to lose this way.

The process to decide what risks should be paid out of pocket is normally done coming from the other end: determining which risks should be funded in one form or another and what is left is automatically financed from available resources. These resources then should be sufficient to cover losses at the time they occur. If that is not the case, money should be obtained from other sources. For example by borrowing from third parties or issuing shares - to not endanger the continuity of the organization. If the money cannot be obtained that way, the company may go bankrupt. In principle, out-of-pocket financing is suitable only for smaller risks/losses that occur with a known frequency.

The fact that losses can be financed from liquid resources does not mean that they are not important. These losses, probably not serious individually, may add up to have a significant influence on operating results. It is therefore essential that these losses are reported and recorded through an adequate information system and further processed as needed. The total amount of loss that is "accepted" this way may be an indication of the quality of the efforts to control unwanted events in particular and of management in a more general sense. And do not forget that actual small losses could be considerably larger if circumstances would deviate from normal.

Often, companies may not really know what the annual total amount of those "smaller" losses is. My experience is that organizations may not have a system to properly identify these losses that are often buried under of maintenance costs, repair, material issuance, overwork etc.

4.4.2. Funding

Risk/loss financing from liquid resources - "out-of-pocket" - has the disadvantage that there may not be sufficient money available at the time the loss occurs. To prevent that and to meet the "just in case" financial requirements, a decision could be made to periodically reserve a certain amount to finance possible future losses. For example: each month a certain amount may be put aside hoping that there will be enough in the fund when the loss occurs. Normally, this method of financing is only suitable for risks that are known with a high degree of accuracy where it concerns event frequency and consequence. If that is the case, this method of risk financing may, for example, be acceptable for payment of medical expenses with a negotiated deductible as part of group coverage with an upper limit and the excess above that covered by commercial insurance. Normally this financing will not be suitable to cover fire and extended perils losses.

In the latter case the damage may be extensive and chances that there is not enough money in the fund may be very real. Only a company with a large number of separate units or locations – such as a major supermarket chain - could decide to finance the fire risk this way. In that case all units will contribute their share into the fund. Adequate spread of risk (large number of separate locations) will make it unlikely that there will be more than only a limited number of units claiming losses from the fund within any period of time. It is also very likely that the head office will require its locations to meet certain minimum risk control requirements such as sprinklers. In this case a form of financing is introduced in which many (units of the same company) periodically pay an amount – the "premium"- into the fund from which to pay losses suffered by individual locations. Selecting this way of funding for future losses depends on the specifics of the company, including its financial capacity. For some companies, this could be the preferred type of funding up to a certain risk/loss level while adding commercial insurance coverage above that. You will note that this type of financing resembles what we would normally call "insurance" where many pay the premium for the loss of some.

In-house funding by reserving for future losses on the balance sheet may only be possible up to a certain limit. Tax authorities will undoubtedly look very critical if the funds for that purpose are excluded from the taxable business results.

A special form of funding can be obtained by setting up a so-called "captive". A captive is an insurance company normally established by a larger company and with only one customer: its own parent. The fund is transferred to the captive while the management of the captive, in principle, remains in the hands of the parent company. Management of the captive insurer can also be put in the hands of a third party and often that distance ("management at arm's length") is desired or necessary, in particular versus the tax authorities to demonstrate that this is a regular structure and not just another method to evade taxation. Captive insurance companies, more often than not, are registered/located in a tax haven, places like: Gibraltar, Mauritius, Belize, Bermuda, The Cayman Islands, Guernsey, Luxembourg and others. Once such a captive insurance company is founded, it can also accept third party insurance. The captive insurance company then has the character of a professional insurer able to accept risk from other parties. Some of the larger insurance companies that we know today were created this way. To limit the loss to the captive insurance company, reinsurance may be sought so the captive will be liable up to a certain level and beyond that the risk will be carried by professional reinsurers.

4.4.3. Insurance

Traditionally the most common way of risk financing is insurance. The underlying principle here is the common interest of many. The mechanism of insurance is really very similar to that of funding: (relatively) small amounts of money (the "premium") are put in a fund which is now owned and managed by a professional insurer. This way, each policyholder purchases a high degree of certainty for future possible losses at a relatively low price.

Several insurance companies were established covering risks of companies belonging to the same type of industry and requiring preventive measures that are common in that type of industry. Some of the largest insurers (the "Mutuals") started that way. Mutual insurance companies are owned by their policyholders in contrast to stock insurance companies that are owned by shareholders and cover risks of organizations or people that have no common interest other than their needs to cover their risks and future losses.

Some insurance companies offer coverage at very low rates based upon extensive protection requirements and a high degree of management commitment to control loss. One of the best known companies in the category of "Highly Protected Risk (HPR)" is the Factory Mutual Company.

Independent of the type of insurance company, the advantage is that uncertainty is transformed into budgetary certainty. Part of the premium is used by the insurance company to cover cost of operation and the remainder is used to pay out claims for losses sustained by policyholders and to invest to generate extra income. Profit is made when the total of operating costs plus claims paid amount to less than the sum of premiums earned plus investment income.

To reduce the premium one may chose different combinations of coverage including a (high) deductible with an aggregate maximum amount to be paid in case of loss and, above that, regular insurance. Or spreading risks across different insurers, possibly by "layering" in which case each insurer will be responsible for paying losses within established lower and upper margins.

4.4.4. The loan

If there is no, or insufficient, insurance coverage at the time of the loss and no other funds available, one way to obtain money might be to interest third parties to provide the necessary finances. Capital can be obtained in various ways, by issuing shares or by getting a loan.

With this type of financing, one should bear in mind that the willingness to make money available will decrease when there are fewer certainties for people to obtain a sufficient return on their investment. Issuing shares or borrowing money to rebuild a company that just burned down may not be that easy; therefore, this method of financing will only be selected in extreme situations when no other possibilities exist.

4.4.5. Combination of alternatives

In practice, a mix of financing possibilities will exist ranging from out-of-pocket payment of smaller losses and within the deductible to regular insurance in one form or the other.

Risk management measures taken will always include a combination of loss control activities and risk financing. Such as precautionary measures to prevent the event and its consequences from happening (fire, liability, damage, etc.), measures to reduce the extent of loss or harm (sprinklers, fire brigade, product identification and recall procedure for products, etc.) and risk financing consisting of one of the above mentioned methods or a combination thereof.

The possibilities for risk financing can significantly depend on the measures taken to prevent the incident and limit potential loss. In the past this, otherwise very logical, principle did not always apply due to the high return on investments which could be obtained by insurers. This was why insurers could compensate a "technical" loss (paying more in damages and costs than premium received) by investing premium on the stock market or otherwise. In that situation preventive measures were not, or very little, rewarded and little incentive was offered by insurance companies to control risk. This situation also allowed deterioration of the quality of the underwriting function within insurance companies – anything and everything was good as long as enough premium was generated to be invested.

The situation of high return on investments does no longer exist today in a market where interest rates are low and investment in stock less reliable. Thus it is expected that more emphasis is and will be placed on prevention and control of risks/loss, opening the gateway to greater professionalism in risk management.

> **Peter Drucker**
>
> The first duty of management is to survive and the guiding principle of business economics is not the maximization of profit – it is the avoidance of loss
> - ooo-
> In case of keen competition and low profit margins, learning from accidents can contribute more to profits than an organization's best salesperson

Peter Drucker (1909 – 2005) – management consultant, educator and author

5.   CONTROL OF LOSS

5.1. Introduction

Loss control management basically has to do with the control of all losses such as, but not limited to:

- Product (safety) accidents
- Criminal acts
- Damage to property, buildings, installations
- Environmental damage
- Loss of key personnel
- Personal injury, fatalities
- Loss of information, knowledge, expertise
- Damage to company image
- Liability claims, product, contractual
- Delivery problems
- Loss or disappearing of goods
- Loss of customers
- Loss of market
- Personnel turnover
- Production delays
- Quality problems
- Waste

It is beyond the scope of this book - and my competence – to discuss all different losses in any detail. However, further on, we will see that these seemingly different losses are, to a large extent, coming from the same or similar "root" causes. Coping with the underlying problems of a specific loss type may also offer opportunities to address the causes of a number of other losses at the same time. When further describing loss control management a generic approach will be suggested. That approach comes from my safety related experience and background but it should not be that difficult to translate this to other business areas where control of unwanted events is desired.

The principle of multiple causes

Accidents and other loss producing events are seldom, if ever, the result of a single cause

---

The generic approach offers aspects that can also be used as a basis for areas of business such as quality, cost control, environmental, etc. In the end, all these areas will include reaching objectives and controlling unwanted events, analyzing causes and solving related problems.

The principle of multiple consequences

More often than not will a single cause result in multiple consequences

---

As mentioned earlier, control of unwanted events is at the heart of risk management. Preventing such events is normally preferred to limiting the (potential) consequences that may result from the event. This is especially so because the actual loss can often not be determined in advance and the reason for this is that the consequences of an event may largely depend on the circumstances that exist when the event takes place.

In the remainder of this book I will mainly discuss subjects related to:

- Prevention of unwanted events and their consequences
- Learning from what caused those events so we can take measures to prevent the same or similar from happening again

First I will discuss a more general concept regarding the causes of these undesirable events and after that I will go into some more detail that may help you to set up a risk/loss control management system. I trust that you will be able to relate these more generic concepts to the specific situation of your organization and your discipline. Given my background, I will look at various issues from a safety management point of view but the concepts are generic and it should not be too difficult to adapt those to your area of concern and expertise.

Risk (or loss control) management is not new and the generic approach to control risk or loss is, in principle, not difficult and has been part of the business world for decennia. Sometimes as "safety" developing from a narrow scope – directed at injury type related accidents only – in the past to a much broader approach to include all the unwanted events that you want to include. There is no basic difference between learning from an injury and learning from any other unwanted event. Controlling loss always takes place, one way or another. The same could be said of risk financing, also nothing new. What could be "new", depending on the specific situation of your organization, could be the more conscious and focused attention to the control of risk/loss through a structured management system. Doing it unstructured, haphazardly does not work. Notice the word "hazard" in haphazardly meaning danger, risk; unstructured means taking chances, like playing Russian roulette.

5.2. Cause – consequence sequence

Controlling unwanted events means controlling the causes that lead to the events. When we control causes, we control events and, at least to some extent, the consequences that they may have. The cause-consequence model, including steps or "phases" that lead to events and their consequences is shown in picture 5.1.

The model was originally developed by W.H. Heinrich during the thirties of last century. At that time "Management System" was labeled "Ancestry - Social Environment" while "Basic Causes" was called "Fault of Person". Not something you could manage very well in an organization.

In the sixties of last century, Frank E. Bird Jr. renamed the phases to suggest the relation between the unwanted event and its consequences on the right and the Management System on the left via direct- and basic causes. Mr. Bird showed the way by making the sequence a manageable and controllable matter.

Bird cause-consequence model

"Central" to this sequence is the (unwanted) event which you may also want to call "incident". The event is between causes and consequences. Between what caused the event to happen and what and how large the consequences are, or could be. As already said, the actual consequences of the event will depend on the circumstances that exist at the time of occurrence and these circumstances often cannot be predicted or controlled. The consequences may therefore vary from nothing (the "near miss" or "close-call"') to catastrophic and can relate to people, machines, materials, environment, product, etc. The results of unwanted events could mean reduced profitability, human suffering, multiple fatalities or bankruptcy.

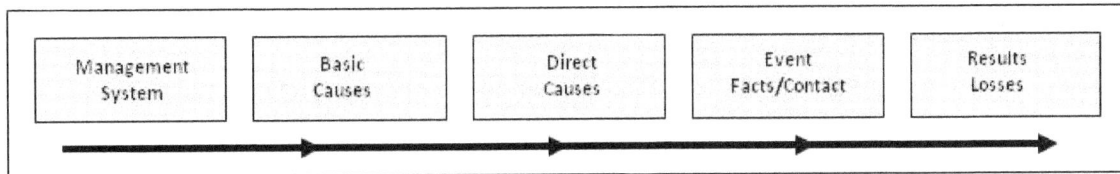

| Management System | Basic Causes | Direct Causes | Event Facts/Contact | Results Losses |

Picture 5.1 – Simple Cause - consequence model

The model above is a simplified reflection of the real life situation but powerful for communication purposes: it relates the management system to the event and the results thereof, either good or bad, depending on the quality of each link in the system. It indicates three cause levels:

- Direct causes
- Basic causes
- Management system

The model shown above can be negative as well as positive. It is negative when the outcome is negative, a loss, and the event then is an unwanted event; coming from "substandard" performance in (one or more of) the three phases to the left of the event. Ultimately, the unwanted event/consequence is related to "failure" of the management system. The model is positive when the outcome is positive coming from desired events and ultimately coming from a "perfect" management system. Both aspects – negative and positive – are always together and to arrive at a positive sequence at all times will normally be utopia. Remember that, while I will refer mostly to the negative side of the model, the model also underlines the role that the management system plays in obtaining the best results with minimal losses.

The Bird/Heinrich model or "domino" model assumes that if one of the dominoes to the left side of the event falls it will trigger the sequence leading to the losses at the right. If you think that this means that taking out one domino, or prevent it from falling, would mean that the losses at the end would not happen, then remember that the model is only a simplification of real life. The dominoes are not separated, they overlap. In all phases, people make things work – or not. Fallible human beings we are. No losses at all times would mean that each domino or phase of the sequence would have to be perfect and remain perfect for the duration of an undertaking.

This model, showing the importance of the management system, is widely accepted in business including such areas as safety, quality, environment and, of course: cost control.

A 3 dimensional cause-consequence model is shown in picture 5.2 and is an extension to show the complexity that may not be realized when looking at the 2 dimensional model above.

In principle both models are the same and both seem to indicate that the unwanted event is caused by "direct causes" – such as an act of a person – directly preceding the event. However, while those direct causes may have triggered the event, it should be remembered that there often are other people - more "upstream" in the organization and further away from the event – that may have had their share in creating those direct causes.

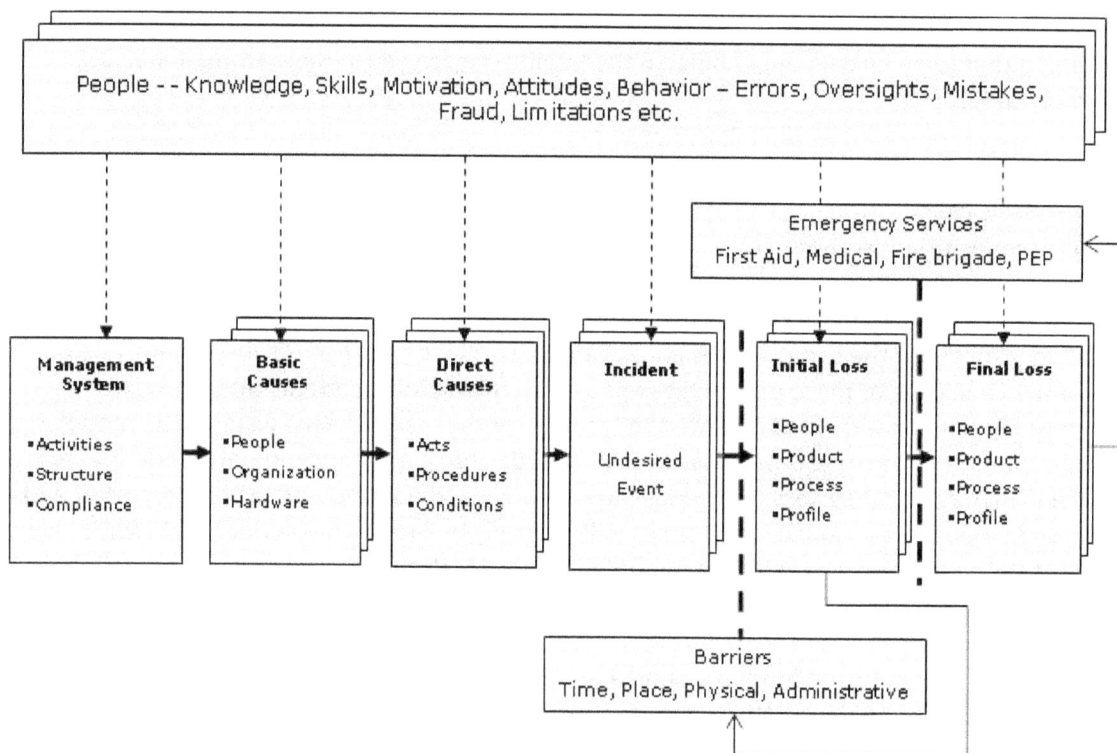

Picture 5.2 - Extended Cause – Consequence model

The text on the dominoes is a little different compared with the 2-D model but, without any further explanation, I think you get the idea about the complexity that unwanted event causation models can have.

I included the "barrier concept" between the event and the initial loss. The barrier concept, used in the area of safety/risk management, refers to using barriers to limit the impact of energy exchange between energy source and the body or object. Simple example: a hard hat to limit the effect of bumping into a low hanging beam.

Barriers preventing or limiting loss include:

- Physical barriers, walls, shields
- Place related barriers, separating energy source and body or object in place
- Time related barriers, separating energy source and body or object in time
- Administrative barriers, procedures, work instructions
- (Personal) protective equipment

I also considered that the final loss will depend on the actions taken to reduce loss and added the emergency services and the Post Event or Post Emergency Plan (PEP) intended to get the operation back to normal as soon as possible.

I made a difference between the initial loss and the final loss after I was involved in reviewing an accident that took place in Indonesia, long time ago. This accident concerned an employee of a mining company falling down a shaft when climbing down a ladder. While this already was a bad injury initially, the person died in the hospital where he arrived one day after the accident took place. The difference between the initial loss and the final loss is depending on the speed and adequacy of the emergency services and if the actions to bring the situation back to normal are less effective the consequences of an unwanted event would normally be more extensive. This is also a reason to evaluate emergency services and actions in each loss case.

Please note that I only have one management system at the far left. Obviously there could be more than one - not preferable but often practice following various certification processes, legislative requirements and customer demands.

The extent of the consequences of an unwanted event depends on the actions taken to reduce loss. Issues that play a role include the (timely) availability of adequate resources: (i) e.g. sprinklers or fire trucks to fight fire, hospitals for treatment of victims and (ii) people with their expertise and experience in disaster management. This should all be included in an effective action plan to cope with possible emergencies. And do not forget the actions to get back to normal operations as quickly as possible to provide the market with services and products and to limit business interruption and potential loss of customers and market share.

Loss occurrences, how disastrous they may be, provide opportunities to investigate and analyze what took place and why and why the consequences are what they are. The consequences are pictured to the right of the incident or undesired event and the final loss depends on the barriers in place and the actions taken to limit loss. When carrying out an accident investigation do not limit yourselves to finding what caused the event but also look at the extent of the consequences to take measures to limit future loss should the same or a similar event happen again.

Preventing the undesired event should normally be given priority over limiting the consequences as we cannot normally predict the actual consequences which will depend on the circumstances that exist when the event happens.

On the left side of the undesirable event we see why the event took place:

- Direct causes
- Basic causes
- Management system - activities, structure and compliance

The direct causes are often divided in:

- (Substandard) acts
- (Substandard) conditions.

Traditionally these acts and conditions were referred to as "unsafe". However, and in line with today's concepts of safety, loss control, risk management and quality, is may be better to call these acts and conditions "substandard" or "less than adequate". This indicates that there should be a correct or "standard" or right way of doing things and proper or "standard" conditions or work environment such that work can be carried out without unwanted events.

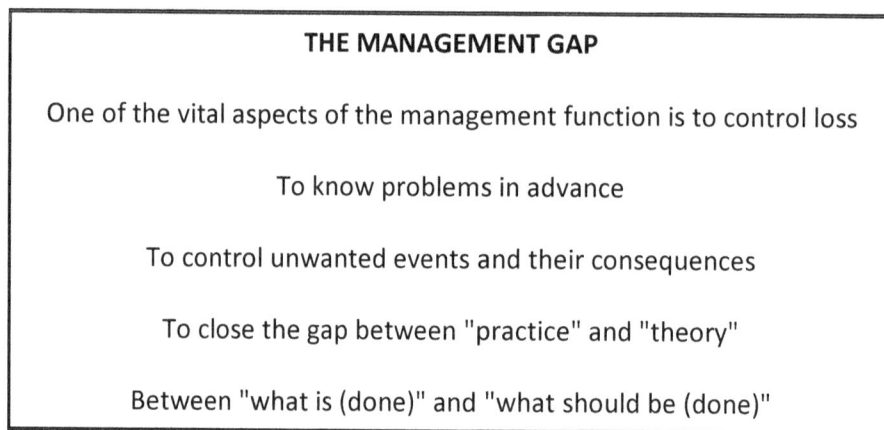

THE MANAGEMENT GAP

One of the vital aspects of the management function is to control loss

To know problems in advance

To control unwanted events and their consequences

To close the gap between "practice" and "theory"

Between "what is (done)" and "what should be (done)"

In the safety world, these substandard acts and conditions are traditionally divided as shown in picture 5.3.

```
Substandard Acts

    •  using of defective equipment
    •  improper use of otherwise safe equipment
    •  servicing equipment in operation
    •  not following proper work instructions or rules
    •  not using or improper use of protective equipment
    •  not using proper equipment
    •  improper loading or stacking
    •  improper placement
    •  improper lifting
    •  taking up improper position for task
    •  games/horseplay
    •  attention distracted

Substandard Conditions

    •  improper guards or barriers
    •  no or inadequate or personal protection
    •  defective tools, equipment or materials
    •  proper tools not available
    •  congestion / restricted action
    •  lack of adequate housekeeping
    •  inadequate warning systems
    •  fire or explosion hazards
```

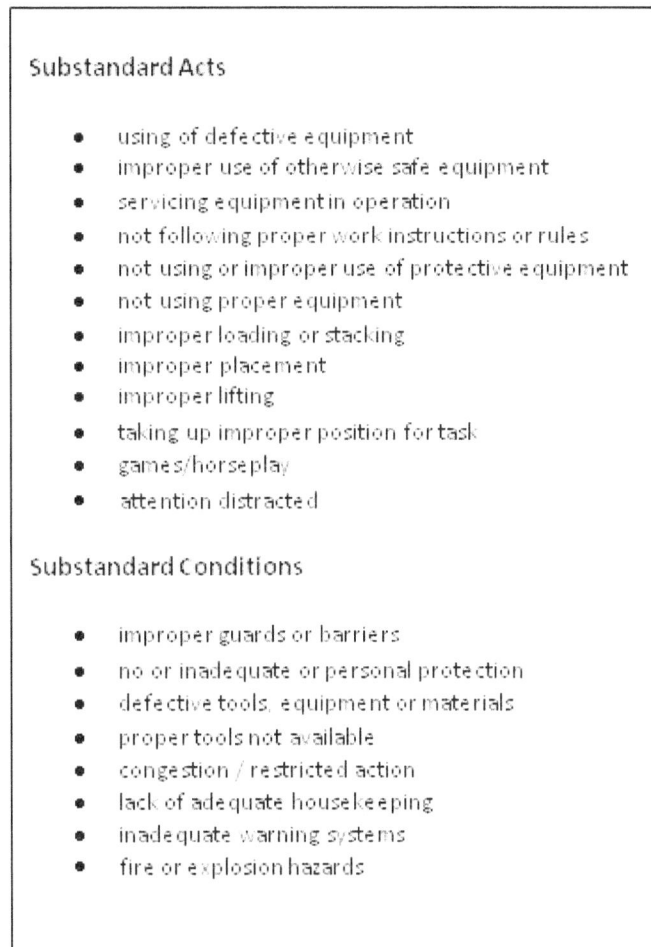

Picture 5.3 - Safety related direct causes: substandard acts and conditions

Traditionally, when referring to substandard acts, this meant the act of the person who is directly involved in the occurrence of the undesirable event - often the victim. However, it is more than quite possible that a substandard act of someone else during an earlier stage of the causation model has contributed to the unwanted event, including the creation of a substandard condition. For example, purchasing materials, tools or equipment may have created a substandard condition that may be involved in an unwanted event later on. Design of installations and the working environment is another activity that could have contributed to the existence of substandard conditions. So the substandard acts may have been by the purchaser or designer. Improper compliance with the Management of Change procedure may be a contributing factor and so would be inadequate training of people to properly carry out the work; safe and without undue unwanted events. Inadequate management or supervision allowing substandard acts and conditions to exist are other important aspects as well as improper or outdated work procedures. So when looking at those direct causes, keep in mind they may have been created or allowed by people further "upstream" in the process (to the left of the model and closer to the management system). Non-existence of a management system, inadequate contents or structure and non-compliance for whatever reason may very well be the real source from which substandard acts and conditions originate.

The principle of multiple causes

Accidents and other loss producing events are seldom, if ever, the result of a single cause

According to the cause – consequence model, the substandard acts and conditions come from the existence of basic causes, consisting of:

- Person related factors
- Job related factors.

The first category is linked to people, while the second category mainly refers to the work environment although, in the end, both aspects depend on, or are, created by people. Picture 5.4 shows examples of safety related basic causes in some more detail.

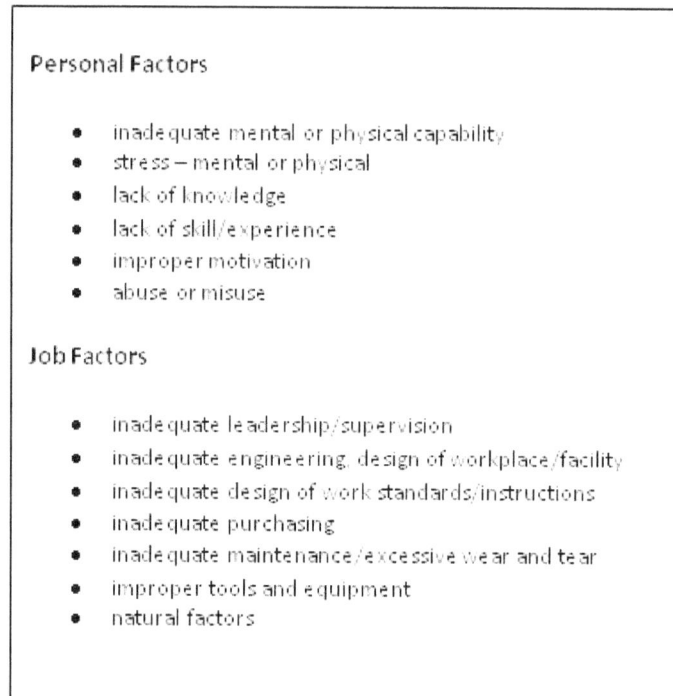

Personal Factors

- inadequate mental or physical capability
- stress – mental or physical
- lack of knowledge
- lack of skill/experience
- improper motivation
- abuse or misuse

Job Factors

- inadequate leadership/supervision
- inadequate engineering, design of workplace/facility
- inadequate design of work standards/instructions
- inadequate purchasing
- inadequate maintenance/excessive wear and tear
- improper tools and equipment
- natural factors

Picture 5.4 - Safety related basic causes: personal and job factors

I pointed at the management system as the real or "root" source of unwanted events. But, if you want, you can take this further as the initiative to make a management system has to come from top-management also indicating how the system is to be build, maintained and improved. So you can point at the people in top management positions; their attitude, their education, the social environment, the management profession. But let us be practical and stop at the management system when we talk about "root" causes. The "lack of control – management" to include:

- Insufficient type or number of management activity areas or "elements" making up the management system aimed at reaching desired objectives while, at the same time preventing undesirable events, limiting their consequences and learning from what goes wrong. Elements including but not limited to: purchasing, design, personnel selection, training, risk assessment, task analysis/procedures, incident investigations, and inspections. Not enough or improper elements will not make it possible to reach the objectives of the overall management system. I will later discus the content of a (safety/risk) management system in some more detail. Some examples of what others are doing are provided in appendix N (page 285).
- Insufficient or unclear guidelines or criteria for element activities. Activities may not be clearly defined concerning what shall be done, why, by whom, when and how.
- Failure to comply with otherwise clear and adequate criteria for element activities. This may be due to lack of training or by the fact that periodic assessment of activities is not carried out to see if work is being done as described in the management system elements. The structure of each element should stimulate activities to be carried out and results to be obtained.

The first responsibility for deviating from the past towards a better future, based on a well build and accepted plan, rests with top management that can play a major role in relation to the quality of the organization, including the prevention of unwanted events and their consequences. This is consistent with what is known in the quality world and should not be a surprise. Accident research also points into that direction, as demonstrated by the investigations carried out after such well-known incidents as the Herald of Free Enterprise, Three Mile Island and others.

But also in "smaller" more recent accidents as the "Moerdijk" fire in The Netherlands where a fire occurred in January 2011 at a chemicals processing plant. An employee used an open flame to defrost a flammable liquid pump with the end result that the total plant burned down and went into bankruptcy later on; no injuries. After extensive investigation DutchNews.nl reported on 16 January 2012: "Management failings are to blame for last year's massive fire at a chemicals packaging company in Moerdijk, near Rotterdam, according to a safety council report on the blaze, NOS television reports. The report, which has not yet been officially published, says Chemie-Pack failed to meet operating permit conditions and did not keep to its own policy or procedures. This led to the company failing to take any safety measures to manage the fire".

Not only does (top) management initiate and agree on requirements for the performance of work and the quality thereof, it also contributes - and this applies to every manager at his or her level – to the extent to which the activities aimed at preventing and reducing losses are being carried out.

Peter Drucker

The best way to predict the future is to create it.

Peter F. Drucker (1909 –2005) - management consultant, educator, and author

The cause – consequence model indicates that the basis for success in reaching desired goals, while preventing unwanted events that are in the way of reaching objectives, can be found in the management system. Success and failure go hand-in-hand. Control of risk is the determining factor to make the difference.

Picture 5.5 shows that "control of risk" is really where risk management comes into action. What is done in that area determines to a large extent what the possibilities are for risk financing and can have a major influence on the profitability and continuation of the organization.

Control of risk can roughly be divided in two areas: (i) organizational and (ii) technical. While technical solutions often are preferred, it is the organizational part that is the actual heart of risk/loss control management. It is in that area that activities and their criteria are set up to reach objectives, to control risks, reduce losses and learn from unwanted events. Technical follows organizational; technical follows the management system.

The risk status of the hardware is determined by the way is designed, purchased, inspected, modified and maintained and the way it will be used (work methods/-procedures). These are all aspects of "the organization", the way things are done, the management system. In order to achieve ongoing control of risks, we must look at those organizational aspects, the presence of loss control management activities, their quality and how they are implemented and approved.

```
┌─────────────────────────────┐
│      RISK MANAGEMENT        │
│  Identification and Evaluation │
│          of Risk            │
└─────────────────────────────┘
```

Picture 5.5 - Main areas of risk management

Late sixties, early seventies, I worked as a technical representative of INA (Insurance Company of North America) in Europe. The work I did was to visit (potential) industrial clients of the insurance company to look at their risk status from a fire/extended perils and business interruption insurance point of view and to make so-called "underwriting reports". Those reports were the basis for the underwriters to make accurate and cost-effective underwriting decisions. While the visit was almost exclusively directed at looking around the facilities to observe technical issues, housekeeping and work practices, I soon realized that what I saw did not come there by itself but was there because of design, purchase, maintenance, inspection, work procedures, training, etcetera; activities that are part of the "management system". So, while going around the premises, I was actually looking at the "products" of the management system. It did help me then that I knew about the Total Loss Control Services that INA was providing to its industrial clients in the USA. This TLC system was an early seventies predecessor of the ISRS – International Safety Rating System that saw the light in 1978.

Aspects that belong under the umbrella of risk management, safety and control of loss management include:

- Establishment of policies and related (implementation) guidelines
- Identification of risks and related risk/loss control measures
- Active participation by, and support from, management and executives
- Training of top, middle- management and supervision
- Training of (support) staff functions
- Training/instruction of operational personnel
- Risk analysis of operational and non-operational work, decision-making
- Design of machinery, equipment and work environment
- Purchasing procedures

- Selection and placement of personnel
- Inspection and maintenance of machinery, equipment, work environment
- Assessment (observation/discussion) of the execution of (critical) tasks
- Preparation for emergencies
- Rules, regulations, permit systems
- Use of protective and rescue facilities
- Occupational health, hazardous substances/environments
- Communication concerning risk aspects
- Promotion of risk- and loss control management, safety
- Safety off-the-job
- Periodic assessment of risk control activities and objectives, feedback.

Some of the practice of loss control management will be further discussed in chapters 8 - 10. But first let me go through the basic model in some more detail and do not forget that this is a model only, an attempt to put real life into a much simpler picture. Let us have a closer look at the cause-consequence model, going from the right – the unwanted event with its consequence - to the management system on the left.

The principle of multiple causes

Accidents and other loss producing events are seldom, if ever, the result of a single cause

---

6. THE UNWANTED EVENT - LEADING TO LOSS

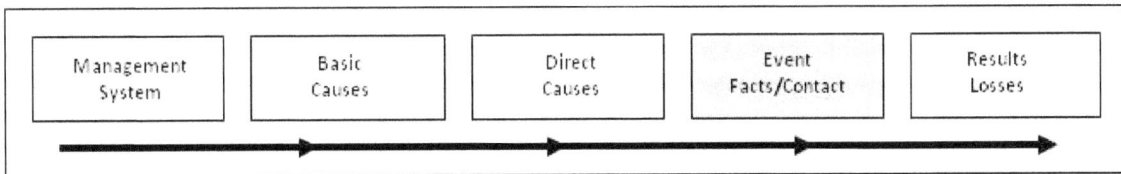

| Management System | Basic Causes | Direct Causes | Event Facts/Contact | Results Losses |

The event in the cause - consequence sequence could almost be anything:

- Fire, explosion
- Flooding, landslides, windstorm, earthquake
- Theft, mysterious disappearance
- Loss of customer or market share
- Not being able to enter new markets (product, geographical)
- Accidents leading to loss: human, property, environment, business
- Unplanned production interruption
- Failure to comply with legislation
- Failure to meet customer expectations – service/product
- Riot, civil commotion
- Loss of key personnel
- Loss of information
- Industrial espionage
- Loss of suppliers
- Loss of resources, energy, water
- Inefficiency, waste
- Etcetera

You may conclude that the list above is a mix of causes, events and consequences and I agree with you. What is a consequence and what is a cause? It may often be difficult to separate them as they are all part of a sequence and in practice the phases of the model above will be overlapping. What is the consequence, the event or the cause? Is the act of defrosting the flammable liquid pump the event caused by lack of training of the operator or lack of supervision with the resulting fire as the consequence? Or is the fire the event caused by the act of the operator leading to destruction of the plant as a consequence? If you look at the cause-consequence model we may conclude that each phase is the cause of the next one with the next one being the consequence of the previous phase. Consequence or resulting event? Confusing? Yes, I think so but hopefully, what comes on the next couple of pages will at least help to bring some structure to it.

Energy trace and barrier concept

In relation to injury, environmental and material damage one of the concepts is the energy trace/barrier concept. The concept assumes a contact between a source of energy and a body or object and energy exchange between those at the time of the event. If the energy exchange is above the threshold limit value of body or object and no adequate barriers are present then the result will be (visible) harm (injury or damage). If the energy exchange is below the threshold value or when adequate barriers are present there may not be any (visible) loss. However, the event may still have to be taken seriously; under the different circumstances the results could be quite different. Risk classification is an issue here.

Within the safety area, the types of contact considered include:

- Electrical
- Kinetic (moving mass e.g. a vehicle, a machine part, a bullet or body)
- Potential kinetic (not moving mass e.g. a heavy object suspended overhead)
- Chemical (e.g. explosives, corrosive/toxic materials)
- Noise and Vibration
- Thermal (heat, cold)
- Radiation (Non-ionizing e.g. microwave, and ionizing e.g. nuclear radiation, x-rays)
- Pressure (air, water)
- Overstress, overexertion, overload

Barriers preventing the event to produce actual loss would include:

- Physical barriers, walls, shields
- Place related barriers, separating energy source and body or object in place
- Time related barriers, separating energy source and body or object in time
- Administrative barriers, procedures, work instructions
- (Personal) protective equipment

6.1. Reporting the unwanted event - learn from the past

The unwanted event can produce visible loss or not and the loss could range from minimal to catastrophic. To prevent the same or similar events from happening again they need to be known so we can learn from them. Once a loss occurs learn from it; learn to be better. For that, unwanted events need to be reported, even if there is no actual visible loss. Use risk classification and establish what the loss results could have been; the loss could be significantly worse under different circumstances.

SANKOFA - "return and get it", learn from the past

Minor or no-loss events may not get reported for various reasons, but they should as results could have been very different if the circumstances would have been different. The unwanted event or accident investigation protocol should indicate what shall be reported, investigated etc. to come up with remedial actions so the same or similar would not happen again in the future or with fewer consequences. See appendix T (page 306) for aspects to be included in an accident investigation protocol or use the search function of my website www.topves.nl and look for "protocol".

Please ….

When reading the next few pages on direct causes, basic causes and the management system or "root" causes, keep in mind that the cause-consequence model is a simplification of real life. If you look closer and think harder, you will see that the lines between the phases of the model may become vague or even disappear.

Just keep in mind that the main message of the model is that it is the quality of the management system on the left that will determine what will come out at the other end of the model.

6.2. Direct Causes – directly preceding unwanted events

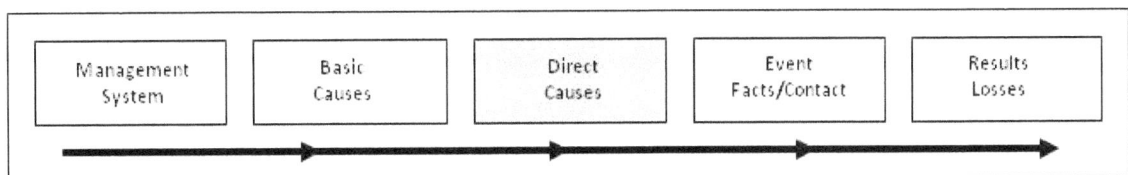

The above picture suggests that events that lead to the consequences that we see are triggered by "direct causes": someone doing something in a certain environment. We divide the direct causes in: (1) causes related to a person – what people do and how and, (2) causes related to the (work) environment - the conditions in and under which the work is being done.

Direct causes of accidents, incidents and other unwanted events are therefore divided in two categories:

- Substandard acts
- Substandard conditions

We use the term "substandard" to indicate that there must be a right or "standard" way of doing things when it comes to acts and right or standard situations or environments when it comes to conditions. "Standard" meaning safe, good, without undue risks and also implying that tasks and conditions may need to be in balance with each other and with the capabilities of the people that need to do the work.

Substandard acts and conditions are in the "management gap"; between what is (done) and what should be (done).

The simple 2 D model above seems to indicate that we are mainly concerned with the acts of people carrying out work directly prior to the unwanted event. But, as I mentioned before, that is because the model is a simplification and you should keep in mind that the actual situation is more complex. Sometimes there is only a thin line between direct causes and basic causes. The substandard act could have been done by a person at a different level in the organization, further away from the unwanted event and at a different time. For example: lack of adequate training to carry out work could be the cause of a substandard act by the person on the job. Could the "underlying" act have been committed by the supervisor or human resource department not providing proper training? Or by higher management not requiring proper training through management system directives? Or did the purchasing department buy the cheaper product to create a substandard condition? Or was the substandard condition created by the person designing the work environment or installation?

Substandard acts may exist because (i) there is no "standard way" of doing things, (ii) there is no initial training on how to carry out the work, (iii) there are no regular observations or discussions to see if the work can still be done according to the standard work procedure, (iv) the standard way to do the work is not being updated, (v) substandard work practices are being tolerated by supervision and management, (vi) carrying out work according to the standard way of doing things is considered "for sissies", etcetera.

From the quality world:

80 % of the underlying causes of quality are due to the improper functioning of the "management system" with the remaining 20% attributable to the people performing the job.

Substandard conditions or situations may exist because: (i) they are designed that way, (ii) there is no proper management of change program, (iii) there is no proper inspection program to find the substandard conditions, (iv) they are not corrected when found, (v) there is no housekeeping program, (vi) substandard conditions are being tolerated by supervision and management, (vii) they are seen as "part of the normal work environment", etcetera.

Substandard acts and conditions are closely related. A substandard condition or situation may be created though a substandard act by a person, operational, managerial or staff. Once the substandard condition is there, the act of another person may be looked upon as substandard while in fact it was the condition that may have been contributing most to the unwanted event.

Direct causes of unwanted events can often be seen at the actual work site and may be found during execution of procedures such as work permits or Last Minute Risk Assessment (LMRA). They can be seen during formal inspections/observations and, preferably, should be noted and acted upon during day-today operations.

Since direct causes relate to acts and conditions that may be there only momentarily, they should also be considered during incident or accident imaging exercises asking the "what if" questions. They can be found during investigation of unwanted events, leading to remedial actions which may include revision of work procedures or changing the work environment.

6.2.1. Substandard Acts – main sources of unwanted Events

Substandard acts may lead to an unwanted event. These substandard acts could be caused by various people at various levels in the organization, close to the unwanted event or further upstream. By operational personnel, by management or staff.

The principle of shared responsibilities

More often than not are accidents and other unwanted events the result of work done by many people at different levels in the organization and at different times. They all share responsibility for the consequences.

Safety related *Substandard acts* as part of direct causes, immediately preceding the unwanted event, include:

- Operating without authority
- Failure to warn
- Failure to secure or to make safe
- Operating at improper speed
- Rendering safety devices inoperative
- Using defective equipment

- Improper use of otherwise safe equipment
- Servicing equipment in operation
- Not following proper work instructions or rules
- Not using or improper use of protective equipment
- Not using proper equipment
- Improper loading or stacking
- Improper placement
- Improper lifting
- Improper positioning for task
- Games/horseplay
- Distracting attention

One of the vital aspects of the management function is to control loss

To close the gap between "practice" and "theory"

Between "how it is (done)" and "how it should be (done)"

6.2.2. Substandard Conditions - hazards in the work environment

Substandard conditions may lead to an accident, incident or other unwanted event. These substandard conditions could be created by various people at various levels in the organization; close to the unwanted event or further upstream. By operational personnel, management or staff and related to such areas as design and modification, purchasing, inspections and maintenance. Substandard conditions, more often than not, are the result of what people do or don't do.

Substandard conditions may be present from the start of an undertaking or develop over time due to lack of proper modification procedures, inspection and maintenance or simply because management and supervision allow such conditions to exist.

Safety related *substandard conditions* as part of direct causes, immediately preceding the unwanted event, include:

- Improper guards or barriers
- No or inadequate personal protection
- Defective tools, equipment or materials
- Proper tools not available
- Congestion/restricted area
- Lack of adequate housekeeping
- Inadequate warning systems

- Fire or explosion hazards
- Excessive noise
- Inadequate ventilation
- Substandard lighting
- Inadequate design of workplace
- Exposure to chemicals
- Exposure to radiation
- Hazardous atmospheric conditions: fumes, dusts, vapors

Direct causes could be temporarily, like someone misplacing a drum or pallet; a substandard act leading to a substandard condition. Assuming appropriate action taken, such direct causes would be there for only a short period of time. If, however, no actions are taken, for whatever reason, those direct causes may become more or less permanent. Is that an indication of culture or not?

There are also other types of direct causes having a more permanent character and they may be more difficult to correct. Those are the acts and conditions that are there by design, because they are purchased or hired and because of lack of supervision and management, lack of training etc. That will bring us to the basic causes.

I was once asked to write an article on "accident prone people". I thought about this and concluded that it all depends on the "environment", the way installations and work areas are designed, the tools purchased, the work procedures, etc. So my conclusion was that, given the limitations that we all have, there are really no accident prone people but there are accident prone environments, the extent of which depending on the people selected to do the work. This ties in with the thinking that, if you wish to reduce losses, the environment may have to be adapted to the people, not the other way around. Can that always be done? Probably not, but you can come a long way. Anyway, I never wrote the article.

Mind you there are risk takers and we all are, one more than the other, and when we take more risks we are bound to have more accidents but that does not mean that we are accident prone. Life without risk may be pretty dull as the saying goes: "A little risk is a joy in life". But then there is also this: "Don't risk a lot for a little".

6.3. Basic Causes – permanent source of unwanted events

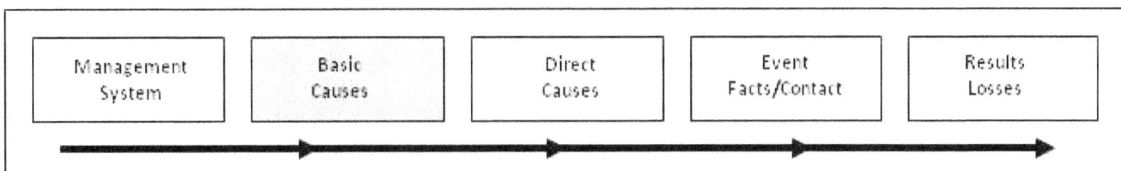

Basic causes are sometimes also called "root causes". As such they are the "source", so to speak, from which the direct causes and unwanted events evolve. Basic causes are also called the "underlying causes".

In my opinion the real "root causes" can be found in the management system. The reasoning behind this is that basic or underlying causes are caused when the management system fails to produce the proper results. This may be due to insufficient content of the system (elements and their activities) and/or inadequate structure of system elements (objectives, evaluation of activities carried out and results obtained) to make sure that necessary activities are being implemented and improved as necessary. Another issue may be non-compliance with the directives/guidelines of an otherwise properly build management system. Of course you could argue that, if the system was really properly built (and maintained and improved), noncompliance should not be an issue. So maybe then, if there is no compliance, the conclusion may be that the system was not build and maintained the way it should have been: with the involvement of all people at all levels. Possibly the system was lacking "emotional ownership"?

Similar to the direct causes, we recognize two main categories here: (1) related to a person, and (2) related to the organization, work conditions and processes.

Basic causes of undesired events are divided into:

- Substandard personal factors
- Substandard organizational or job factors

Basic causes form the breeding ground from which the direct causes can develop that may result in unwanted events with consequences such as: injury, material damage, quality problems, liability claims and other losses.

Basic causes are more directly related to the management system and to the quality and implementation of the activities contained therein. They can be found through activities such as design reviews, risk identification, inspections, task observations/-discussions and accident imaging.

6.3.1 Substandard Personal Factors – the real causes of loss

Personal factors are related to people. This could be the person involved in the actual work during which the unwanted event occurs. Or this could be people contributing to the substandard act of the person doing the work or to substandard working conditions by their decisions or by the quality of their work. These may have been people responsible for such areas as design of installations or work procedures, for purchasing, maintenance, training or people in supervisory and management positions. Their skills and motivation are absolutely relevant when considering why unwanted events happen.

Personal factors have to do with people; people doing the actual work or people creating the work situations for those who have to do it.

The personal factors listed below may apply to people at all levels in the organization and in all functions at various phases of the causation model. These personal factors may be temporarily or permanent and may be reasons for existence of substandard job factors mentioned in 6.3.2.

Substandard personal factors that may lead to basic as well as direct causes include:

- Inadequate mental or physical capability
- Stress – mental or physical
- Lack of knowledge
- Lack of skill/experience
- Improper motivation
- Abuse or misuse
- Sabotage

Come to think of it, these personal factors may also be involved when setting up the management system which is to the left of the basic causes. The 3-D model (picture 5.2 on page 84) shows that at the top of the model: the personal factors run along the entire cause-consequence sequence.

6.3.2. Substandard Job Factors - organizational threats to loss

Job factors are related to "the organization". Job factors often have to do with people further away from the unwanted event.

Substandard organizational or job factors that may lead to basic as well as direct causes include:

- Inadequate leadership/supervision
- Inadequate engineering, design of workplace/facility
- Inadequate design of work standards/instructions
- Inadequate purchasing
- Inadequate training of management and operational personnel
- Inadequate maintenance/excessive wear and tear
- Improper tools and equipment

Substandard job factors may occur due to not complying with management system activities or because of gaps in the system allowing substandard practices to develop and remain. Substandard organizational factors are often the result of personal factors mentioned in 6.3.1.

6.4. The Management System – source of good and bad

While some consider the basic causes as the "root causes" of unwanted events, these causes are there because they are created. They are there because controls that should have prevented their development were: (i) either not there, or (ii) not adequate, or (II) not properly implemented or complied with. Those controls precede the creation of basic causes and are part of the management system that should have been in place to prevent unwanted events to occur.

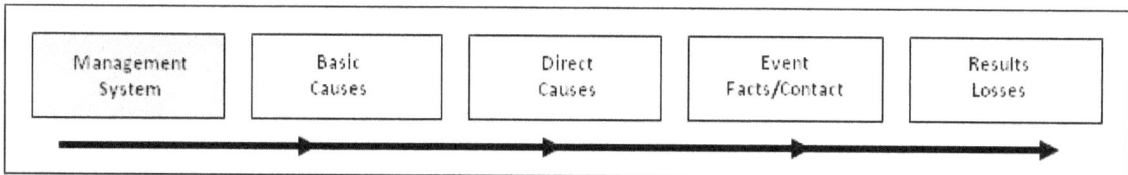

Management System	Basic Causes	Direct Causes	Event Facts/Contact	Results Losses

Basic causes - and, of course, the rest of the cause consequence chain - can be seen as "failures" of the management system and can be prevented and controlled by the management system, provided that:

1. The content of the management system is sufficient in terms of activity areas or elements that are relevant to reach the management system objectives and control the causes leading to unwanted events
2. The content of each element is adequate in terms of specific element activities to reach the objective(s) specific to the element concerned
3. The elements have the proper structure to make sure that element activities are properly carried out and improved as necessary to reach element objectives

Remember that "control" really has two sides: (i) development and improvement of activities to reach objectives and (ii) correcting deviations from "what should be (done)" and learning from the consequences of unwanted events.

Management system shortcomings or failures can be found through regularly carrying out audits to make sure that element activities are being carried out as intended and element and overall management system objectives are being achieved. These shortcomings also come to light through the unwanted events that we witness through the losses that are ultimately the end product of management system failure.

The way a management system is build, maintained and improved is crucial to continued success. The process to build a management system to include the necessary content and structure is discussed in some more detail in chapter 8.1.

7. LOS CONTROL MANAGEMENT – A SYSTEMS APPROACH

Concerning the underlying causes of accidents, losses and unwanted events, it is in line with international experience to put the emphasis on management and organizational aspects. Those experiences include the Health and Safety Executive in the UK, investigations conducted in response to the disasters that we know from the media (including the Three Mile Island and Herald of Free Enterprise disasters) and data available to us from the quality world.

From the latter came the experience that 80 % of the underlying causes of quality problems are due to the improper functioning of the "management system" with the remaining 20% attributable to the people performing the operational work.

In the safety world it used to be said that 20% of accidents are caused by "technical issues" and that 80% is attributable to human error. I wonder what this means. Technology is designed by humans. Plant and equipment are placed in a certain environment by people and maintained by people. It is "safe" to blame technical conditions or "the computer" or "the system" but it is also incorrect to do so. Leaving aside the "acts of God", it may be is more correct to attribute 100% of accident causes to people and focus on the work we do while recognizing that, yes, we are fallible. But we can also learn and should, even though history may sometimes seem to indicate otherwise.

The 80% of human error then often used to be attributed to people involved in the work from which the accident originates. Fresh from the Internet: "80 out of every 100 accidents are the fault of the person involved in the incident." While this may be true in some cases, it is almost an insult and a grave error. If you would accept that it will bring us back 80 years ago when the Heinrich model indicated "fault of person" as what we now call "basic causes". The quality world tells us that causes (of "quality problems") are to be found mainly in the management system and this is where management plays an important role. Are quality related unwanted events really different from safety related unwanted events? Don't they come from the same sources, from the same jobs? The same work? From the same causes and the same people?

> **From the quality world:**
>
> 80 % of the underlying causes of quality are due to the improper functioning of the "management system" with the remaining 20% attributable to the people performing the job.

We can, and should, ask ourselves: "Which people are really involved in laying the foundation from which unwanted events, damage or accidents originate?" The persons who are directly involved in doing the job? Or the persons who have been responsible for designing and/or maintaining substandard systems, installations, work environment or procedures? The guy who was to see if the doors of the Herald were closed or the person who did not provide the proper

interlocks? Or those who did not make the resources available to install the interlocks?
What is the worst thing that can happen on a single line railroad track? Does not take too much imagination, does it? Two trains moving towards each other. What do we do to prevent that? We put a station-master in charge of preventing such disaster! A fallible human being as we all are and then we blame this person when the tragedy happens as it did in 1985 in the tiny village of Flaujac-Gare, about 300 miles south of Paris, and killing 35 people.

Who causes the accident? The person who did not properly perform the job? Or the person who did not provide the necessary training or instruction? The person who did not provide the necessary supervision or the person who did not select the right person for the job? Or he or she who did not provide the necessary resources or made the proper decision? The station-master dozes off and two trains collide. If that happens to the president of the company it is very likely that nothing will happen.

Preliminary information concerning the May 4, 2013 Schellebeke, Belgium derailment of the train transporting acrylonitrile indicated that the accident – at 02:00 hours - was caused by the train driver missing a slow-down sign 1,5 km before the place of the accident. The driver realized his error when he saw the next sign 100 meters away from the derailment area. So, who is to blame? The train driver? The people who designed the safety system? Or maybe those responsible for making sure that the system should have been designed to operate "fail-safe"? The safety manager? Risk manager? The president who dozes off and wakes up again when his secretary comes in with the afternoon tea?

Who caused the accident? The driver of the train that derailed on July 14, 2013 at Santiago de Compostella? Or those who designed the train system? Or those who were aware of the problems but failed to take action and left the responsibility of life and death of many in the hands of one fallible human being? The train driver has to live the rest of his life thinking he caused the death of many people and the sorrow of many more. The CEO of the train company declared that the train was safe.

Are there messages in this? I think there are many but two may be more important than the others:

1. You cannot leave the lives of many people in the hands of one and depend on his/her alertness. People are distracted from their work from time to time for whatever reason and that happens to you and me as well. .

2. You cannot blame the person doing the actual work whenever the systems – technical or otherwise – are not designed and maintained properly. Creating unwanted events and their consequences is often the result of the work of many people. Don't blame "the system" either but learn to make the future better.

There may be many people who share responsibility for the unwanted event and its consequences. But those with the greatest influence on the left part of our cause-consequence model may share the bulk of it.

7.1. Three phases

The question whether control of risks and losses is needed seems rather irrelevant: this is a must for lasting, optimal, business results. More important is the question how to effectively control risks, unwanted events and losses.

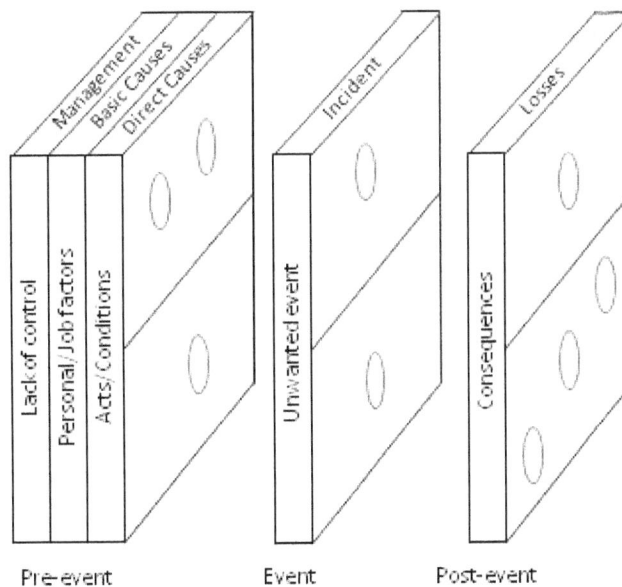

Picture 7.1 - Three phases to control loss

I will discuss this later in more detail. For the moment let me just point at the three control phases that are part of the cause-consequence "domino" model.

These phases are shown in picture 7.1:

- Pre-event phase
- Event phase
- Post-event phase

These three phases will be discussed briefly below and I will do that in reverse order, from post-event to pre-event, from event consequences to event causes, from the loss to the management system.

<u>7.2.1. Post-event phase</u>

You may also want to call this the post-contact phase which may be more applicable when you consider the cause-consequence chain from a safety point of view. This assumes that – in the safety chain – there is a contact between an energy source and a body or object.

The post-event phase includes activities directed at limiting the event consequences. This includes all or part of the activities that are within the emergency plan and the PEP (Post- Event Plan) which should have been prepared in advance and include:

- Care of injured or ill
- Terminating the emergency situation in such cases as fire, flood, loss of containment, natural disasters etc.
- Salvage of materials, data, equipment
- Restoring production and service capabilities

It is also important in this phase of the sequence to consider any possible secondary events. In this post-event phase the attention and efforts may be exclusively directed to fighting the incident and providing first aid to victims. The Sandoz fire that happened in 1986 is an example where the secondary losses were considerable following pollution of the Rhine river by water used to extinguish the fire and containing toxic materials. As a consequence, Sandoz extended its Health, Safety & Environment activities and introduced new procedures for risk & emergency management including auditing.

As so often was and is the case, measures to prevent similar events and limit their consequences are often taken AFTER losses have been experienced. This could be due to a lack of imagination answering questions such as: "What could happen?", "What if?" Or it could just be carelessness or misplaced optimism like: "It won't happen to us." Remember Murphy's law: "If anything can go wrong, it will" or:"What can happen, will happen".

7.2.2. Event phase

This phase is all about limiting the energy exchange - which often occurs in property damage and injury related events. This concept assumes that accidental damage (to a person or object) occurs when the energy exchange (kinetic, electrical, chemical, thermal, etc.) is above the threshold value of person or object. (The "threshold value" is the energy value of the impact above which damage or harm will occur.)

When the unwanted event cannot be eliminated, it is important to limit the possible consequences, to limit loss by reducing the energy exchange and the effects thereof.

Measures that help to reduce the energy exchange and/or limit the consequences include:

- Elimination of the energy source, such as replacing combustible material by non-combustible.
- Reduction of the energy level, such as replacing high tension voltage by lower voltage, limiting maximum speed of vehicles, using less combustible material or limiting weights to be lifted manually.
- Separation of the energy source and the person or object in place/distance (such as remote control of a machine located in an isolated area) or in time (work done overnight when there are fewer people present or less traffic).
- Placing a barrier between the energy source and the person or object. For example safety helmets, crash barriers, sound insulation, and the heat shield of the Challenger.
- Reinforcing the object or body; fireproofing of supporting structure or improving the condition of people exposed to physical effort.
- Changing the surface structure of objects. For example by applying an anti-slip layer or by grinding sharp edges on a work surface or machine.

7.2.3. Pre-event phase

This concerns all activities and related aspects aimed at preventing the unwanted event such as: purchasing of goods and services; design of installations, work environment and products; personnel hiring and placement; training; task risk assessment; maintenance; job observation; inspections; incident investigation; communication and promotion of safety. These activities all have to do with creating the organization (including people, machines, materials, work environment, work methods, management and supervision) and maintaining it at the desired (quality) level. This phase in particular is related to the management system having such a great influence on the existence of basic and direct causes.

7.3. To measure is to know – is it?

Being able to quantify and measure performance is important if you want to know where you are and where you want to be.

You have probably read or heard the expression "What gets measured gets done". While this is true, it also may not be entirely right. If you measure the wrong things, the attention may go the wrong way. I like to think that: "What gets measured gets the attention".

What gets measured gets:

Done?
Valued?
Managed?

ATTENTION!

An example is the way that safety is traditionally measured: in terms of accident frequency rates. But - look closer - it is in reported lost time accident injury rates. Look again at the accident triangle on page 46 and you may conclude that the traditional, and often still usual, way to measure safety is only based on the top of the triangle. Depending on where you are this measurement may not even include personal injuries with less than 3 days of absence. So the attention goes to injuries that result in lost time and often to the person involved in the accident, most likely the victim. This is why traditional accident investigation did not go much further than the direct cause: substandard act and "person did not follow rules". It does not tell much about the safety performance (input) level and is an after the fact, end of pipe, output measurement and relates only to a small part of the unwanted events that occur.

In line with the above: people will not fall from the roof because they do not wear fall protection and if you recognize them for not having an accident indicating: "you did a good job so I give you a reward", you may stimulate unsafe behavior (not wearing fall protection). The same is true when putting (financial) bonuses on having less than a certain number of accidents – sometimes measured in fatalities – on a project; the result of that may be that (minor) accidents will not be reported and valuable information to improve may be lost.

Measurement is important: it directs attention to what is measured. But be sure to measure what is relevant or you may send people in the wrong direction. Measurement gains value if expressed quantitatively. When we can put things in numbers it gains in value and objectivity and facilitates communication.

William Thomson, 1st Baron Kelvin (1824 – 1907) British mathematical physicist and engineer

Measurement is normally done based on an agreed upon reference and this is also true for issues that are normally considered subjective such as the quality of an inspection report, the quality of an accident investigation report, safety management efforts and the quality of an improvement process. Subjective but still measurable; we will see examples of this in the text further on and in appendixes I (page 271), M (page 284) and R (page 302) at the end of this book. What is important is that people agree on the reference used which could be people belonging to a specific professional group or people being part of the same organization.

Considering the cause-consequence model (pictures 5.1 and 5.2 on pages 83 and 84), we can see opportunities to measure:

- Consequences
- Direct and basic causes
- Control
- Opinions/behavior

Different areas of measurement are schematically shown in the picture below in which both the forward control (via a management system audit) as well as the backward control (via inspections, observations and incidents/losses) can be recognized.

HWE MU DUA - the measuring stick, symbol of examination and quality control

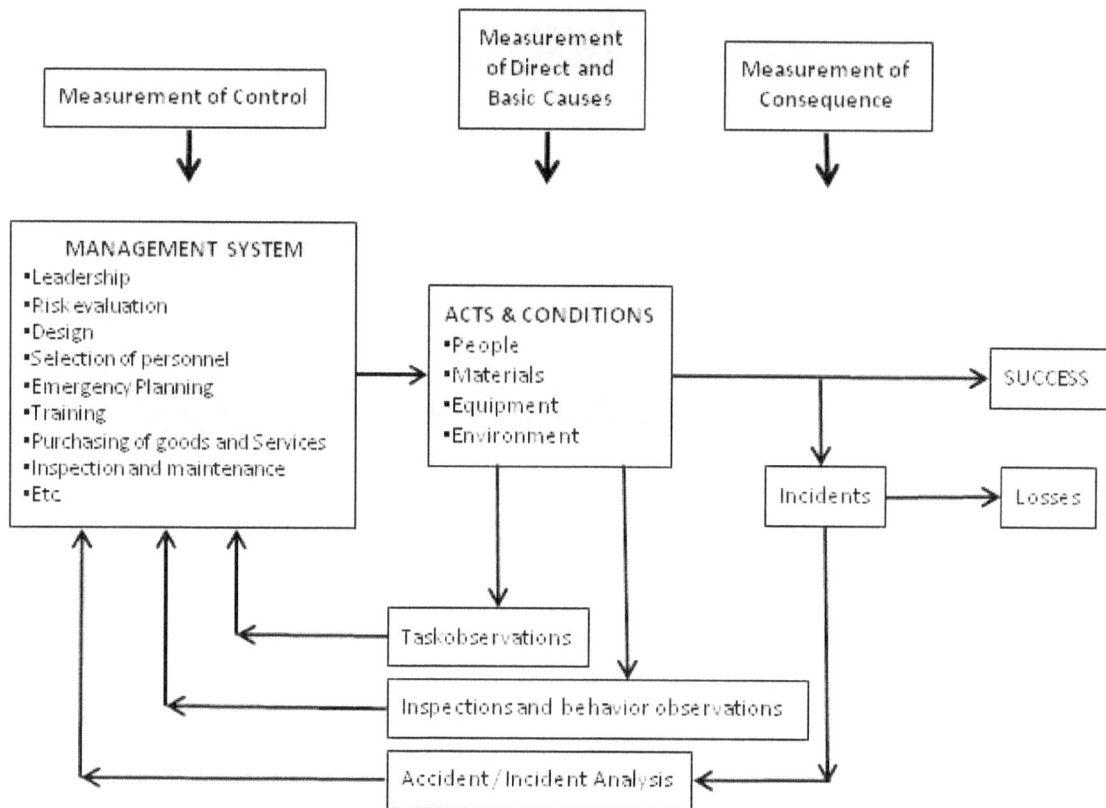

Picture 7.2 - Schematic illustration of measurement opportunities

7.3.1. Measurement of consequences

This is a common and important measurement of the end results of what we are doing. In terms of the Kaizen quality concept these measurements are results (R) criteria. You can also call it "end-of-pipe" or "output" measurement. Common and important, but maybe not the most important measurement as it does not provide a direct insight into the quality of management activities, the Kaizen Process (P) criteria. The most familiar type of consequence measurement is the number of accidents, or rather the "lost time injury frequency rates" (LTIFR).

The advantage of the consequence or result measurement is that it is relatively simple. In the safety area this usually consist of measuring the number of injury type accidents that occur during a certain number of hours worked. It is, however, quite possible to include other consequence measurements such as property damage rates. This would broaden the scope of safety. Determination of absentee rates could also fall into this category and could be an indication of issues such as attitude and culture. However, practice shows that even today and in high hazard industry it is quite common to measure safety based on lost time accident rates.

LTIFR's are also used for comparing safety efforts between companies and between different types of industry.

There are also disadvantages: to measure safety by LTIFR's only gives a very limited idea of what really happens as we can see in the accident triangle. And LTIFR's may very well be the only end-of-pipe indicators concerning safety, loss control and risk management. Limited measurements may lead to limited attention and remedial actions that will have limited application.

End-of-pipe measurements say very little or nothing about what has been going on in the organization and is after the event. Managing a process or management system based on output information alone is like driving a car by getting the occasional look in the rearview mirror.

Talking about LTIFR's as a measuring stick for safety reminds me to a report that was made quite a while ago, in 1982 if I remember correctly. This report - "Safety to which price?" - was about the safety efforts/situation of a location in The Netherlands of an international organization that was known for its low accident rate. What I remember was that the location had indeed a low accident frequency rate but it also had an absentee rate that was higher than the national average at that time. While the report did not comment on this, it would not be too difficult to make a scenario that would produce this, rather contradictory, situation. Could you? The question that arises then is this: "Does a low accident rate reflect a good safety culture?" I don't know about you but I would be very hesitant to say "yes".

Another shortcoming of measuring consequences is that this may relate to a low organizational level. In relation to safety for example, the measurement is linked to the occurrence of injury and directs attention to the victim who is often also involved in activities immediately prior to the unwanted event. This usually involves operational personnel. The measurement directs the focus to the workplace level where most accidents take place. But we have seen that what goes on at that level may very well be the product of what is done at a higher or different level in the organization and, possibly, at a different time. More to the left in the cause-consequence model. It does not make sense to correct workplace issues while hazardous situations may still be created through purchasing or design. Or through higher level decision-making.

To be effective we need to be able to measure on a "higher" organizational level allowing management to intervene and take corrective measures to prevent/reduce or mitigate unwanted and their consequences. Proper investigation and analysis of unwanted events shall not be limited to direct causes and shall go all the way to the root causes and the management system.

Safety or quality systems may have the objective to prevent "all accidents" or "zero defects". While this should be the correct attitude, in practice this may be utopia. But it may be possible to limit certain types of unwanted events and reduce those to (close to) zero, such serious or fatal injury accidents. This means decreasing the accident triangle as is shown in picture 7.3. If one wants to achieve this it will mean that attention (in reporting and investigating unwanted events) should also go to first aid cases, property damage accidents and near-misses or close-calls.

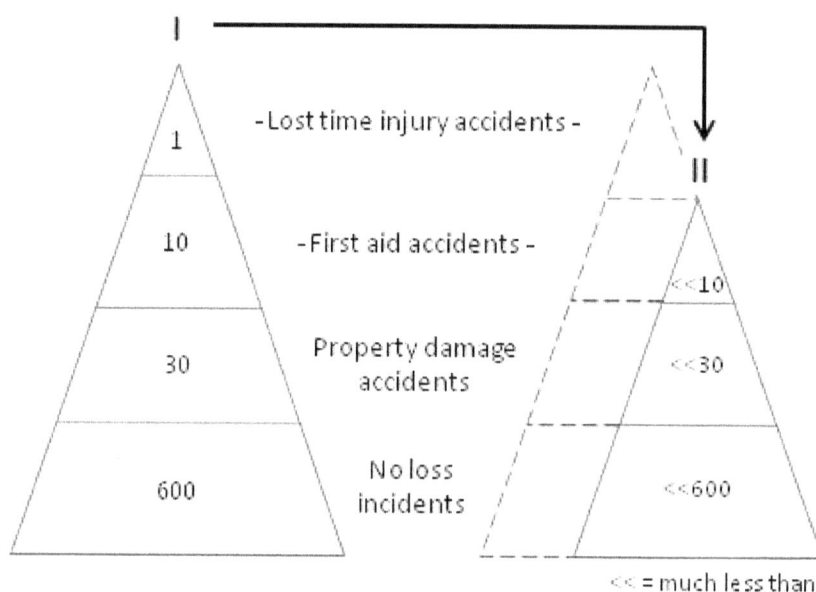

Picture 7.3 - Reducing the accident triangle

Measurement of consequences could include:

- Various injury rates (frequency/severity)
- Material damage rates
- Abnormal/normal maintenance rates
- Insurance claims
- Absenteeism rates
- Client complaints
- Environmental incident rates

The measurement of consequences does not only have to include the consequences mentioned above but could be further subdivided in relation to the severity of actual or potential loss. Use a risk classification system as discussed earlier and shown in appendix B (page 241) to quantify potential loss. Consequences could be expressed in terms of workdays lost as in the case of absenteeism or lost time accidents, in monetary terms or otherwise. Preferably, monetary presentation should be included to obtain the attention and involvement of higher management levels and include all unwanted event consequences, not just injury related accidents alone.

In relation to injury type accidents the ILO (International Labor Office) accident classification lists the following headings:

- Type of accidents
  - Struck against (running or bumping into)
  - Struck by (hit by moving object)
  - Fall to lower level
  - Fall on same level
  - Caught in (pinch or nip points)
  - Caught on (snagged, hung)
  - Caught between or under (crushed or amputated)
  - Contact with (electricity, heat, cold, radiation, caustics, toxic, noise)
  - Overstress, overexertion, overload
- Type of injury
  - Fractures
  - Dislocations
  - Sprains and strains
  - Concussions and other internal injuries
  - Amputations and enucleations
  - Other wounds
  - Superficial injuries
  - Contusions and crushings
  - Burns
  - Acute poisonings
  - Effects of weather exposure, and related conditions
  - Asphyxia
  - Effects of electric currents
  - Effects of radiations

- Multiple injuries of different nature
- Other and unspecified injuries
- Type of body part
  - Head
  - Neck (including throat and cervical vertebrae)
  - Trunk
  - Upper limb
  - Lower limb
  - Multiple locations
  - General injuries
  - Unspecified location of injury
- Type of agency
  - Machines
  - Means of transport and lifting equipment
  - Other equipment
  - Materials, substances and radiations
  - Working environment
  - Other agencies, not elsewhere classified
  - Agencies not classified for lack of sufficient data

These measurements would allow identifying specific problem areas that may require attention. The "type of agency" measurement could indicate possible problems related to equipment, tools, the working environment and operating procedures related to the use of such agencies. The above mentioned categories are further subdivided by ILO – for more detail visit the ILO website.

7.3.2. Measuring direct causes

One step "higher up" (to the left) in the cause – consequence model is the measurement of direct or immediate causes:

- Substandard conditions
- Substandard acts

Substandard conditions

This measurement, directed at substandard conditions/situations, basically is the use of an inspection program that looks at the condition of machinery, plant, equipment, installations, working environment, etc. The objective is to determine how many of the hardware situations observed deviate from what is considered "standard" meaning "safe", "proper", "the way it should be (done)". The more deviations, the more substandard conditions and therefore more opportunities for the occurrence of unwanted events. In fact, such deviations should also be considered unwanted events and are opportunities for improvement. These measurements should be conducted by people knowing what the right (standard) conditions should be.

> **Lord Kelvin**
>
> Anything that exists, exists in a certain quantity and can be measured.

William Thomson, 1st Baron Kelvin (1824 – 1907) British mathematical physicist and engineer.

As inspections – either formal or informal – would normally result in visible deviations (or damage) the potential loss should be estimated using a risk classification system. I consider the use of a risk classification system a must, not only to put a value on what could happen but also because not all deviations represent the same risk and first attention should go to those with the higher loss potential.

This measurement gives us no insight into how the substandard condition was created. This could have been due to the purchase of "unsafe" material or equipment with unnecessary risks. Substandard conditions may also be introduced by design, via modification of plant or work environment, by inadequate maintenance or otherwise.

Substandard conditions can persist through improper functioning of departmental or other type of inspection programs which should early detect and remedy unwanted situations. Remember that inspection activities are often corrective in nature and directed at bringing the situation back to what it used to be; without looking for the causes that led to the deviation. Correcting deviations from standard without cause analysis may very well form the basis for the same or similar situations in the future, possibly with (more) serious consequences.

To get an overall picture of the situation and to see any development, either up or down, the number of deviations found should be related to the total number observed. An alternative may be to compare the number of deviations found based on the duration of the inspection.

Appendix I (page 271) shows an example of a method to evaluate conditions.

Substandard acts

Measuring substandard acts originates from observation of what is being done and how. These observations of work and behavior can take many forms and are discussed later in a separate paragraph. Here too, the quality of the measurement largely depends on the experience of the observer and his/her knowledge of what standard behavior or the standard way of carrying out the job or task is or should be. The more deviations from the standard, the more possibilities for the occurrence of unwanted consequences, but, of course, also more possibilities for improvement.

The observation of behavior and the way work is being done is also a method to determine whether training, instruction and supervision are properly executed. It is also a possibility to determine whether changes in work environment have been introduced – for example via procurement or design - which made it no longer possible to carry out the work as intended via standard work instructions or -procedures. Observations can also be used to improve existing instructions and procedures.

As is the case with inspections, the observations are often corrective in nature with less attention going to why the behavior is what it is. A major "challenge" when carrying out observations lies in the fact that there is a direct line with the person performing the work or showing the specific behavior. Because of this, observations may not be the proper tool for organizations in which the underlying causes – of substandard behavior and task execution - have not been properly addressed.

Carrying out behavior- and/or task observations requires a culture of open and positive communication between management and operating personnel and between operating personnel. When such culture is not present, periodic discussions of how work is actually done may replace the observations and people performing the actual work should then take part in these discussions. Such discussions may include "at location" visits and may even be a better way leading to improvement of procedures than actual one-on-one observations as they will include the opinion of several people and remove the "personal issue".

Same remarks about risk classification and relative numbers of deviations as mentioned under substandard conditions above.

7.3.3. Measurement of basic causes

Direct causes are, in principle, the result of the underlying or basic causes which include:

Personal factors such as:

- Inadequate mental or physical capability
- Stress – mental or physical
- Lack of knowledge
- Lack of skill/experience
- Improper motivation
- Abuse or misuse
- Sabotage

and

Job factors, such as:

- Inadequate leadership/supervision
- Inadequate engineering, design of workplace/facility
- Inadequate design of work standards/instructions
- Inadequate purchasing
- Inadequate maintenance/excessive wear and tear
- Improper tools and equipment

Personal factors, by the way, are part of basic as well as direct causes. At the direct causes level they may be a reason why people are not following rules or work procedures or showing particular substandard behavior. At the basic causes level, they may be the reasons why job factors as listed above exist.

I consider that basic causes are so intertwined with direct causes that this measurement (of basic causes) does not really make much sense.

That does not mean that I am saying that issues as mentioned above shall be ignored. On the contrary, the development of major guidelines such as for design, purchasing, maintenance, training etc. are most important to guide work and to control unwanted events and their consequences. These guidelines are made by people and the issues under personal factors apply when considering the quality of job factor aspects. How to make these guidelines and the criteria involved in making, approving and updating them should be part of the management system.

The result of existing basic causes – personal/job factors – can often be seen at the shop floor as substandard conditions and acts/behavior. The selection of management and support staff personnel with responsibilities for the quality of management system elements and resulting procedures plays a very important role here.

7.3.4. Measurement of control

A higher level of measurement is the management system audit assessing management activities to reach objectives and control unwanted events and their consequences. In relation to safety this is the safety audit and I am using a broad definition of the term "safety", meaning control of loss. And "loss", of course, is the risk of the past. The safety audit could then also be called a loss control management audit or a risk management audit, whatever you prefer. Note that a safety audit does normally not include risk financing issues that should be included in an audit related to risk management. Financing of unnecessary loss should be an important consideration no matter what.

I trust that you will be able to find more definitions and more "scientific" definitions of "safety audit" when searching the Internet, but here is one:

"A (periodic) assessment of the (management) activities in an organization directed at controlling risk, loss and unwanted events with the aim of taking action to maintain those activities at a desired level and improve them as appropriate."

The (safety/loss control) audit may include management activity areas or "elements" such as:

- Leadership and administration
- Hazards to the environment and identification of critical issues
- Organizational rules and permits to operate
- Analysis of critical tasks/work activities
- Hiring and placement
- Training
- Communication and motivation
- Engineering controls
- Purchasing controls
- Health control
- Formal inspections
- Environmental performance monitoring and assessment
- Personal protective equipment
- Emergency preparedness
- Reporting/investigation and analysis of undesired events
- Safety system evaluation

During an audit, activities are compared with a reference that could be internal or external to the company undergoing the audit. When an internal reference is used, the audit would be directed at assessing whether the activities and objectives set by the management system are properly met. In other words: are we doing what we should be doing and are we reaching the objectives/targets that we set? Using an external reference could lead to the addition of elements or activities to the company system to bring the company's control efforts to the next level. External references could also be used to determine if external requirements are being met such as set by legislation, -industry or -certification standards.

Audit systems could be provided with criteria value factors which would allow quantification of audit results and facilitate communication to stakeholders and help to set objectives for further improvement. See appendix R (page 302) for a limited example of safety audit criteria using value factors.

Measurement of control has the disadvantage that it takes time and involvement of many. I personally have been doing audits using the ISRS (International Safety Rating System) and its predecessors, between 1974/5 and 1991. Normally I would spend one full week on site doing the audit. This did not include the reporting which would take another couple of days also including the results of opinion surveys which I had done prior to the onsite visit.

The big advantage, however, is that this type of measurement is focused on "organization" and "management activities". In the cause-consequence sequence, this measurement is to the extreme left, ahead of the two measurements mentioned earlier and allows taking action prior to the occurrence of substandard acts, conditions and unwanted events. It allows "forward control" and can be an effective "tool of management" to achieve further improvement of the organization by meeting objectives and controlling unwanted events and losses

The (safety) audit can be seen as a measure of the "level of control", a measure of management system activity indicating the "way we work" or "organizational behavior". This measurement may reflect organizational culture and (top) management attitude one way or another; good or possibly not so good depending on how the system is embedded in the organization.

When reading the above, please remember that it is the <u>function</u> of management that I mostly consider. This function is carried out by all in the organization, not just by those we normally refer to as "managers". The freedom to act within that function is greater at the top of the organization than at the lower levels. The responsibility for the performance of the organization parallels that freedom but the function of management is present at all levels. With the objective to close the management gap.

The audit measures the "root causes" of unwanted events, the real problems referred to in the "principle of definition":

The principle of definition

A logical and proper decision can be made only when the basic or real problems are first defined

---

Louis A. Allen, management consultant and writer. Founder of Louis Allen Worldwide

7.3.5. Measuring opinions, behavior

The degree of "safety" or "control of risk" depends on what and how people do in the organization: their behavior. The average combined behavior of people then becomes the behavior of the organization and is the visual part of "culture". How people think and feel determines to a large extent what they do and how. It is their attitudes as individuals, combined as an organization and depending largely on top-management, that will be the basis for success, or failure.

> **Vincent T. Lombardi**
>
> Winning is not a sometime thing; it's an all time thing. You don't win once in a while, you don't do things right once in a while ... you do them right all the time.
>
> Winning is a habit.
>
> Unfortunately, so is losing

Vincent Thomas Lombardi (1913 – 1970) was an American football coach

What is more important, attitude or behavior? My opinion? I think attitude as the "driving force" behind behavior. Attitude and beliefs are more basic and the best "guarantee" for ongoing behavior, either good or bad. But, in the end, it may be behavior that counts.

In the end, attitude, behavior and culture belong together and are interrelated. Having said that, it is easier to observe and measure behavior than attitude or culture; the latter being reflected by the combined behavior of many or all in the organization.

Measuring attitude? I am probably going to disappoint you here. I am not a psychologist so I rather talk about measuring opinions instead of measuring attitude and leave it to greater spirits to make the difference, if there is any.

Opinion surveys may be of interest to understand how people experience, think and feel about the safety, loss control and risk management efforts in their organization. They can also be sending an important message to the people subject to the survey, like: "Hey they are asking my opinion". But be careful, if the opinion surveys are not part of a serious effort to improve and nothing really happens after the survey then they may be counterproductive and work against you.

You may not be able to do much with the opinion survey results unless you know what to do next. You may want to combine the survey with finding out what is being done to control risk and losses and how this is being done. So, do an audit. Slogans like "safety first" may be looked upon as reflecting attitude but it tells little about behavior. It also tells little or nothing about the culture. It may not tell much about attitude either. Actions count, management system elements and activities count. Whether control of risk/loss is really considered of importance can, to a large extent, be checked on the basis of an audit assessing the quality of related management system activities. Does it make sense to ask people what they think about their safety system or their safety training if you can establish – via an audit – that there is no system, no training or that what is done is far from effective? Yes it does, provided that you combine survey and audit in a process like the one I will discuss in section 8.1.6 (page 151).

At some time in my career and for a short time, I used to be the managing director of a fire fighting training center located in the Rotterdam area. That was kind of a "sidestep" as my career really has been prevention oriented whereas the fire fighting training school was focused on … fighting fire which I consider a necessity when things go wrong.

Anyway, when working with the fire fighting center, I was asked to evaluate the safety efforts of one of the parent companies. I remember looking at the safety manual of the company, in particular at the first page which was the management SHE policy statement. Really this policy statement gave me a warm feeling – which does not happen often to me – but turning the page, the feeling disappeared quickly as the rest of the manual consisted of do's and don'ts instructions directed at the lower levels of the organization telling the people what they should and should not do. So what started as expecting a safety culture based on sharing and involvement of all, allowing emotional ownership at all levels, quickly changed to a more traditional culture in which the boss was telling what to do and not.

Do I think that the policy statement by top management is important and that it reflects the culture of the company? Not really, the policy statement may very well be a piece of paper hung on the wall or on the publication board in the cafeteria or a statement on the website. If you really want to feel and see the safety culture, look at the (safety) management system, how it was build, the involvement of people when making, maintaining and improving it. Look at the results of opinion surveys to find out how people in the organization feel and think about the system – is it really THEIR system?

Is a low accident frequency rate a reflection of the safety culture of an organization? My answer? Not necessarily so! The low frequency may be there for other reasons.

I used to do safety audits with the International Safety Rating System (ISRS) and when starting to do this, mid seventies of last century, I also used to have opinion surveys done at three levels in the organization: top-and middle management (see appendix H, page 262), first line supervision and operational employees. The survey questionnaires to a large extent contained the same questions at all three levels and in addition also questions specific for the level concerned. They contained yes/no questions, valued weighted questions (between 0 and 10), factual questions and open questions. These surveys gave me a lot of information before going to the site to do the actual system audit and go through some 20 elements together containing about 600 questions or reference points. My experience was that I never, during these audits, found any real controversy between the survey results and the outcome of the audit. To me that indicates the relation between input and output; the input being the system activities and the output being what people feel and think about it. What I did find, however, was that people, depending on their level in the organization, could feel quite differently about their safety system. I remember one case in which and on a scale between 0 and 10, management gave an 8 for their efforts while these were given a 4 at the receiving end of the organization, the shop floor. The audit results, by the way, were more in line with the lower score.

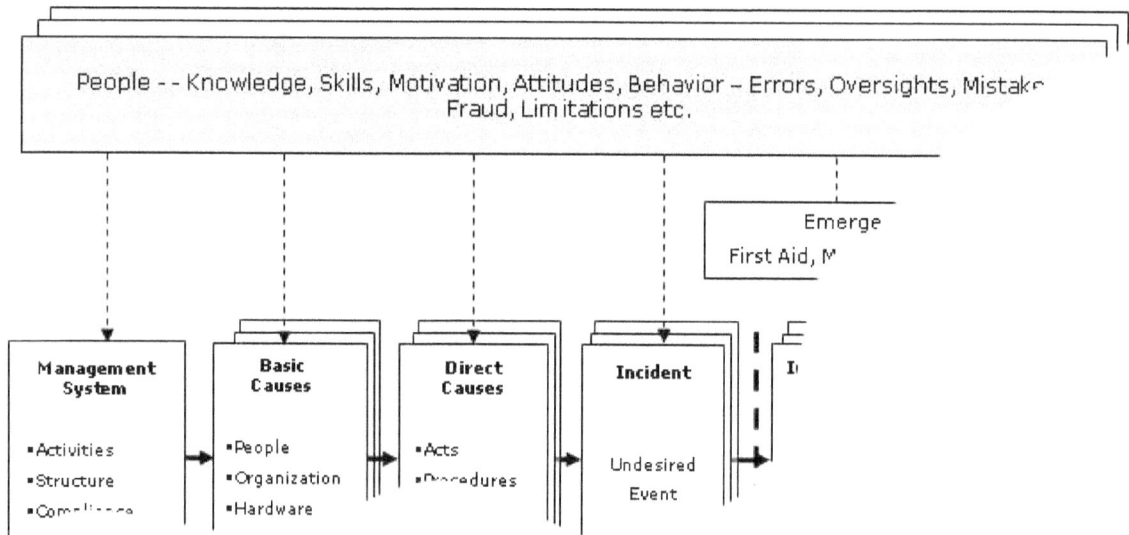

Picture 7.4 – People issues are at the basis of an effective approach to control loss

As I tried to indicate in the above picture, attitude and behavior are important in all phases of the cause-consequence model and relate to everyone in the organization. Behavior is easier and more effective to observe and measure; behavior is the mirror of attitude and culture.

Measuring behavior of operational personnel can be divided in:

- Work specific behavior – task observation carried out using related work procedures
- General behavior

General behavior items include:

- Proper use of personal protective equipment
- Proper position or posture for task
- Complying with permits
- Proper lifting, bending
- Following general rules, no-smoking etc.
- Proper use of equipment
- Etc.

See also 9.2.3, page 202.

Measuring behavior of management and supervisory personnel is somewhat more difficult although it is reflected in the behavior of people doing operating work. However, the "behavior" of people in leadership positions can be evaluated by the way they comply with criteria that are part of the management system. In relation to safety and loss prevention in their area of responsibility, such criteria may include:

- Evaluate departmental compliance with safety and loss prevention program
- Contact each of their people as deemed necessary on important safety matters.
- Assist in investigations to determine causes and corrective actions
- Include sand loss prevention in meetings with their subordinates.
- See that compliance with rules, regulations and procedures is maintained.
- Analyze safety and loss prevention compliance problems
- Review task procedures and practices program
- Arrange for safety training as required by company and departmental needs
- Instill, through action and example, a sincere safety attitude
- Participate in the management safety committee, as scheduled.
- Contribute in the development of the annual HSE plan.
- Participate in a management safety and loss prevention audit
- Carry out performance appraisals of the persons directly reporting to them
- Participate in training programs set up for management

Safety Culture

Culture receives quite a bit of attention these days, so a little more about that now.

A company always has a (safety) culture. But you may not have the culture that you want.

Company culture is related to societal culture, often depending on the country in which the company is located. So what works in one country may not work in another country; keep that in mind when reading the next sentences.

Many of us often consider having a desired culture as the holy grail of safety, or quality or whatever. If culture is simply defined as: "The way we work here", I would probably agree. The question then is not whether you have a (safety) culture but rather: "How do you get a desired culture and keep it?" That, in principle, may not be so difficult but you will have to work at it and it will help when you have people in your organization who are willing and able to work together to get the desired culture; it would just make it easier. Having said that and depending on your situation, it may take a long time to get the culture that you want. But when the situation looks complex, my advice is: go back to the basics.

```
┌─────────────────────────────────────────────────────────────┐
│                     GETTING RESULTS                          │
│                                                             │
│      In a complex situation always go back to the basics:   │
│                                                             │
│           Make a PLAN to change, to include:                │
│                                                             │
│                 The PROCESS to build it                     │
│                      Its CONTENT                            │
│                     Its STRUCTURE                           │
│                                                             │
│            DO IT TOGETHER – INVOLVE PEOPLE                  │
│                                                             │
│  Use available knowledge and experience – allow emotional ownership │
│                                                             │
│             YOU CAN'T DO IT ALONE ANYWAY                    │
└─────────────────────────────────────────────────────────────┘
```

So, back to the question "How to get the culture you want?" Actually, I already gave the answer: do it together. If you want a desired culture you will have to involve "all" people to create that culture by having them participate and take responsibility in making, maintaining and improving a plan to change, a management system, directed at safety or quality or something else. Preferably you do that from the beginning when making the organization and after you have determined where to go with it, what your objectives are. Let people know what you want to do, where you want to go, how, when etc. and how they will be involved in making the system THEIR system by sharing responsibility for the outcome. If you do it much later after the start of the organization you may have developed a culture that you do not want. When that happens, it may be more difficult, even impossible, to get where you want to be.

The 17-step process mentioned in this book (section 8.1.6, page 151 and appendix L, page 280) shows you the process to make a management system that will have a high chance of success, provided you work at it and do not give up. Making and executing a management system and involving all people in the process is almost a guarantee to obtain the desired culture for success. The "secret" of the 17-step process? Really there is no secret, just do it together and work at it.

Remember this: the process to get a desired culture is relatively simple but to get there may take more than just a little bit of effort. Peter Drucker said it this way:

Peter Drucker

What you have to do and the way you have to do it is incredibly simple.
Whether you are willing to do it, that's another matter.

Peter Drucker (1909 – 2005) – management consultant, educator and author

He also said this:

Peter Drucker

The best way to predict the future is to create it.

Peter F. Drucker (1909 –2005) - management consultant, educator, and author

Culture relates to behavior relates to work procedures and rules. How you make those procedures and rules is vital to getting the behavior that they are supposed to produce. Appendix K (page 275) gives a guide to make procedures and rules with a high degree of compliance and desired behavior. Again, the "secret" is to involve the people that have to apply and use the procedures/rules. "Emotional ownership" is the key word.

The principle of emotional ownership

People tend to be more willing to participate in planned change when they have an opportunity to participate and influence the process leading to change

---

So what I really am saying is that if you want to have a desired culture you should consider setting up a management system with the involvement of all in the organization. If you would have the choice you may want to start with safety. The advantage of safety is that it is closely related to the wellbeing of people and the work that they do. It shows to them – and their family members - that management, "the company", cares about them. Starting with safety makes it relatively easy to extend the scope from injuries to include property damage, environmental incidents and beyond that to control "unwanted events".

When looking at the above principle, please also look at this version:

The principle of emotional ownership (2)

The more ownership people have in the way a present situation has developed, the more difficult it is to change.

7.3.6. Measure what is needed and practical

It is not my intention to exclude any form of measurement and you should measure what you think is worthwhile measuring.

Having said that, I would recommend that you measure at least the following:

- Output – result criteria
- Input – process criteria

Dr. H. James Harrington

Measurement is the first step that leads to control and eventually to improvement.

If you can't measure something, you can't understand it. If you can't understand it, you can't control it. If you can't control it, you can't improve it

---

H. J. Harrington (1929), American author, engineer, entrepreneur, and consultant in performance improvement

The result criteria include frequency rates related to injuries, property damage, unwanted events and related actual and potential severity rates (number of lost workdays, amount of financial loss). Include inspection and observation results as desired and needed. Use the result criteria that will allow you to determine the effect of what you put into the management system to reach objectives. If you have a low lost time injury (LTI) rate, measuring only those makes little sense and you may want to extend your measurements to still be able to track the results of the efforts you put into the process to improve.

The process criteria relate to the activities that you undertake to reach your goals. These include the control activities that are part of the management system, at the extreme left of the cause-consequence model. The (safety) audit is a measurement of the (safety) management system and probably the most important measurement. A good audit methodology (such as the International Safety Rating System - see chapter 8.2.1, page 165) would include other measuring methods such as inspections and observations, the measurement of results and statistics.

7.3.7. Communicate what you measure

There are two important measurements when it comes to safety and loss control:

1. Measurement of consequences (output)
2. Measurement of control (input)

I put them is this order on purpose as I feel that the measurement of consequences could help to motivate top management to provide their leadership when making a management system to control the actual and potential consequences.

Whenever possible, put the consequences in financial terms as (top) management is used to think in monetary terms and not in odd figures such as LTIFR's (lost time incident frequency rates). It may not mean much to them when you talk lost time accidents per million hours worked.

> **The principle of economic association**
>
> A manager will usually pay more attention to statistical or general information when expressed or associated with cost terminology

In the book "Loss Control Management" (Institute Press 1976) Frank Bird and Bob Loftus provide us with some interesting information. During a period of about 2 ½ years they started collecting opinions of people attending courses that were run by ILCI and IAPA using what they called the "Motivational Scale Exercise". In total they received the opinions of over 2.300 safety professionals from eight countries asking them to consider what would really be important to their management and place the following issues in order of importance:

- Provide personal satisfaction
- Improve labor relations
- Enhance public relations
- Increase production rate
- Give legislative compliance
- Improve product quality
- Reduce injury rate
- Improve operating costs
- Increase job pride
- Reduce liability potential
- Improve customer relations

The thermometer pictured below gave the average outcome.

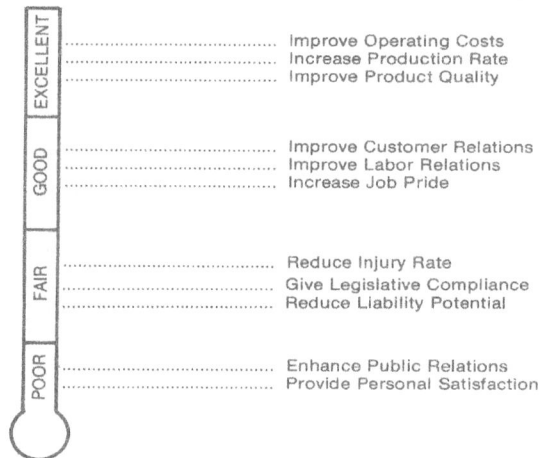

MOTIVATIONAL SCALE
FOR
RECIPROCATED MANAGEMENT INTEREST

EXCELLENT	Improve Operating Costs
	Increase Production Rate
	Improve Product Quality
GOOD	Improve Customer Relations
	Improve Labor Relations
	Increase Job Pride
FAIR	Reduce Injury Rate
	Give Legislative Compliance
	Reduce Liability Potential
POOR	Enhance Public Relations
	Provide Personal Satisfaction

Picture 7.5 - Motivational scale for management interest

In some more detail, the outcome was as follows:

- 92% of respondents placed improving operating costs at the top of the list
- Increasing production rate came second with 87%
- Third place was for improving product quality
- Reducing injury frequency rate was placed between 6th and 8th position by 47% of respondents
- 96% placed provide personal satisfaction at the bottom
- Enhance public relations came second before last with 94%

So, even though these opinions are from a long time ago, consider what would attract attention better to obtain for management action: LTIFR's or (total) costs of unwanted events including accidents? Relate that to the accident triangle (picture 3.4 on page 46) the cost iceberg (picture 3.3 on page 45) and the incident costs – sales table (picture 3.5 on page 46).

7.4. Cause – Consequence matrix

I already mentioned that risk/loss control management deals with the management of different losses (see picture 3.2, page 43). While this may seem so at first sight, one needs to realize that these different losses are bound together by their underlying causes. I try to clarify this with the help of the cause – consequence matrix as shown in picture 7.6. Just ask yourselves if there is a relationship between the losses at the top of the matrix and the basic/underlying causes on the left.

Losses / Business Areas	Product Loss	Quality problems	Property Damage	Waste	Liability Claims	Occupational Illness	Personal Injury	Environmental Damage	Personnel Turnover	Loss of Customer	Loss of Market share	Information Loss	Loss of Image	Etcetera
Training /Instruction														
Design of Installations, Workplace														
Purchasing of Goods, Services														
Hiring of Personnel														
Management/Supervision														
Inspections														
Learning from Unwanted Events														
Emergency Preparedness														
Post Emergency Plan														
Change Management														
Work Procedures/Instructions														
Communications														
Task Observation														
Risk/Problem Identification														
Etcetera														

Picture 7.6 - Cause – Consequence matrix

My guess is that you probably will tick off most boxes indicating that you too feel that most losses have one or more basic causes in common. If you do not come to this conclusion, the least we could have would be an interesting discussion but I take my changes and assume that you and I will be on the same wavelength when I say that:

- One type of loss can result from more than one basic cause
- Seemingly different losses share the same basic causes

The principle of multiple causes

Accidents and other loss producing events are seldom, if ever, the result of a single cause

---

Should we agree it is most likely that we also agree that, when improving for example the underlying causes of injury type accidents, we would at the same time also be able to improve in other loss areas. At least we would have the opportunity to do so. If we find that training was one of the basic causes of an injury type accident, should we not also look at eliminating or reducing other types of risk associated with the same job? Quality issues, for example? If done the right way, structuring risk/loss control or safety activities – via a management system – can lead to an improvement of the organization in many aspects. And, by doing so, we would almost "automatically" extend our safety management system towards an integrated system.

While the above principle relates a single consequence to multiple causes, the principle below makes the relation between a single cause and multiple consequences. Just do the exercise above in reverse order starting with a particular root cause to see what the consequences could be.

The principle of multiple consequences

More often than not will a single cause result in multiple consequences

---

7.5. Information – starting point for controlling risk/loss

In each approach to (potential) problems, relevant information is necessary to arrive at the correct action. The question then is: "Where to get the necessary information?"

To obtain this information I consider a limited number of sources or "levels":

The incident level

At the incident level, information is collected about what happens or has happened; the unwanted events that occur or have occurred. Losses, damages, near misses and other deviations from "what should be (done)". What has occurred in the past will be repeated in the future unless we take action to prevent that. What happens now will happen again, unless …..

To obtain a sufficient amount of relevant information, attention should also be given to the relatively small losses or no-loss incidents which, under slightly different circumstances, could have been serious or even catastrophic. Use a risk classification system (matrix, Fine/Kinney or other) to determine what the consequences of an event could be.

The risk level

Here the questions are: What could happen? What could go wrong? What losses, damage, etc. may occur? How large will they be? How large could they be if circumstances would be other than normal? Here we consider losses that have not yet materialized. In practice we will be looking at the bigger risks assuming that the smaller ones already have come up at the incident level. Again: a risk classification method (appendix B, page 241) should be used to find the events that need serious attention.

Peter F. Drucker (1909 –2005) - management consultant, educator, and author

The control level

The questions at the (management) control level are to obtain information concerning the existence and effectiveness of activities to reach objectives and prevent and limit unwanted events and their consequences. What is being done to optimize the organization, without undue interruption and loss?

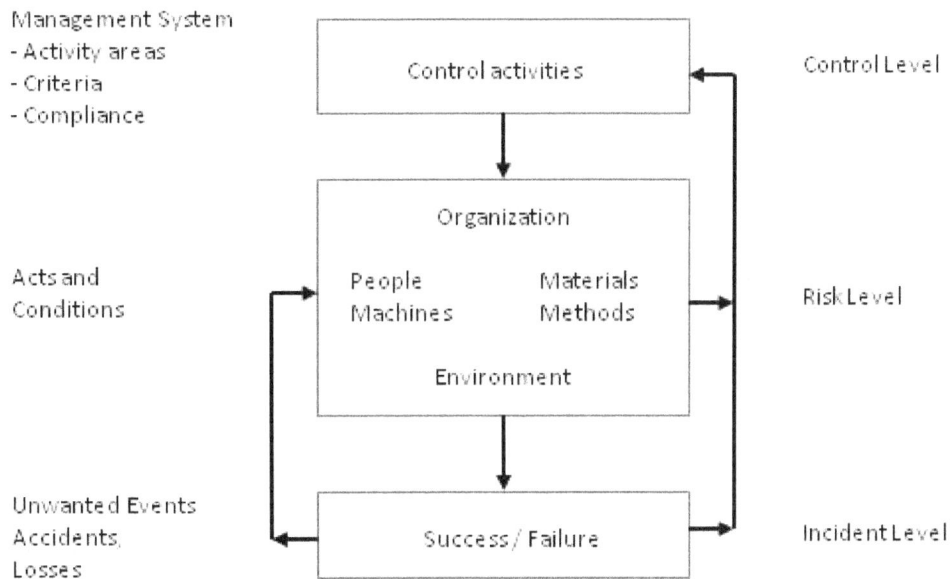

Picture 7.7 - Information levels to control unwanted events

The above picture provides a schematic illustration of the levels and their interrelationships.

It is not difficult to relate these three levels to the cause–consequence model which you can see on the left side of the picture. Please remember that the picture is no more than a reflection of real life and that in practice these levels will overlap. In the next couple of pages, I discuss the information that may be obtained from these sources in some more detail.

At the incident level the objective is to obtain information from losses, damages, accidents and other unwanted events that have occurred and occur. In practice, the situation may be that we need to obtain the information from several sources in different ways. This situation may exist due to the fact that part of the losses that occur may not be reported or registered as such. They may not, formally, be seen as "loss" or referred to as "unwanted events". In certain industries losses may just be considered "part of the job". The saying: "You can't make an omelet without breaking eggs" seems to suggest that it is only normal to have accidents. But that cannot be an excuse to ignore valuable information that may help to improve what you are doing.

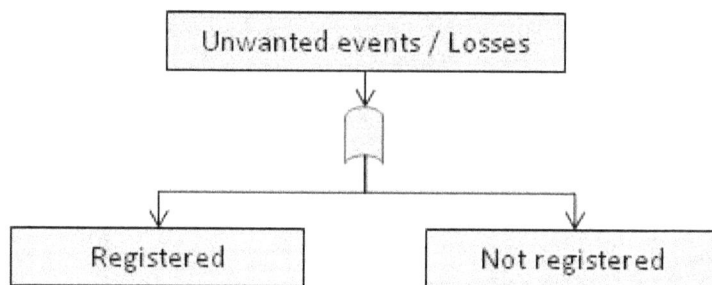

Picture 7.8 - Unwanted events and losses: registered or not.

Registered losses are usually easy to identify from relevant files, paper or electronic. The value of the information will be determined by what has been or is being recorded. Registered losses usually include absenteeism rates, lost time injuries, property damage and claims reported to the insurance company, quality problems and customer complaints. Losses that are not registered may include repairs and maintenance other than normal wear and tear and non-insured claims. Losses may not be registered because people are not asked to report them or for whatever other reason.

Unregistered unwanted events and losses can often only be found by asking people who should be aware of failures and work interruptions that take place without being recorded. A survey like that can be done written or through interviews, either on an individual basis or in a group, depending on the culture of the organization. A combination of methods will usually produce the best result which would probably be no more than 70-80% of what is actually happening. A survey like this needs preparation to properly select interviewees and communicate purpose and follow-up to obtain the necessary cooperation. Blame-fixing should be avoided.

At the incident level we look for incidents and losses as mentioned in picture 3.2 (page 43) plus others depending on the specific situation of your organization. For example, in the offshore oil and gas production the occurrence of oil in water may be an important category of incidents.

Information regarding the incident level can be obtained from production and support staff departments but should include supervision and operational personnel at the point of control.

The principle of point of control

The greatest potential for control tends to exist at the point where the action takes place

---

Louis A. Allen, management consultant and writer. Founder of Louis Allen Worldwide

Suppliers of goods and services and certainly our customers are sources of information not to be forgotten when it comes to quality issues and product related incidents.

In addition to obtaining information concerning the past, it is very important to know about what is happening now. Investigating and analyzing current losses often provides us with more, and more accurate, information and can therefore be a better source to improve our loss control efforts. This information is up-to-date and we can easily obtain any missing data necessary for proper cause analysis. In practice, we are talking here about analysis and investigation of accidents, incidents, damage, etc. and the unwanted events that have led to the losses that we experience. I will discuss some of the more important methods to investigate and cause analyze unwanted events later on. You will find an indication of what should be included in an unwanted event or accident investigation protocol at the end of this book (appendix T page 306).

Concerning the investigation and analysis of incidents, the experience is that this is often not done optimally. One of the reasons may be that the question is being asked "who did this" and then the attention goes to the person (who must have done something wrong). This may lead to blame-fixing interfering with finding out what went wrong and why and information to improve may be lost. Having said this, I realize that some type investigations may be limited on purpose to finding the person who did it – the culprit - such as investigations by authorities and in the context of insurance involving establishment of guilt and liability. From a company management point of view such blame-fixing investigations may be ineffective and inefficient because they may not be directed at learning from what went wrong. As a result of this, analysis and remedial actions may be limited to the lower levels of the organization without ever reaching the management system. Blame-fixing may also reduce the willingness to report unwanted events. As a manager, when finger pointing at who did it, don't forget that there are three fingers pointing back at you.

<u>7.5.2. The risk level</u>

At the risk level the attention does not go so much to what has gone wrong but is directed at what COULD go wrong. This looking at what could go wrong also plays an important role when investigating actual losses and no-loss events. What has happened will happen again, unless you do something about it. Even when the actual loss is small, the question that always needs to be asked is: "What could the consequences have been if the circumstances would have been different?"

The experience of people involved in design of installations, products, processes, work procedures and the work environment is important when considering what happened in the past to others, in other situations or other processes. What happened once before to somebody else could possible happen again …. to you.

When determining what can go wrong you need to look at the entire system (e.g. the production process or installation) and at parts thereof. You can work from the outside in (i.e. from system towards subsystem and components) as well as from the inside out (i.e. from component to subsystem to system). The boundary of the system under consideration is determined by the circumstances and this can sometimes be very far away, both in place as well as in time, as evidenced by the attention to the depletion of the ozone layer of our planet or the climate changes that are taking place.

As a rule, the limits of the system considered should be broad enough to also take into account the risks that may be more distant - in time and in place. This certainly applies to activities or products with a very long lifespan or processes with potential environmental issues.

The question "What can go wrong?" with the aim to bring risks within acceptable limits, should be asked at a very early stages of process or product design and then be repeated during the design process, and beyond that. The objective here is to design and construct a system that is "safe-to-operate" in accordance with the prevailing and (expected or assumed) future standards and knowledge.

A systematic approach should be followed with regard to the (manufacturing) process, the final product and its application. The phases that should be considered include:

- Feasibility- or conceptual phase of process or product: the idea is born
- Conceptual design phase: first elaboration of the idea
- Detailed design phase: further development and testing
- Construction and start-up phase, production facilities are built and brought online
- Operational phase: production and delivery of products or services to the market
- Demolition phase: termination of production, installation and products.

See appendix F (page 255) for further subdivision of the phases mentioned above.

Analyzes carried out at the risk level will generally focus on more serious and catastrophic risks. This is especially so when existing systems are being analyzed as it may be assumed that the smaller and more frequent risks would already have materialized and taken care of during production and product application over a longer period.

Methods of risk level investigations and studies include:

- Process studies
- Layout studies
- Information from the incident level
- Product inventory
- Inventory of functions and tasks
- Inventory of contracts

Process studies

Apart from investigating any "absolute risks", the focus of our attention here is to find out what could go wrong with the (proposed) operation or process. An "absolute risk" in this context is a risk that is not acceptable no matter what controls available. These risks include, for example, the use of certain pesticides (such as DDT) or the use of halons (halogenated hydrocarbons in relation to the ozone layer) in other than specific risks that exist in, for example, the aviation industry. As a rule these are risks that are considered socially unacceptable; for all of mankind or a large part thereof.

Process studies focus on uncovering potentially unwanted process situations and their consequences. This includes external effects (e.g. possible environmental problems and products use issues) as well any impact within the organization itself, ranging from serious personal harm and property damage to extensive interruption of production causing inability to supply product or services to the market.

In process studies, the entire system should be considered from suppliers (and possibly from suppliers of suppliers), through transportation, storage, production, handling, storage, transportation, etc. to customers (and possibly customers of customers and consumers). Studies need to identify possible failures, mishaps, etc. that may occur in the components and sub-systems of the system and what the consequences could be, in order to take appropriate measures to reduce the risks to an acceptable level. Such studies should take place during design phases and when modifying the original process and facilities (ref. management of change/modification management procedure).

The depth of the process study depends on the nature of the process but, in principle, the process study can – and should - be used for any operation, process of procedure in any organization. In any case, the techniques used are not reserved to the chemical/process industry but can likewise be used in administrative organizations.

Lay-out studies

Layout studies are based on the location of a company or organization and the position of the facilities, installations, and buildings. The aim of a layout study is to determine the risks that may arise from that particular location. It serves both to ascertain what damage could result from: (i) the company to its surroundings and the environment and, (ii) from the surroundings to the company. Issues that should be addressed are those covered by nuisance legislation, including transportation to and from the location. But also fire spreading to or from the environment, environmental pollution, flooding, landslides, etc. Consider normal and abnormal operation conditions as well as possible emergency situations including location of emergency services (hospital, fire brigade), availability of adequate water supply (volume and pressure) to fight fires and any special equipment necessary in case of an emergency.

During the late sixties and early seventies of last century, I used to carry out inspections of (potential) industrial clients of the American insurance company that I was working with. Purpose of those inspections was to provide information to the underwriters to allow them to set premium for the risks involved and to structure the coverage to include own risk, co-insurance and re-insurance. Carrying out the inspections we used to acronym COPE, covering the main areas to consider (risk) criteria important to the underwriter:

- Construction – the way the buildings/installations are constructed and the materials used
- Occupancy – what activities are carried out on the site and inside buildings/installations
- Protection – private as well as public protection
- Exposure – from the plant to the surroundings/environment and vice versa but also exposure between onsite buildings/facilities/installations/outside storage

Information from incident level

What happens today or happened in the past may happen again, unless adequate measures are taken to prevent recurrence. Knowing what went wrong in the past is crucial to learn about what could go wrong in the future. This could be the past in another organization – you should learn from what happened to others being in the same or similar situation. When considering the past, keep in mind that small losses could lead to much more serious, even catastrophic, losses in the future due to possibly different circumstances when the same or similar event occurs again.

Even in case the actual loss is small, consider what could have happened. I will get back to this later on when discussing "learning from unwanted events" - see section 9.3 on page 212.

see section 9.3 on page 212.

The principle of future characteristics

The past performance of an organization or unit tends to foreshadow its future characteristics

---

Louis A. Allen, management consultant and writer. Founder of Louis Allen Worldwide

The above "Principle of future characteristics" simply means: "if you do nothing, the future will probably be the same as the past". Or worse, as the environment in which you operate will change and put more requirements on you and your company. However, the principle also indicates that you should learn from the past so the same errors, mishaps and accidents will not take place again. I think this principle – and some others given in this book - came from Louis A. Allen, management consultant and author of award winning book "The Management Profession" (McGraw Hill, 1964). A book that I bought early seventies and which gave me a good insight into the process of management.

Product inventory

The inventory of products in the company can give you an idea about the potential risks. All products should be considered: raw materials, finished products and auxiliary products, intermediate products, waste etc. Not only under normal production conditions but also when the process is not running as expected. During transportation, storage and handling. During emergency situations. What products can be formed? What products can be formed when unwanted contact occurs or under the influence of fire? And what will be done with those products, will they be allowed to contaminate surface or ground water? Can rivers be polluted so the contamination goes downstream endangering wildlife or the drinking water of people living there? Examples include disasters such as Seveso, Sandoz, Bhopal, Love Canal, etcetera. Those were events from the past but similar may happen again today and tomorrow.

Also consider what could happen during product use – by customers and end users – and during disposal.

Job and task inventory

This inventory includes two issues:

- What is the importance of the various functions in the organization? What will the consequences be if a person is no longer available? What if he/she accepts a job with a competitor? The aim is to determine what the "key" functions are in the organization and the risks if persons fulfilling those jobs are lost.

- What tasks are being performed within certain functions in the organization and which of them are "critical" in the sense that serious loss may occur if the work is not performed properly? Because of the importance of this subject when setting up an effective loss control system, I will discuss this "control of critical tasks" later in section 9.1.4 on page 188).

Contracts inventory

The aim here is to examine what contractual obligations exist and what risks they may represent. This specialist subject is not further discussed here. However, it is important to determine what risks currently exist and to ensure proper coordination of contract development so all the interests of the organization are properly represented resulting in contracts with known, acceptable, risks.

By definition, legislative requirements should also be considered here; permits to operate may be vital to the ongoing existence of the company/organization.

Under "contracts" you may also want to consider any marketing, sales and instructional brochures and media activities via which promises are being made to the (end) user. Promises that are not based on reliable test data may work against you. Do not forget: bad news travels faster – and wider – than good news; especially today with increased media communications.

Repeat

Even in highly hazardous undertakings risk assessments will seldom, if ever, be 100% at any point in time. So the assessments need to be repeated periodically. Use of different risk assessment methods and involving other people may help to uncover risks that were not identified before. And I repeat: use the small losses that could be much bigger under different circumstances. Use "accident imaging" during design phases, during operations and during modifications. Reap the benefits that can come out of physical inspections and observation/discussion of critical tasks, by asking the question: "What if?"

The above studies or inventories need to be reviewed periodically and modified as needed. They need to be carried out again when changing circumstances could possibly introduce risks that were not there before. Preferably, risk assessments should be "built-in" when carrying out day-to-day activities such as inspections, maintenance, management of change, purchasing, design and when carrying out tasks with elevated risks. Risk assessment, one way or another, should be part of the daily routine.

7.5.3. The control level

This "highest" level includes the (management) activities in the organization directed at:

- Creating the best possible organization: has the organization been set up such to optimally control problems, risks, damage, etc.? Has the risk management system been developed with the on-going involvement of all people that should be involved? Including decision-making, operational work, design, purchasing, hiring and placement of personnel? Have risk assessments been carried out as needed? Is the organization "safe-to-operate"?
- Maintaining the safe-to-operate status of the organization: keeping this status at all times making use of such approaches as abnormal situation management (ASM) and management of change (MOC). Are risk assessment activities periodically repeated? Accident imaging as part of the inspection programs? What could happen if?
- Learning from what goes wrong. What can happen will happen! What has happened will happen again! Is the unwanted event investigation protocol adequate and operational? Don't let the opportunity get lost to become better.

The control level is on the extreme left of pictures 5.1 and 5.2 (pages 83 and 84): the management system: activities – structure - compliance.

What is done in the organization to control risks will determine the loss level of the organization. Obviously, this should be considered over a longer period; a risk with a frequency rate of once every 10 years may not happen tomorrow. This is why control activities have to be there "forever", as long as the organization will exist or even longer than that. The level of the control activities that are mentioned below is an indication of the quality of management and of the "problem solving power"' of the organization as a whole.

I have divided the control activities over the three issues mentioned above: (i) creating the organization, (ii) maintaining it, and (iii) learning from what goes wrong. My assumption here is that an organization will be build "safe-to-operate"; that all risk aspects will have been considered and dealt with prior to going on stream. If that is not the case you will have an inherently unsafe or risk prone organization from the start and the extent thereof depends on the thoroughness of your risk assessment processes. If you have not done it properly before you start operation, you will have more work later on and you may be caught by surprise and, depending on your role in the organization, you may not sleep that well wondering what will bring tomorrow.

Please note the "management activity areas" mentioned below are examples only; your actual choice of those "elements of a management system" will depend on the specific situation of your organization. In the appendix N (page 285), I give some examples of actual (safety) management systems and their "elements".

Creating the organization – starting "safe-to-operate "

- Risk assessment, to include:
    - Process studies
    - Layout studies
    - Information from the incident level
    - Product inventory
    - Inventory of functions and tasks
    - Inventory of contracts
- Design of installations, work environment, work procedures, rules etc.
- Purchasing of equipment, tools, services
- Selection and placement of personnel
- Initial training of management/supervision
- Initial training of operational employees

Maintaining the organization – remaining "safe-to-operate"

- Policy statement
- Inspection of hardware
- Observation and/or discussion of work carried out to update work procedures
- Re-training of people
- Instruction and training of new personnel
- Medical examinations
- Maintenance of installations, work environment
- Abnormal situation management
- Modifying of process/equipment, installations, work procedures
- Communication and promotion
- Personal protection
- Periodic evaluation of management activities

Learning from what goes wrong – turning back to "safe-to-operate"

- Emergency preparedness
- Investigation and analysis of unwanted events: accidents, damages, losses, etc.

Keep in mind that all elements under "maintaining the organization" and "learning from what goes wrong" should be up and running from the early start of the organization. And all activities under "creating the organization" should continue during the entire lifespan of the company or undertaking. So all elements or activities mentioned above actually have to be part of "creating the organization", part of the "organizational design" phase. Your management system should be up and running from the start; to be maintained and improved during the lifetime of your organization depending on results obtained and ever changing external conditions.

8. RISK/LOSS CONTROL STRATEGY

8.1. Strategy for control of unwanted events

Developing or improving risk management in an organization follows a process that is generic to every organizational change. The approach is true for safety, risk management, loss control, quality or any other business aspect and includes the following:

1. PLAN – making a plan or "management system" containing the necessary content: the elements and their specific activities embedded in a structure to reach objectives; elements that will contribute to reaching the objective(s) of the management system
2. TRAIN – inform/instruct/train people to carry out the plan activities, including assessment of activities carried out and of objectives reached compared to those set
3. DO – carry out the activities and periodically assess execution and progress compared to objectives

Basically the three aspects are: (i) know where to go and how to get there, (ii) knowing what to do and how to do it, and (iii) do what is necessary to reach objectives. That is the basis and it is relatively simple.

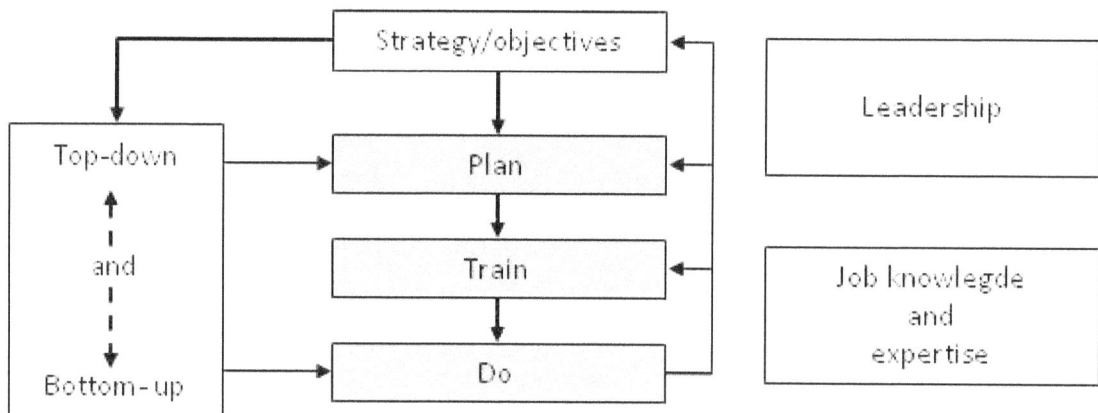

Picture 8.1 - Three fundamental issues to better performance: Plan – Train – Do

Picture 8.1 really puts everything together in which the basic process is indicated by the grey boxes following strategy and related objectives and combining leadership with knowledge and expertise in a top-down/bottom-up cooperation. Central to the process is the making of a plan.

In principle it is simple to get where you want to be:

- You need a plan, what do you have to do to get where you want to be
- You need to have the knowledge/skills and means to carry out your plan
- From time to time, you need to check that you are doing what you should be doing and that you are getting closer to where you want to be

The above process can be used in business as well as in private life and for any purpose, any objective, anywhere you want to go; on your own or with others. A simple formula but first of all: you need to have at least some idea of where you want to go.

If you are not getting closer to where you want to be, you are either not doing what you should be doing or you are not doing the right things.

Basically simple – is it not?

Peter Drucker

What you have to do and the way you have to do it is incredibly simple.
Whether you are willing to do it, that's another matter.

Peter Drucker (1909 – 2005) – management consultant, educator and author

Relatively simple but doing it may be complicated and complex. Not because the process is that complex but it is the people who may, and often will, make it complex. And that may be because you have waited too long to do things right and meanwhile got into a culture that is less than cooperative. Even so, the process remains simple – you need to keep an eye on the basics that are in the picture above and further detailed in the next couple of pages.

In a complex situation?

Always go back to the basics!

And get the results that you are looking for

8.1.1. PLAN – (re)directing the organization

What comes out of an organization in terms of success or failure depends on what goes in: (i) the (structured) activities directed at obtaining success and, at the same time: (ii) control unwanted events that could be in the way of getting desired results.

This applies not only to risk or safety but also to quality, cost- and loss control, etc. These seemingly different aspects of business share a number of management activity areas (ref. picture 7.6 on page 129) and can - to a large extent at least – be served by the same management system. Those management activity areas – which should be "elements" of a management system or plan – include:

- Design of installations, products, work environment, work procedures
- Hiring and placement of personnel
- Purchasing of goods and services
- Training of management and operational personnel
- Inspections of installations, equipment, tools
- Risk identification – identifying potential problems
- Preparation for emergencies
- Abnormal situation management - early detection of deviations
- Learning from deviations, what went wrong
- Etc.

To control losses/risks it helps to consider the unwanted events as (potential) loss sources that should be prevented or controlled. It really does not matter whether an event is categorized "safety" or "quality", an "injury" or "damage" as this classification is often determined by the outcome of the event, the type of consequence. Separating events and their consequences based on their outcome should be avoided as it may lead to sub-optimization during execution of work as well as when considering effective controls.

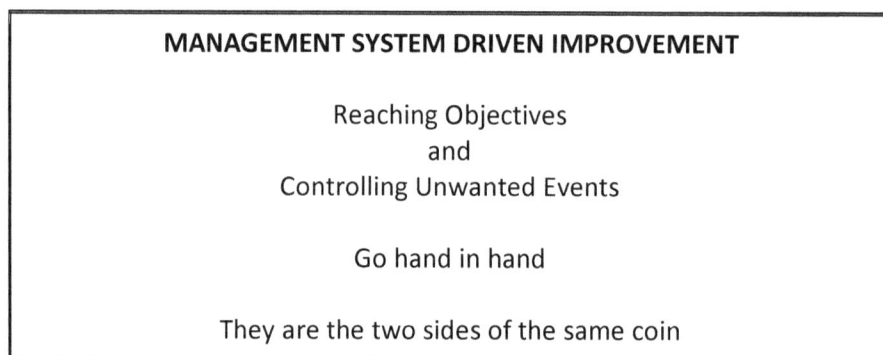

MANAGEMENT SYSTEM DRIVEN IMPROVEMENT

Reaching Objectives
and
Controlling Unwanted Events

Go hand in hand

They are the two sides of the same coin

In principle, you could be able to obtain improvement based on just learning from unwanted events. While that may be tempting, it may also not be the right way to go as you may be caught by surprise. Statistics may work against you – you may get the larger losses first even though their frequency may be low. A combination of activities to reach objectives and learning from unwanted events should be the proper approach and you may build your management system to reach objectives without becoming too large and cumbersome: lean and mean.

Making or changing an organization really means: which activities should be carried out, why, by whom, when and how. If properly selected and accepted, executing those activities will make or change the organization, its behavior and its culture. It is only when everyone knows what needs to be done and what requirements should be met that lasting results will be possible. A good standard or audit reference can prove its worth to determine what needs to be done.

As simple as it seems, experience shows that people may look for solutions in the wrong direction. People may "feel" that something is not entirely working as it should in relation to "safety" and attack "the problem" by running courses on communication techniques, motivation and so. At the same time it can often be established that it is far from clear what is required of people. How can communication be good if people do not know what should be done, why and how?

What gets measured gets:

Done?
Valued?
Managed?
ATTENTION!

One example from my own experience includes a power station in The Netherlands that tried to improve safety related communication by running courses on transactional analysis (then costing about Fl. 90 000 – this was during the eighties of last century). However, this company only scored 9% in the ISRS element "Leadership and Administration". I never was invited to do a proper ISRS audit there which would have cost about 15% of the amount spent to the transactional analysis training but it would have been much more effective as it would have revealed what was missing to allow effective communication.

Or it is assumed that "accidents are mainly caused by unsafe behavior". And a lot of money and effort is spend on training managers in observation techniques in order to observe and change the behavior of the people doing operational work. That would be change from the bottom up while the real problem may be from the top down, including how the management system was build and the way rules and (work) procedures were made. What is the logic behind looking at employee behavior when it is not clear what the risks involved are, when no task risk analyses have been carried out, no proper task instruction has been provided, no management of change procedure, no proper accident investigation and so on? Besides that, is the behavior of operational workers not also a reflection of the behavior of their supervisors and managers?

Transactional analysis and observation techniques may be appropriate for an organization. But only AFTER it has been clearly determined what and how work should be done and AFTER appropriate instruction/training has been provided and when this is done right, transactional analysis and behavior observations may not be necessary anymore.

Training people in relation to reaching objectives and controlling unwanted events should only be provided AFTER a clear plan has been setup including what shall be done, why, by whom, when and how. It does not make sense to train people how to carry out inspections when the company has not first established a protocol on how and when to do this. The result would be that people go back to their workstations and will not be asked to practice what they just learned which will probably not help much and may even be demotivating. The plan comes first, then the training and only after that the implementation of what needs to be done to be successful. And that with the involvement and consent of those who need to be involved which will definitely include the "point of control" people – at the level of "where the action is".

8.1.2. Train – knowledge and skills to do what needs to be done

After it has been determined what needs to be done, people need to be instructed and trained so:

- They will know what it is they are expected to do and when, why they have to do this and how this relates to their job
- They will acquire the necessary knowledge and skills how to carry out the activities

Training is essential to carry out the activities contained in the plan or management system. To optimize success, this should be done top-down. Information on what needs to be done, why, when and how should first go to senior management and then further down the hierarchy so that the responsible manager or supervisor will know what should be done and how in his or her company or department. Training needs should be adapted to the level in the organization and the qualities and competencies of people at those levels. In principle it should be: leadership, policy and direction at top management level and coaching, stimulating, execution and controlling at the levels of middle management, direct supervision and operational personnel.

> **The principle of point of control**
>
> The greatest potential for control tends to exist at the point where the action takes place

Louis A. Allen, management consultant and writer. Founder of Louis Allen Worldwide

8.1.3. Do – Carry out the work to get results

In the end it comes down to doing the work that needs to be done in such a way that success will be inevitable. Discipline is necessary to obtain and maintain lasting results. This discipline needs to be manifest at all levels and the argument "no time" to not carry out a planned inspection, not to investigate an accident or not correct an undesired situation will easily be understood as "not a priority", apparently not important (enough). And that may very well be the first step of a good culture going down the drain; or possibly one more step in a process that is already there?

Managing risks and losses is not something that can be done once and then be forgotten. The activities to control risks should, if not continuous, at least be periodically and repeated frequently enough in line with preset criteria. They cannot be stopped. For example, we cannot decide that inspections do no longer need to be carried out "because we never have deviations." That would be like having no fire insurance because "we never had a fire". Remember Murphy: "What can happen, will happen".

8.1.4. The Platform model

Basically, the model provides the main ingredients to improve.

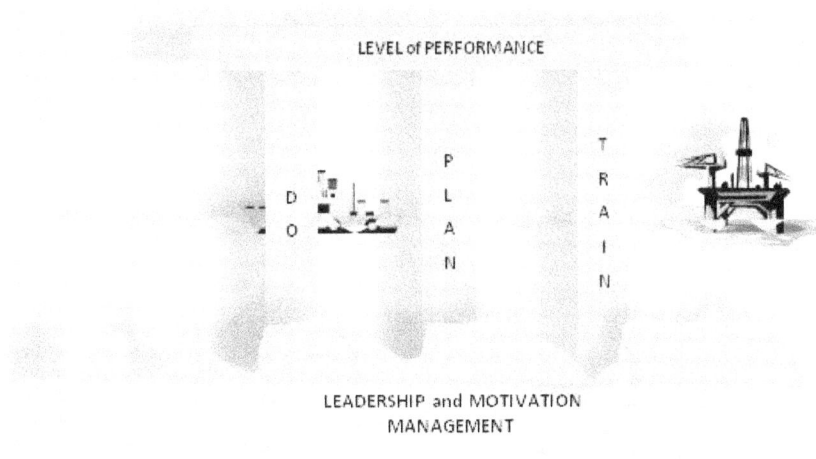

Picture 8.2 - "Platform" model including ingredients for improvement/change

Picture 8.2 is based on the schematic illustration shown in picture 8.1 on page 142. The "Platform model", the concepts of which I first published in my 1988 book "Risk/Loss Control Management", shows the performance level resting on three columns - Plan, Train and Do - which are based on the foundation of management leadership and motivation. You may want to compare this to the Deming PDCA (Plan, Do, Check, Act) circle and observe the following:

1. The Platform model shows three important areas that are not readily seen in the PDCA circle: (i) the "level of performance" or the objective to be obtained, (ii) training and (iii) the leadership role of (top) management.
2. The Platform model does not show the Check and Act that are indicated in the Deming circle. I left those out because I find that periodic evaluation of activities and results are so much integral parts of implementation (Do) that they do not need a separate place in the model. But I did put those two issues in the structure of the management system elements as you will see in section 8.1.7 on page 154.

There is another reason why Check and Act are not in the Platform model. I wanted only three columns under the performance level to highlight the fact that Plan, Train and Do need to be in balance with each other. If those three aspects are not developing together it would not take much imagination to see what will happen to the performance level resting on the three columns. That is why you need to build your management system (Plan) over a period of time; building it quickly, because you need a certificate as soon as possible, may just not work if you are looking to become better. Just let it grow in balance; Plan-Train-Do, element by element depending on their priority. Plan precedes training precedes doing.

Seen from above the Platform model looks like this:

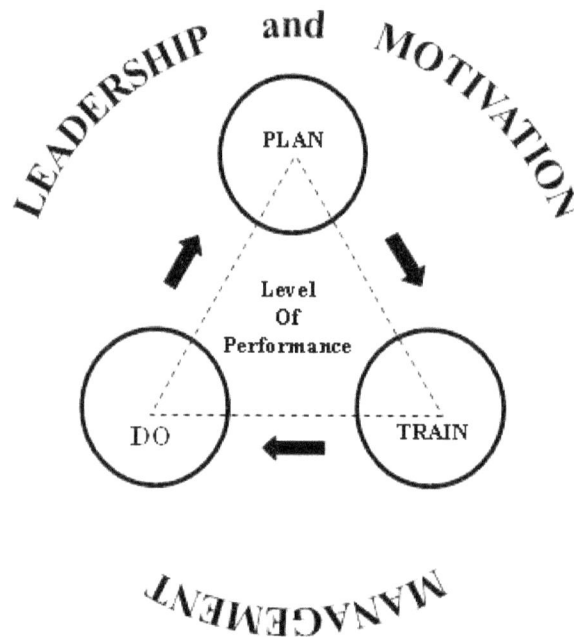

Picture 8.3 – Platform seen from above – notice the Plan-Train-Do cycle

8.1.5. Implementing the strategy for success

To allow improvement of what is being done, it is essential to: (i) actively demonstrate leadership and support by management from high to low, and (ii) continue carrying out the activities necessary to reach objectives while controlling unwanted events that may make that difficult or impossible.

It is important to periodically assess and measure (or "audit") these activities to see if they are at the required level and if desired results are being obtained. Feedback should be provided to stakeholders and is important at every level, either done formally or via personal communication between, for example, supervision and employees (e.g. via toolbox meetings). Feedback is necessary for adjusting the overall risk/loss control system or parts thereof, as well as in relation to specific "substandard" acts and conditions.

Of great importance is that the three columns of the platform stay in balance. In other words, that there is a balance between what people are asked to do, their training for this and the execution of the required work. Training/instruction of people has to come after it has been decided what must be done, how and why and before they are asked to do it.

Best and lasting results of management system activities can be obtained through a combination of top-down and bottom-up involvement, during preparatory stages and when activities are being carried out.

Top-down is setting objectives to be obtained by the overall management system while indicating what activities are required, how risks should be controlled and how the organization should be redirected ("Plan"). Top-down also indicating which training ("Train") people should receive such that people know what to do, why they should do it and how ("Do").

Top-down support for the execution of the work to be done. By making important items, truly important. By implanting in the organization a system for (self-) management of what is to be done and the results that are to be obtained. By providing feedback and commending people and workgroups whenever possible. By making sure that undesired situations or acts are being addressed in order of priority. By asking about performance and progress at relevant meetings. By being pro-active rather than re-active. And above all: by example when possible and appropriate. By action, not just words!

The principle of self management

Self-management is generally the most effective method of management

---

Louis A. Allen, management consultant and writer. Founder of Louis Allen Worldwide

Bottom-up involving people at lower levels of the organization in problem-solving within their area of operation. Using the expertise that is available in relation with the work to be done, to develop and execute and improve control activities in their area of operation.

Bottom-up does not mean having rather vague meetings where everyone can have their say about anything and everything. No, it means knowing what should be done, what criteria should be met and what objectives to be reached. It means improvement of what is being done, making agreements, keeping schedules and having concrete communications.

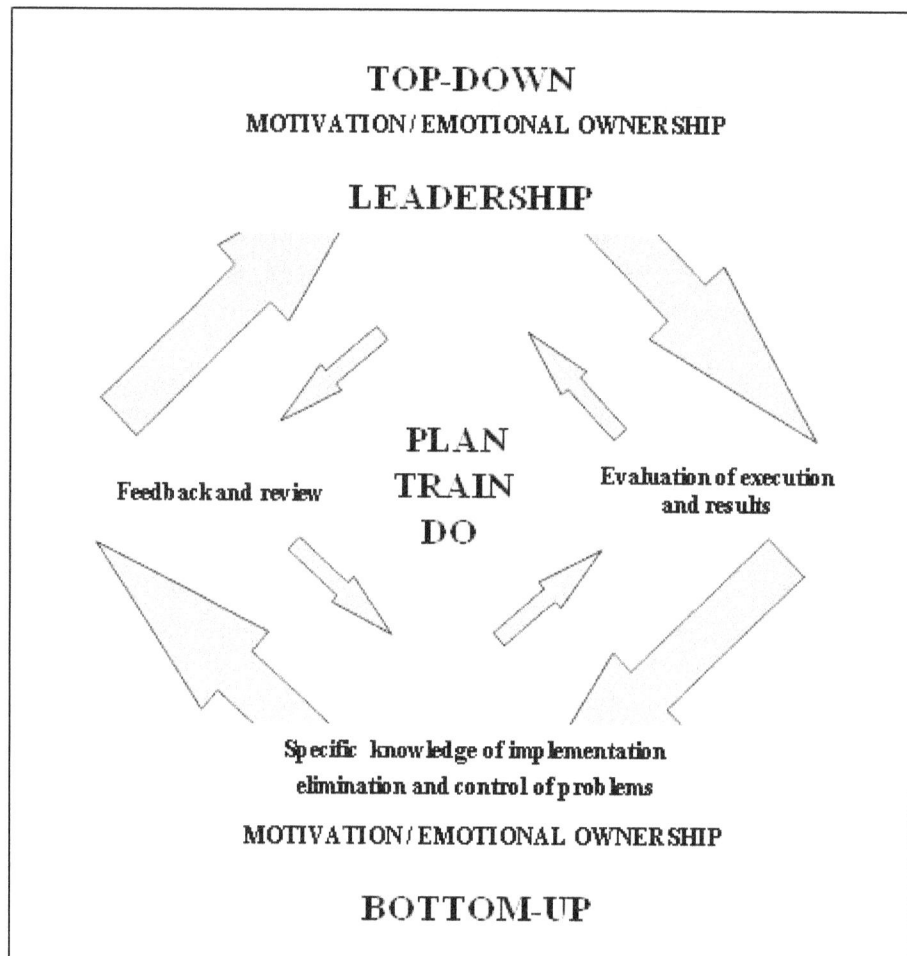

TOP-DOWN
MOTIVATION / EMOTIONAL OWNERSHIP

LEADERSHIP

PLAN
TRAIN
DO

Feedback and review

Evaluation of execution and results

Specific knowledge of implementation elimination and control of problems

MOTIVATION / EMOTIONAL OWNERSHIP

BOTTOM-UP

Picture 8.4 - Success through a combination of top-down & bottom-up

Involvement of employees and lower management levels may include:

- Setting up, maintaining and improving the management system
- Design and modification of installations and workplace

- Identification of workplace hazards
- Identification of "critical" tasks, analysis of those and the establishment of task procedures or work practices
- Periodic review and improvement of existing procedures
- Conducting planned inspections in their own department
- Analysis of accidents and incidents
- Establishment of rules and regulations
- Selection of protective equipment

Considering bottom-up involvement, you have to realize that this does not come by itself. Positive bottom-up involvement should be introduced top-down into the organization while establishing effective two-way communication channels. In fact, top-management should want and encourage bottom-up involvement to make it truly effective. Adequate (prompt, correct, positive) management response to problems, solutions and suggestions originating from lower levels of the organizational hierarchy is necessary.

Key word in picture 8.4 is "emotional ownership" meaning that people experience the plan or management system as "our" system, our plan. This ownership should be present at all levels.

8.1.6. The 17-step process towards success

The three platform columns or legs: (re)directing the organization (Plan), training (Train) and implementation (Do) should be combined in a process to gradually grow from where you are to where you want to be. This process involves the making and execution of a plan, a management system or "standing plan" containing the management activity areas or "elements" considered essential to reach the overall objective(s). These elements contain specific (element) activities to reach specific (element) objectives contributing to the results of the overall system.

This process should include logical chronological steps and start at the top of the organization going down in line with the two-way top-down/bottom-up approach. During my consulting practice I established a process consisting of 11 steps, later to become 16 steps and finally 17, to include:

1. Top manager leadership – management leadership and motivation
2. Management team leadership – management leadership and motivation
3. Management improvement team – management leadership and coordination
4. Internal expertise - internal expertise to guide the process
5. Project communicated – communicating the process to all in the organization
6. Opinion surveys – finding out what people think and feel.
7. Base-line assessment (audit") – assessing present activities.
8. Selection of elements/activity areas - selection of critical elements for success
9. Introduction training – information to all levels.

10. Establish element coordination (teams) – to coordinate element development
11. Element coordination (team) training/instruction – to coordinate element development and execution
12. Element development – making of the element plan(s); activities to reach the element objective(s)
13. Element implementation training – training of people to carry out the work
14. Management briefing – leadership, support and motivation by managers and supervisors
15. Carry out element activities – implementation and assessment of element activities and results; do what needs to be done
16. Review by the management improvement team - overall management system results
17. Extend project, repeat process – to reach, maintain and improve level of performance

The above process, based on the Platform model, shows the path along which to build a management system on the way to success. It includes all levels in the organization, the making of the system or plan, training of people, execution of plan activities and periodic assessment of what is being done and what the results are. See appendix L (page 280) for a further description of these 17 steps.

When using the 17 step process, keep the four management principles below in mind.

The ones that will work for you to get people involved:

The principle of emotional ownership (1)

People tend to be more willing to participate in planned change when they have an opportunity to participate and influence the process leading to change

---

The principle of participation

Motivation to accomplish results tends to increase as people are given opportunity to participate in matters affecting those results.

Louis A. Allen, management consultant and writer. Founder of Louis Allen Worldwide

And the principles that you have to be aware of as they may work against you:

The principle of emotional ownership (2)

The more ownership people have in the way a present situation has developed, the more difficult it is to change.

> **The principle of resistance to change**
>
> The greater the departure of any planned change from the accepted ways
> of the past, the greater the potential resistance by the people involved

Louis A. Allen, management consultant and writer. Founder of Louis Allen Worldwide

The reason why I developed this process was simply that I realized that at some time my customers would or could say: "Hey, Willem, we have been paying you for improving our safety record but where are the results?" I also realized that it was not me improving their safety record; it could only be the customer creating their own success from their own efforts. My main role was to let them know what they should be doing so they could get what they want.

And so I did, I made the process but unfortunately and due to several circumstances, I was only able to get limited experience with the practical application of this process. One of the reasons why I could not get the experience that I was looking for was that the company I was working for between 1991 and 1999 did not accept the process as a common reference for consulting activity. Possibly because the consulting of that company was mainly directed at helping customers to get a certificate which is quite different from consulting for actual improvement.

BOA ME NA ME MMOA WO - symbol of cooperation and interdependence

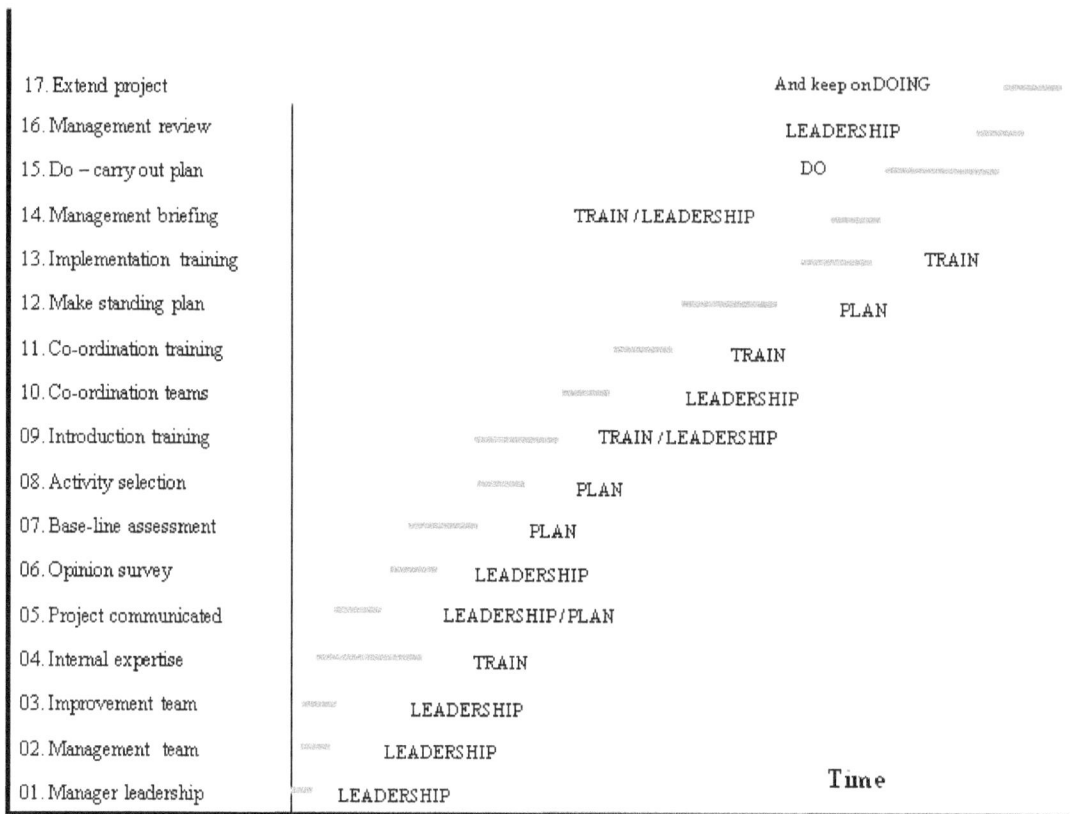

17. Extend project	And keep on DOING
16. Management review	LEADERSHIP
15. Do – carry out plan	DO
14. Management briefing	TRAIN / LEADERSHIP
13. Implementation training	TRAIN
12. Make standing plan	PLAN
11. Co-ordination training	TRAIN
10. Co-ordination teams	LEADERSHIP
09. Introduction training	TRAIN / LEADERSHIP
08. Activity selection	PLAN
07. Base-line assessment	PLAN
06. Opinion survey	LEADERSHIP
05. Project communicated	LEADERSHIP / PLAN
04. Internal expertise	TRAIN
03. Improvement team	LEADERSHIP
02. Management team	LEADERSHIP
01. Manager leadership	LEADERSHIP

Time

Picture 8.5 - the 17-step process towards success

8.1.7. The structure towards success

The management system is the plan to be executed towards success. To stimulate this, each element of the management system should have the structure to motivate execution of activities to reach element objectives. The assumption behind this is that the elements are vital to reaching the objectives of the overall system. In other words if elements objectives are not obtained then the overall objective will not be reached. It also works the other way: if the overall objectives are obtained while some of the element objectives are not then those elements may not be essential for the whole system.

I developed the following structure that should be in all elements unless there are reasons to deviate from this.

The structure (see also appendix O, page 289):

1.   Element policy and management statement including:
       - Reason for element activity
       - Goals and objectives of element
2.   Coordination of element development
       - Training/instruction of people involved in element coordination
3.   Element plan development
       - 3.1. Review of legislation/standards for minimum requirements
       - 3.2. Additional element activities as indicated by other sources
       - 3.3. Employee participation in development of element activities
       - 3.4. Employee training to execute element activities
       - 3.5. Employee participation in execution of element activities
       - 3.6. Communication needs to internal/external parties
            o   Data collection and analysis
       - 3.7. Assessment of activities and results
            o   Periodic evaluation of element activities
            o   Periodic evaluation of element results in relation to element objectives
4.   Review and improvement

Does the structure have to be as indicated above? In principle, my answer is "yes" but you may be able to combine certain items so in practice it may look different. Not a problem, as long as the essentials are there.

One example: I am presently involved in suggesting an update of a certification scheme that exists for about 20 years now. The suggested overall structure of the scheme - consisting of 8 chapters or elements is provided in picture 8.6.

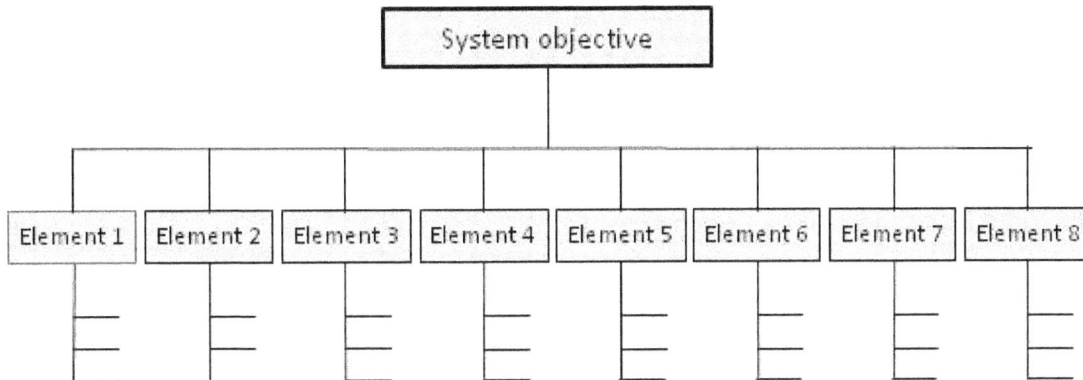

Picture 8.6 – Suggested structure of management system reference

The proposed structure of each element then looks as follows:

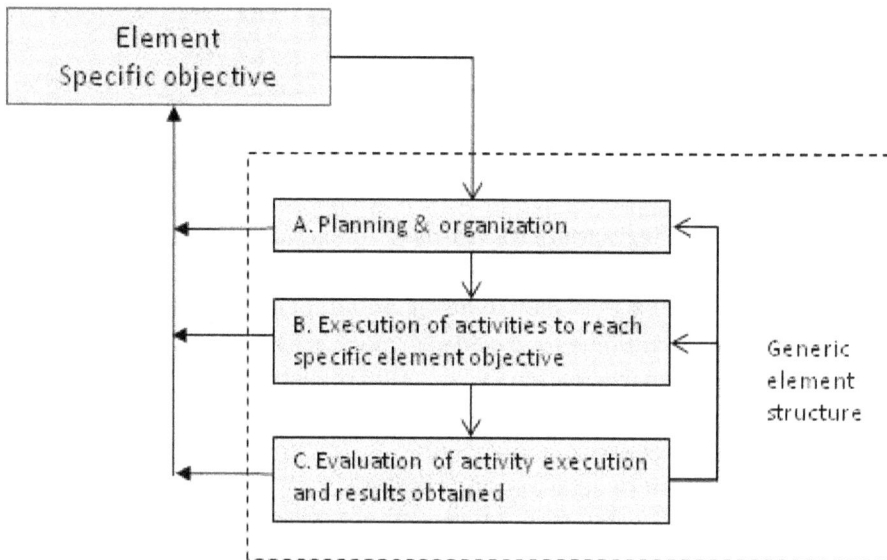

Picture 8.7 – Suggested generic structure of management system elements

The proposed structure as indicated in picture 8.7 includes the elements specific objective and the generic structure including:

A. Planning and organization includes three levels:
   1. Management (leadership) – why the element is there and the objectives to be obtained
   2. Coordination – assignment of responsibility and resources for element coordination
   3. Operational - involved of operational levels in developing and executing element activities
B. Execution of activities including the specific elements activities – what, whom, how and when – to reach the element objective
C. Periodic assessment of what is being done and what results are being obtained. Reporting findings including any suggestions for improvement when desired results are not being obtained

The structure basically includes the cycle for improvement and is, as you can see, based on the Platform model for change and improvement. The picture below shows this cycle as the "Improvement Wheel" where the element- or "standing" plan is contained in the axle which is driven by the "engine" built around it and fuelled (pushed and pulled) by management leadership, the foundation of the Platform model: Plan – Train – Do.

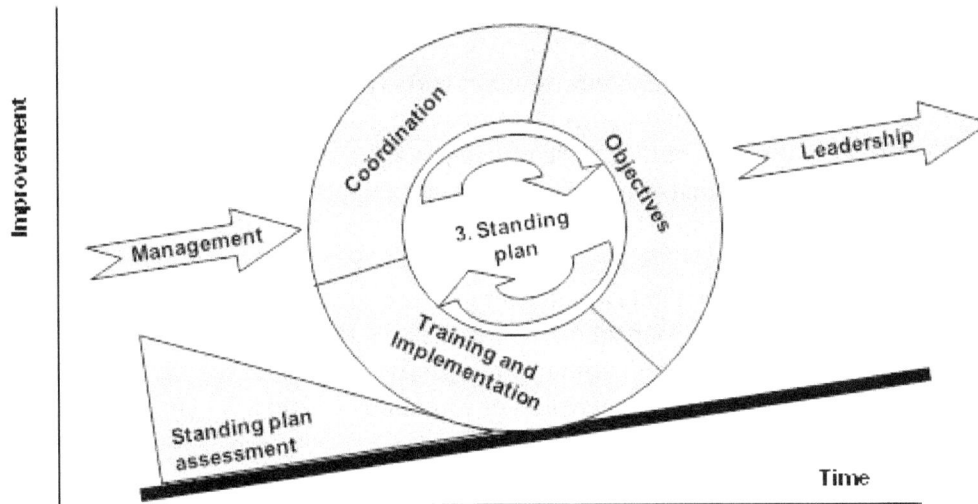

Picture 8.8 – The "improvement" wheel

8.1.8. Evaluating the process towards success

I think assessment is pretty important - of what is being done and what results are being obtained. It should therefore not be a surprise to you that I set up a method to evaluate the use of the 17-step process. I called that "17-step rating". Basically, making that was relatively easy. I gave a maximum of 100 points – easy when you want to express results in percentages – to the entire process and then divided those 100 points over the 17 steps. The result of that you can see in appendix M (page 284). The rating is based on my thinking; you may want to distribute the total score (100) differently over the 17 steps.

Unfortunately, due to circumstances, I was only able to use the rating once during mid nineties and involving a chemical company in The Netherlands that had a not so good accident rate. In 3 to 4 hours we – 4 people of the company including the safety, quality and environmental managers, their boss, the QESH manager and I – evaluated the efforts of the company in those three areas. Their average score was just over 30% with safety scoring highest at 42%. Of course, the score is relative, not absolute, but it may help communication while showing areas that may need additional attention.

Using the 17-step process will involve all levels in the organization and help to create the behavior and culture desired. But be aware: there are no guarantees - the process shows the way and you will have to work at it to make the success that you are looking for. If you do not get that success, look again at what you are doing and do if different, do it better. And remember: there are no quick fixes, no magic wands, when it comes to lasting success.

8.1.9. Risk/loss control and (safety) legislation

Legislation regarding safety, health and environment varies per country. Having said that, I consider that these legislative requirements largely have the same objectives: to reduce (certain type of) accidents in industry. To obtain those objectives, legislation requires industry to do just that: reduce unwanted events that (can) result in harm to people, (property) and the environment.

In 1978 and trying to make a point in favor of safety/loss control, I wrote an article that was published in the Journal of Safety Management of the NSMS, the National Safety Management Society, with the title: "Loss Control – Societal Implications". The article message I tried to convey was this: "Either you regulate yourselves or somebody will do it for you".

From the article:

"One of the major risks threatening our free enterprise business system is the increasing influence of government and the subsequent loss of management autonomy. Unfortunately this is a long-term development and is not recognized on a large scale. Some government guidance is good, too much government control and regulation isn't. It is difficult to draw the line in some cases but it is certainly worthwhile to consider, for the individual organization as well as for business management as a whole; either you self-regulate or the government will do it for you. Besides that, a number of the activities that can be taken to prevent too much government involvement are just sound business practices.

If we want tomorrow's society to be a place to live in, in freedom, it requires long term vision, self-regulation, commitment, justice and excellent performance. It is there where a major part of management's attention should be focused and energy be spent and where the loss control/safety manager can assist rather than just trying to bring the accident rate down, living within the context of the law."

Anyway, I am not sure that the message got across. So far, we have seen increase in legislation because at least part of industry and its management have failed to take appropriate measures. So we end up with Seveso legislation which was named after the Seveso incident in 1976. Is it different now or will it be in the future? I don't think so. As I mentioned at the beginning of this book, we just experienced the fertilizer plant explosion in Texas and the acrylonitrile train derailment in Belgium. Not to forget the disaster train derailment in Spain on July 24, 2013 killing at least 80 people. Those events alone may very well lead to additional regulations or to stricter application of existing ones. And they should – if you do not regulate yourselves, somebody else will do it for you, eventually. It has always been that way and always will be so. And, by the way, the main message of my 1978 article does not apply to business alone; it applies to all aspects of life and society. Anywhere. For example: think about the worldwide financial crisis that became evident in 2008, the role of the financial world and the increased regulations by governments further limiting the freedom to the operation of financial institutions – and rightly so!

Am I pointing at (top) management just to blame them? I am pointing at them, "yes" but "no" not just to blame them. Blame only, if they have not made sure that their organizations have proper management systems installed. After all, those management systems are (also) their management systems; they should have taken the initiative and they have the greatest influence on how well management systems operate. The other side of the coin is that they can have a major impact on creating safe systems by initiating and making possible that management systems reach desired objectives while, at the same time, preventing unwanted events and their consequences, sometimes disasters. And, not to forget: limiting government influence!

This management influence is not limited to industry but applies to all leaders – top managers and politicians - in all societal organizations and structures: industry, banks, (non-) governmental organizations. Including all type of systems, not just production. Just ask yourselves this question: "Who were the people that had the main influence on the occurrence of the financial crisis that became so evident in 2008?' Not "banking", not "politics". Those are institutions. It is always people who are responsible and often those we call "leaders".

It is not my intention to discuss legislation in any detail and within the purpose of this book it is sufficient to show the overall relation between legislation and the objectives and principles used in this book with regard to safety, loss control and risk management. The detail of the legislation is determined by the legislator filling the gaps that are left by industrial management. I am not trying to say that legislation is bad; a good aspect of legislation is that it creates a level playing field for all. That process has been going on since the beginning of the industrial revolution and even way before that. Unfortunately the bad companies – from a "safety" point of view – probably will have a greater impact on legislation that the good ones.

In picture 8.9, I have tried to highlight the main issues you can find in international safety, health and environmental legislation. The picture shows that legislation basically has the same objectives as risk management, loss control and safety and that should not come as a surprise.

```
┌─────────────────────────────────────────────────────────────────────┐
│                                                                       │
│        Safety and Environmental Legislation – some common denominators│
│                                                                       │
│   Purpose                                                             │
│                                                                       │
│   Improve safety, health, wellbeing, environment                      │
│           ▪ establish present situation ...................... audit  │
│           ▪ establish objectives ...................... (annual) plan │
│           ▪ execution of plan                                         │
│           ▪ feedback ...................... assessment, annual report │
│                                                                       │
│   Industry obligation                                                 │
│           ▪ execute an active  SHE policy                             │
│                   o establish and execute policy                      │
│                   o periodic assessment of policy execution           │
│                   o training/instruction to carry out work            │
│                   o communication management - employees              │
│   Execution                                                           │
│           ▪ continuity ................ integration in organization   │
│                                                                       │
└─────────────────────────────────────────────────────────────────────┘
```

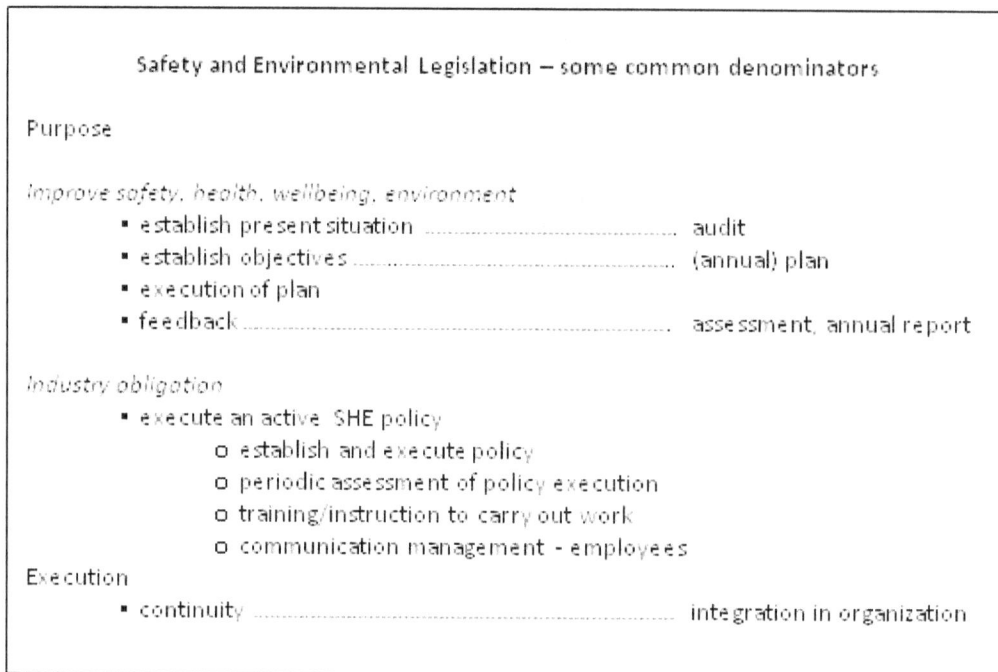

Picture 8.9 - SHE legislation, some main points

The relation between legislation and risk management becomes apparent when looking at the heart of risk management, the control activities embedded in the organization: the (safety) management system. With the twenty elements of the ISRS in mind it will not be difficult to see how a good safety audit system as the ISRS, or similar, is well fitted to live up to legislative requirements. In picture 8.10, I have tried to briefly show the relationship between the scope of safety and health legislation and the possibilities that a good audit system has to offer when it comes to compliance.

```
┌────────────────────────┐        ┌────────────────────────┐
│     Legislation         │        │  Safety audit system    │
│                         │        │        (ISRS)           │
│  Improving (industrial) │        │                         │
│  safety, health and     │        │   Means to improve      │
│   environment.          │        │  activities directed at │
│                         │        │     the control of      │
│  Reduction of unwanted  │        │ accidents, losses, risks│
│   events such as        │        │   and other unwanted    │
│  accidents and incidents│        │       events.           │
└────────────────────────┘        └────────────────────────┘
             │                                  │
             ▼                                  ▼
        ┌──────────────────────────────────────────┐
        │  Planning                                  │
        │                                            │
        │  • establish present situation             │
        │  • setting objectives                      │
        │  • preparation of (annual) plan            │
        │  • execution of plan                       │
        │  • assessment, feedback, report            │
        └──────────────────────────────────────────┘
                          │
                          ▼
        ┌──────────────────────────────────────────┐
        │  Policy and execution                      │
        │                                            │
        │  • adaptation of organization              │
        │  • training, instruction                   │
        │  • communication                           │
        └──────────────────────────────────────────┘
```

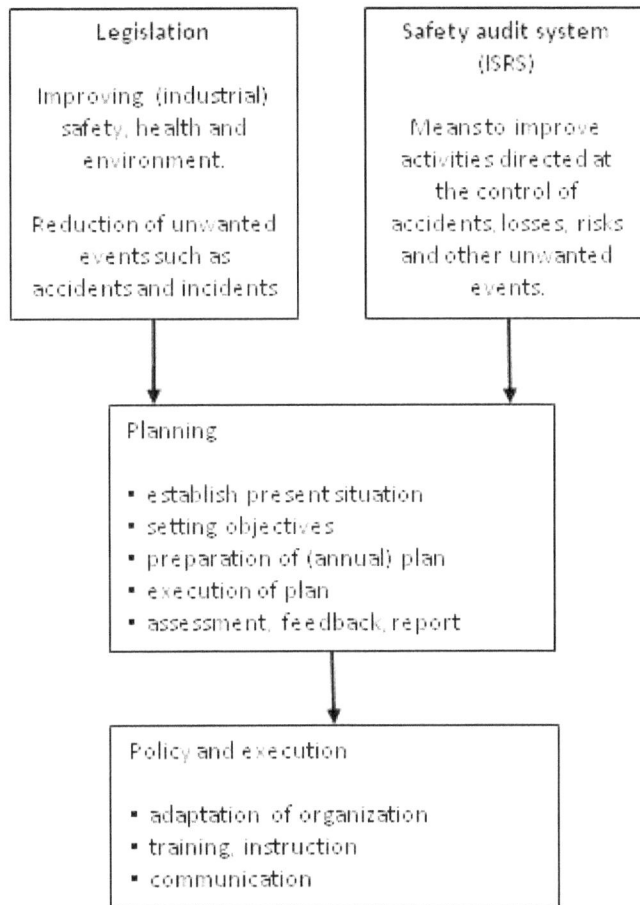

Picture 8.10 - Safety audit and legislation

8.1.10. How to obtain a desired culture

I do not want to spent too much on this subject but want to address it anyway as the subject receives quite a bit of attention these days. That in itself is not so strange. People want to improve safety – or quality or anything else, for that matter – and think or feel that they need to focus on "the culture" which they consider the reason why the behavior of people is not what it should be. That seems a bit like finding that the main cause of accidents is "behavior" or "communication".

I am not saying that culture, behavior and communication are not relevant. But putting the focus there is like putting the horse behind the cart – at least that is how I look at it. I consider these issues as end products of what you put into the system; remember Hyman on page 16. Asking people what they think about their safety system – that too is a result of what is put into the system and how it was set up. But I think doing opinion surveys (see appendix H, page 262) can be a good thing. It is also included as step 6 of the 17-step process that I suggest. An opinion survey can help to prepare the organization for changes to come but only if the survey is part of the entire change process; it should not stand on its own. Look again at the 17-step process and see which steps are before and directly after the opinion survey (see page 280, appendix L).

As I said before, I used to do safety management audits using the ISRS (International Safety Rating System) and had opinion surveys done prior to the audit. Those surveys helped me to the get a lot of information from different levels in the organization related to the safety management efforts that I was about to evaluate. I never found any (major) discrepancies between opinion survey results and the result of the audit. And that was one reason why I stopped doing these surveys prior to audit. Another reason was that doing these surveys was not part of the ISRS audits done by others including my US colleagues what made my audits were more expensive to the customer. But I still think that doing opinion surveys prior to the audit was, and is, a good idea.

When wanting to improve culture, the attention often goes to finding out what people do, feel, think and then work backwards. While that has its value, my preference would be to put more energy in obtaining the desired culture by involving everyone in building the management system, carry out its activities, maintain and improve it. Changing the culture should start at the top of the organization.

If behavior is an issue, should you carry out behavior observations using teams of managers to observe the behavior of people at the shop floor? Focusing on behavior that way may be contra productive and may enlarge the gap between management and operational personnel. So be careful and if you really need to do those observations, do them only for a limited period of time and after proper preparation. Observation programs, directed at operational personnel, start at the wrong level and could be seen as a failure of (top) management and the management system.

If behavior is an issue, have you made a serious effort to get the behavior you want? Is culture not a product of the shared behavior of many? In particular of the behavior of (top) managers? Have procedures, rules, work instructions been set up involving the people that are expected to work and behave in line with these procedures and rules? Are these behavior guidelines updated with their help? Look at appendix K (page 275) for a guide to prepare rules etc.

If communication is an issue, have you identified what the communication should be about?

I think that to obtain a desired culture, you need to work at the management system in a way I described in this chapter (8.1) and involving all relevant personnel at all levels. I like to believe that the suggested 17-step process forms the pathway to obtain the culture that you want. But you need to work at it and do not wait too long or your culture may have gone down the drain and beyond the point of no-return.

If you want this chronological, I think in this order: communication – behavior – culture and they all can come from a properly build, maintained and improved management system. That simple? Yes, I think it is. It boils down to making a plan, involve knowledgeable people and do what needs to be done. But you need to do it with the people, not for them.

Peter Drucker

What you have to do and the way you have to do it is incredibly simple.
Whether you are willing to do it, that's another matter.

Peter Drucker (1909 – 2005) – management consultant, educator and author

Picture 8.11 shows it schematically; success being obtained through the repeated application of Plan – Train – Do. And the leadership to fuel the process. If you do not get the wanted results, you are obviously not doing the right things in the right way; so change what you are doing, do it over, do it different and do it again.

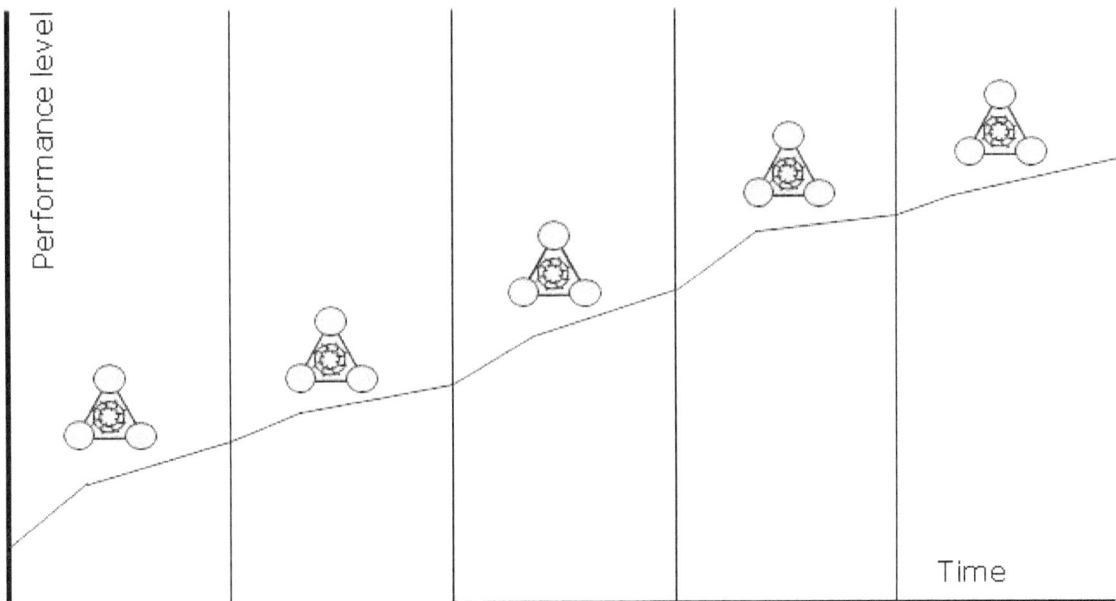

Picture 8.11 - Arriving where you want to be: Plan-Train-Do and keep on doing

8.2. Auditing to maintain and improve your management system

In chapter 8.1 we basically looked at how to make a management system so that you can expect results to be what you want them to be.

Irrespective of how you came to the management system, once you have decided that you will have one, you also need to make sure that activities are being carried out properly and that the system is being maintained and improved as necessary.

Basically there are two "instruments" that are available:

- Carry out audits of (part of) the management system
- Learn from unwanted events

While "audits" are discussed in this chapter, "learning from unwanted events" is the subject of chapter 9.3 (page 212).

As I previously mentioned, the basis of risk management/loss control management and safety lies in the way in which management activities are set up, structured and carried out.

There are these three important issues to remember:

- The way the management system is built (Process)
- The content or "elements" of that system (Content)
- The structure of the system, or rather of its elements (Structure)

In chapter 8.1.6 (page 151), I discussed the process to make a management system and in 8.1.7 (page 154) the structure of the system elements got some attention. Both subjects are extended a bit in appendices L (page 280) and O (page 289) respectively. You will find some examples of the possible content of a (safety) management system in appendix N (page 285).

To allow desired changes and to achieve effective control of the organization and its current and potential losses it is advisable to look at what is being done at the moment. Actually this is part of the process that I suggest to build a management system. To find out what is being done and how, it is recommended to use a "measuring stick"; a reference to which the actual efforts of your organization are compared. Called an "audit", I will refer to the safety audit system that I have been working with in the past; the ISRS (International Safety Rating System) that has been on the market since 1978.

In principle, you may use any available audit system as long as it meets the necessary criteria. One of those criteria is that your reference or measuring stick should be sufficiently detailed and comprehensive. Measuring against a (very) limited reference does not make much sense and may not help you to build or improve your own management system. Using an external reference may help you to learn from the experience of others.

You may also be able to use certification scheme criteria that are available in the market, such as the contractor safety certification scheme (SCC) that exists in The Netherlands and some other European countries or schemes such as OHSAS 18000 or the new ISO 45001 (safety), ISO 9000 (quality), ISO 14000 (environment) and ISO 31000 (risk management).

Whatever your choice, the best audit systems to use to build your own management system should be extensive and contain sufficient detail from which you can select activities to be included in your system.

The limits of a "safety" audit are set by the organization defining what is meant by "safety". The more traditional approach "preventing lost time injury accidents" or the much broader concept of "loss control" to also include other types of unwanted events. The broader approach will shift the focus from traditional safety to risk management and may lead to a more integrated approach to include safety, quality, and environment.

In principle, an "audit" can be used for two reasons:

- To maintain your management system and make sure that activities are being carried out as intended and results are being obtained
- To improve your management system

For maintenance you would use an audit reference that reflects your own management system. For improvement you would probably use an external system that goes (way) beyond your own system.

8.2.1. The ISRS – International Safety Rating System

To discuss the subject "auditing" in some detail, I am using the ISRS as I have been working with that system and its predecessors between 1974 and 1991 and have known the ISRS until 1999.

What I will say when referring to the ISRS is, in principle, also true for other systems. The difference between ISRS and other systems may be in the detail, the number of questions and reference points and the presence of an award system based on a quantitative score of elements and their activities. In the discussion below, please remember that I have known the ISRS from before the first edition until, and including, the sixth. Since 1991, ISRS is owned by DNV (Det Norske Veritas, now DNV-GL) and is presently in its 8th edition.

The development of, what later became, the ISRS was started in the early seventies under the leadership and direction of Frank E. Bird, Jr., at that time Director of Engineering Services of INA (Insurance Company of North America). This first development took place under the "Total Loss Control" umbrella, a service that INA offered to its insureds. After INA, Frank Bird set up his own company (ILCI – International Loss Control Institute) where he developed the ISRS system and brought it to the market in 1978. Since then, ISRS became one of the most comprehensive methods for assessing and improving safety and loss control management systems and -activities. It served as an auditing reference and award system, was used to develop safety management systems and was an excellent way to introduce risk management into an organization. (I think that ISRS is still used in those capacities; if you want up-to-date information contact DNV-GL at www.dnvgl.com).

The ISRS, as I knew it, contained 20 activity areas as the "elements" of a safety and loss control management system. Picture 8.12 below shows the elements as they were at the beginning of the 1990's.

ISRS Elements

1. Leadership and administration
2. Leadership training
3. Planned inspections and maintenance
4. Critical task analysis and -procedures
5. Accident/incident analysis
6. Job observations
7. Emergency preparedness
8. Rules and work permits
9. Accident/incident analysis
10. Knowledge and skill training
11. Personal protective equipment
12. Health and hygiene control
13. System evaluation
14. Engineering and change management
15. Individual communications
16. Group communications
17. General promotion
18. Hiring and placement
19. Materials and services management
20. Off-the-job safety

Picture 8.12 – Elements of edition 6 of the ISRS (International Safety Rating System)

Since 1978, the ISRS has been updated based on market developments and international experiences. This way, the ISRS remained up-to-date and attractive for users as a means to set up and improve their risk/loss control and safety management efforts.

Through periodic updates – 8 editions between 1978 and 2009 – the ISRS remained a top of the line auditing system and reference moving from mainly safety directed to the present integrated approach including safety, health, environment and quality. The ISRS up to the 6th edition did not include the structure in each of its elements that I mentioned in section 8.1.7 (page 154). I feel that structure is crucial in any management system and should be included in related audit systems. The reasoning behind this is that all elements of a management system should be important to reach the objective(s) of the total system. For this reason each element should have its own – specific - objective and the structure to drive implementation of activities and periodic assessment of activity execution and results obtained.

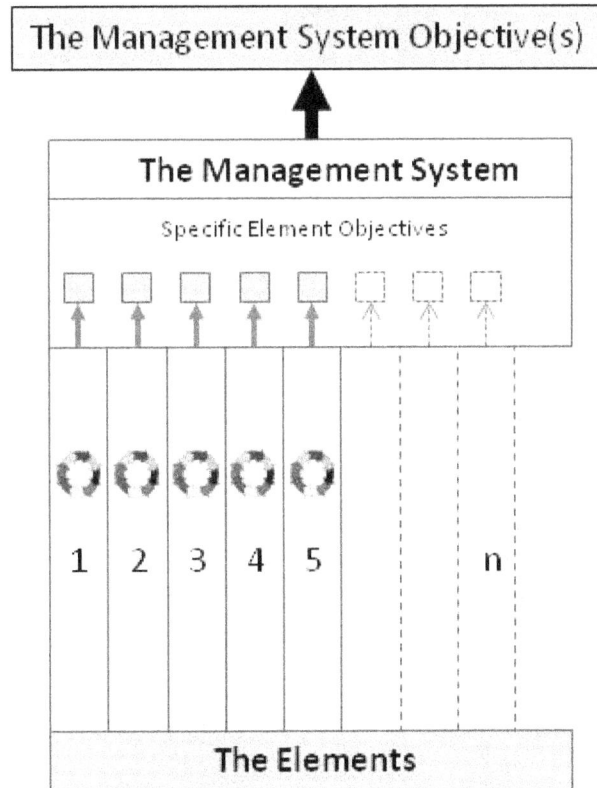

Picture 8.13 - The management system with its composing elements

An interesting experience included the ISRS and a process industry version (IPSRS, in which P= Process industry) that I helped making in 1993. The process industry version included the element structure mentioned on page 154 while the original edition did not. Both audit systems included scoring opportunities resulting in a level recognition for the entire management system ranging from 1 to 10 with 10 being the highest possible level. Both audit instruments were used parallel to each other when auditing a chemical plant in Spain. The audit using the original system resulted in a level 8 rating while the rating with the process industry version did not go beyond level 1. A precondition using the latter version was that the improvement cycle, as represented by the structure, had to be there and had to form a closed loop. Whether the comparison (level 8 vs. level 1) was right is hard to tell, yet I was convinced then and am still now that the structure should be included as the driving force of element application toward system success. As you has seen in chapter 8.1.7 (page 154), the structure includes involvement of (multiple) people responsible for the work to be done. Would it not be logical to include the improvement loop when you want results from your management system or plan?

The activity areas as mentioned in picture 8.12 (page 166) existed in the ISRS at least till and including the sixth edition; the present – 8th edition – has 15 elements but I do not think that this will make a difference for the discussion below.

In principle, the ISRS is based on the management concept of Louis A. Allen and consists of the first two steps of the ISMEC acronym mentioned in paragraph 4.2 (page 50), the "I" and the "S":

- *Identification* of (management) activity areas or elements to reach the objectives of the system while, at the same time, controlling of risks, unwanted events and their (potential) losses
- Establishing *standards* or criteria for element activities to arrive at desired element results

The ISRS I used to know contained about 600 questions/criteria divided over the 20 activity areas mentioned in picture 8.12.

An important aspect of the ISRS was, and probably still is, that each element was provided with a maximum (relative) score (number of points) divided over the element criteria and allowing scoring of the element activity in a numerical and percentage value. So, for example, it became possible to express the accident investigation efforts of a company as 50% in comparison with the related ISRS element maximum score. The same was possible for all elements allowing a total score for the overall management system which was then expressed in a "level" ranging from 1 to 10 with 10 being the highest.

```
5.      ACCIDENT/INCIDENT ANALYSIS/STATISTICS (45)

5.1.    Procedure for investigating/analyzing  accidents/incidents  (8)

        5.1.1.   Is there a procedure for reporting and analysis of
                 accidents/incidents? (2)                                    yes/no _____

        5.1.2.   Does this procedure include:

                 •   reporting of accidents/incidents by employees? (1)      yes/no _____
                 •   system for evaluation of accidents in terms of potential severity
                     and frequency of occurrence? (1)                        yes/no _____
                 •   methods to be used for analysis? (1)                     yes/no _____

        5.1.3.   Is this procedure made known to all managers, supervisors and
                 workers? (2)                                                 yes/no _____

        5.1.4.   Does the procedure include worker involvement in the
                 analyzing/investigation process? (1)                        yes/no _____
```

Picture 8.14 – Example of audit system questions with value factors allowing activity scoring

Being able to properly carry out an audit of a management system would boil down to knowing the right questions to ask and knowing what, within a certain margin, the proper answers should be.

In 1996, when working with DNV, I contributed to making a reference document that was later included as one of the publications used in making OHSAS 18001: 1999 – "Occupational health and safety management systems – Specification". Making the document - "DNV standard for certification of occupational health and safety management systems (OHSMS):1997" was not really that difficult as it was based on the ISO 14000. Making the questions to be asked during an audit was not difficult either as it practically meant putting documents sentences into questions. Making a reference for acceptability of answers, however, took more effort. In practice, this meant to indicate what the "right" answers could be to the questions asked. Very essential in any process in which various people are involved to come up with end conclusions such as is the case of certification.

When making an audit system, agreement between professionals about what the accepted answers to the audit questions should be, is critical. If not done properly, it leaves too much interpretation to the auditor to decide what is acceptable. That decision would then largely depend on the knowledge, experience and attitude of the auditor, his or her integrity and any commercial or other aspects that may influence the decision-making. Too much freedom of interpretation, due to the lack of clarity as to what is acceptable, will ultimately affect the quality and results of an audit. In case of certification this would affect the quality of the certificate and its acceptance by stakeholders. Providing a description of "right" answers will limit the interpretation margin between auditors and the (minimum) level of the certificate will be better "guaranteed". It will also help companies – and consultants - to better set up their management system to meet certification requirements.

Once proper questions and answers have been agreed upon, the audit will help to establish what an organization is doing by:

- Reviewing documents to verify contents and structure of the management system
- Reviewing registrations containing data in relation to the execution of management system activities
- Interviewing people expected to have adequate knowledge of the system and execution of its activities
- Site/location visits to observe physical conditions, the behavior of people during their work and to further interview people that are at the receiving end of the management system

It is important that strict rules are setup and followed by knowledgeable people (the auditors) in order to get maximum objectivity and uniformity in performing audits and their results.

The result of an audit may graphically look as shown in picture 8.15 on the next page. A picture like this may be the starting point to take action to further improve the management system activities. Improvement suggestions should be part of the audit report.

Let me stop here and say something about the difference between two categories of audit systems:

- Proprietary audit systems with or without some sort of recognition
- Audit systems falling under an accreditation regime and leading to accredited certification

ISRS and similar audit systems belong to the first category while audit questionnaires originating from certification standards and used to obtain an ISO, OHSAS or other certificate are of the second category.

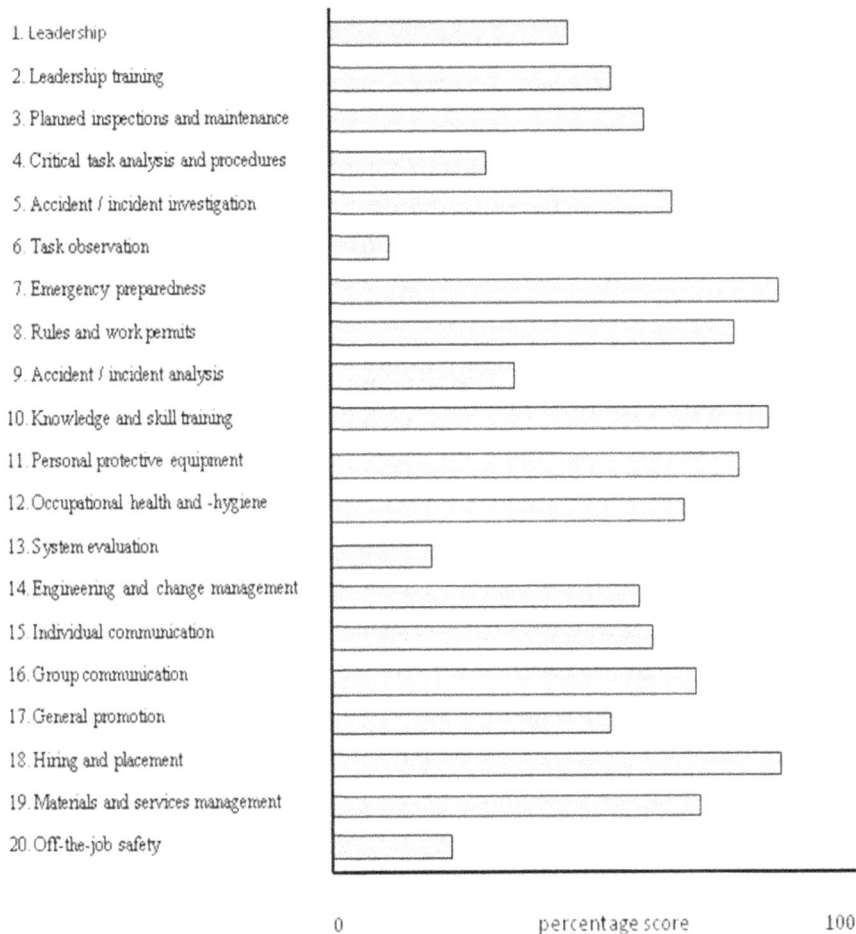

Picture 8.15 - Graphical summary of a safety program

While these two types of audits share a number of issues, they are also different in some aspects:

- Proprietary audit systems have controls set by the owner of the system while ISO and similar audits are supervised by Accreditation Societies. In case of proprietary audit systems it is up to the owner of the system to determine audit process, auditor qualifications, award levels etc. In case of accredited certification the same rules, procedures etc. apply to all organizations issuing certificates. These "certification institutes" are competing in a commercial market in which all provide the same product: the ISO or OHSAS certificate. They are like bakers competing for a market share while all are selling the same bread and price may be an important item for the customer when deciding where to buy.

- Proprietary audit systems are not so much subject to competitive pressure as accredited certification. Certification audits and certificates are subject to competition between certification institutes all making use of the same reference. This may lead to seeking the lower interpretation margins that are always there when (professional) judgment is an issue.
- Proprietary audit systems may have more than one award level allowing companies to grow in time while still using the same reference. ISRS, for example used to have, and probably still has, 10 award levels. (These levels used to be identified by stars, by the way, 1 to 5 green stars for the lower and 1 to 5 gold stars for the higher levels of the award system.) Certification schemes normally have one award level only, the minimum level at which a certificate will be issued. A proprietary audit system – like the ISRS – may provide percentage scores per element and for the entire management system which can be important for communication to stakeholders. An accredited certification system does not have that; you either meet the (minimum) certification level or not.
- Proprietary systems would normally include recommendations for improvement which may be within the scope of the audit reference or not and include suggestions of how to implement the recommendations. Accredited certification does not, formally, allow recommendations to be made although not meeting certain criteria to reach the required level, of course, indicates where improvement is possible. Although I can see some reasons why auditing (for certification) and consulting should not formally be mixed, I also think that you cannot be a good auditor if you are not a good consultant and the other way around. So where to draw the line and why?
- Proprietary systems have their own characteristics, own niche, own "captive" market. They stand separate from accredited certification and are appreciated for that. However, the possible award level – such as is the case with ISRS – may not be fully understood by the market that wants to make use of the audit results in decision-making, for example which contractor of supplier to select.
- Proprietary systems allow growth over a longer time period. Accredited certification systems function in an environment in which external (commercial) pressure plays an important role; possibly leading to spending less time to reach the certificate level. Less time could very well mean less involvement of company personnel at all levels which is one of the cornerstones of reaching and maintaining organizational success.

The main difference between the two audit categories may really be the purpose for which of the organization is undergoing an audit; is it to improve or to get the certificate? If the intention is to get a certificate, practice is often that further efforts stop when the certificate is obtained. Does it have to be that way? No, and a good consultant – either internal to the company or external – should know how to guide his or her company or client after the certification level has been reached. Whether he/she will be able to use that knowledge of course is a different matter – that depends largely on the company/client. By the way, I have nothing against certification as such; certificates are often required by third parties such as legislator or customer. Just keep in mind that certification and improvement may not necessarily be the same.

Quantifying and visualizing audit results are advisable for communication of relevant information to - in particular – higher management levels. A percentage score may mean more than a lengthy report. Even when the audit instrument is not fully understood, a percentage score showing what the situation is in comparison with a - more or less - objective reference drives home a message. Doing 50 % of something that is important to control loss means something and may be an incentive to take action. A certification audit does something similar but does not provide a (percentage) comparison to the reference used and is basically a "go or no go" situation; a certification system does not really offer a look at what is beyond the certificate level. It stops at the level of the certificate and may create the idea "we are doing pretty well, we got the certificate" which may be a reason why companies may not see an incentive to improve beyond the level at which the certificate has been issued.

Quantifying activities provides the possibility to communicate efforts, internally as well as externally. It can be used for setting improvement objectives and for comparing units within a corporation. But quantifying can also lead to negative reactions as not all people want to be measured; they may disagree with the method used which may indicate that the proper attitude to become a top league player is not there. Providing scores and award levels may also create a situation in which reaching the award level may be considered more important than the actual improvement. Doing ISRS audits between the mid seventies and early nineties gave me that experience and I know that puts a lot of pressure on the auditor. This, of course, also applies to any certification process where the company is mainly interested in getting the certificate.

An audit is like a mirror of the management system that is the heart of any structured risk-/loss control or safety management activity. Without proper control over the organization sound (risk) management is not possible. Proper control means control at all levels in the organization; by those at the "point of control" – where the action is – and by those whose decisions and work will affect work procedures and –environments that have an (in-)direct influence on the point of control activities.

Picture 8.16 below is based on my experience with the ISRS between 1978 and 1989. The picture shows the average values obtained from audits covering about fifty companies in the Netherlands and Belgium. Most likely this is not a representative sample of the total population concerned (industrial companies in those countries).

ISRS Elements	Average % Score
1. Leadership and administration	43
2. Leadership training	26
3. Planned inspections and maintenance	35
4. Critical task analysis and -procedures	22
5. Accident/incident analysis	38
6. Job observations	7
7. Emergency preparedness	57
8. Rules and work permits	35
9. Accident/incident analysis	41
10. Knowledge and skill training	39
11. Personal protective equipment	57
12. Health and hygiene control	64
13. System evaluation	30
14. Engineering and change management	37
15. Individual communications	33
16. Group communications	35
17. General promotion	37
18. Hiring and placement	61
19. Materials and services management	37
20. Off-the-job safety	5

Picture 8.16 - Loss control/safety management "state of the art" (1978 – 1989)

I already said that there are two different types of audit systems: (i) proprietary, and (ii) certification. Audits can also be used in two different ways:

- Internal audits – usually based on the company's own management system and used to assess if a location or department is meeting the requirements of the organization as set forth by its management system. Internal audits may also be done as a requirement prior to an external audit for certification. In that case the external reference – the certification scheme - will be used.
- External audits – used to assess meeting external requirements such as for certification, legislation, industry standards or otherwise. External audits may also be used to find possible improvements to the company's management system; in this case the external reference should be more extensive/detailed than the company's own management system.

9.   CONTROLLING LOSS

Under this heading I will mention a number of aspects that I consider important as part of a management system to control loss and which should be considered within a structured approach to control risk/loss. These aspects will be discussed within the framework that was mentioned earlier:

- Creating the organization
- Maintaining the organization
- Improving the organization
  - Learning from unwanted events

I will not discuss the situation where an organization will be taken out of business, including disposal of all physical evidence, installations, buildings etc.

9.1. Creating the organization

The assumption here is that the objective is to make the organization "safe- to- operate". Once that is the status at the start, efforts during the operational phase of the organization will be directed at maintaining that status while adapting it to changing external conditions and expectations – technical, legislation, social, commercial and environmental.

Under the heading "creating the organization" I will discuss the following:

- Design
- Control of critical tasks, work-methods and -procedures
- Rules/regulations
- Selection and placement of personnel
- Purchasing
- Training/instruction of (operational) employees
- Training/instruction of management and supervision

9.1.1. Design

The design of an organization or industrial process is one of the most important features when it comes to controlling risks and loss. Not only with regard to the prevention of substandard conditions (hardware) but also when it comes to preventing substandard operations and acts (work procedures).

Design is important for procurement, not just hardware but, maybe even more so, in relation to people. Design determines what the criteria will be for selecting and purchasing materials, goods, services, personnel, etc. and has an important role with respect to production facilities, work environment and products. Which regard to products, there is a direct relation between design and issues such as product safety/liability and market acceptance/success.

Several aspects to be part of the design phase that may be of great significance concerning risk reduction include:

- Policies and guidelines regarding design and how safety and risk management aspects should be considered. Indicate who should be involved in the design and include end users when it comes to installations, work environment, products and, not to forget, work procedures and operating instructions. Include the safety support functions in the design process and other staff services as applicable such as: insurance, marketing (in case of product safety), etc.
- Designers with experience to include use of methods to identify risks and eliminate or control them. Such methods may include: HAZOP (Hazard and OPerability) studies, FMEA (Failure Mode and Effect Analysis) or failure analysis, fault- and event tree, and the Operational Readiness Tree. Some of these methods are briefly discussed below.
- An experienced safety expert to coordinate the risk identification/-evaluation activities. Although the role of the safety expert may be questioned by some, my opinion is that that the identification of risks requires a certain mindset which normally may only be obtained after years of practice. This mindset basically comes down to consistently seeking answers to the questions: "What can go wrong?", "What are the possible scenarios?", "What consequences could there be?" Technical people may not have this mindset or not sufficiently. Safety people will normally more often deal with these questions and thus may have acquired the proper risk oriented attitude. Having said this, it is not my intention to suggest that the safety expert should solely be responsible for all decisions regarding risk assessment and acceptance. This should be a multidisciplinary process also involving design, construction, maintenance and operation, end users, human resources, insurance and, of course: (top) management.
- Regular review of the design guidelines and criteria and how risk aspects should be involved when verifying existing drawings, progress reports etc.
- Necessary inspections during construction of installations and work environment to ensure that this is carried out in accordance with approved drawings and specifications.
- The inspection before transfer of installations, equipment etc. to the owner or end user (for example: production department operating personnel)
- The inclusion of design-related aspects in operational guidelines. This can be done through procedures regarding: inspections, maintenance, modifications ("management of change"), task observations and incident investigation.

Should certain expertise not be available in-company, related work can be contracted out. In that case it is advisable to also have company personnel on the design team.

9.1.1.1. Some risk assessment methods in the design phase

Below, I briefly mention several methods to be used for risk control during the design phase. Please note that these methods can be used in combination, they are partly different but also partly overlap.

Keep in mind that design is an ongoing issue during the lifetime of an organization, not just initially. The methods mentioned below should also be considered during change processes; change meaning anything different from the original design: installations, tools, procedures, products, materials, software, hardware, humanware. A management of change (MOC) procedure should be available in any organization to maintain or establish the "safe-to-operate" status.

HAZOP

HAZOP studies (HAZard and OPerability) are used in the process industry for qualitative risk assessment.

The method considers the system concerned (e.g. a reactor with inlet and outlet streams) based on parameters and guidewords. Each aspect or parameter of the system is analyzed using guide words and, if the possible consequences are assumed to be unacceptable, further study is done; to uncover possible causes of the unwanted event or situation and to find out what needs to be done to bring the risk to an acceptable level.

Hazop parameters used include:

- Flow
- Pressure
- Temperature
- Level
- Time
- Reaction
- Etc.

Hazop guidewords include:

- No or not
- More
- Less
- As well as
- Part of
- Reverse

- Other than
- Etc.

Design questions are raised through a combination of guidewords and parameters to uncover possible risk sources and consequences and take measures to prevent potentially unwanted events.

For example:

- Combination "other than" and "reaction" What is the possibility that other than intended product enter the reaction vessel? What can happen and what could be the consequences?
- What is the possibility of too high level in the vessel and what would be the consequence? If unacceptable, what should we do to prevent this?

The following table gives an overview of commonly used guide word - parameter pairs and common interpretations of them.

Guideword -- Parameter	More	Less	None	Reverse	As well as	Part of	Other than
Flow	high flow	low flow	no flow	reverse flow	deviating concentration	contamination	deviating material
Pressure	high pressure	low pressure	vacuum		delta-p		explosion
Temperature	high temperature	low temperature					
Level	high level	low level	no level		different level		

Picture 9.1 - HAZOP study guidewords and parameters

Although normally used in the process industry, the principles of the method can also be used in many other processes and situations. I remember the 1989, Hillsborough stadium disaster where close to 100 people lost their lives pressed against high fences blocking the likely escape route to the field. Looking back at this, use of the guideword "more" could have prevented the catastrophe in combination with parameter "people". And in the Heizel, Belgium disaster (1985, 39 dead) the guideword "other than" could have helped to prevent other than neutral (Belgian) supporters buying tickets for the section separating Juventus and Liverpool supporters.

The HAZOP-study can easily be combined with other methods, such as those mentioned below, to arrive at a more complete risk analysis combining event frequencies with potential consequences.

FMEA

Failure Mode and Effect Analyses (FMEA) or failure analysis is an analysis based on the failure of a particular component of a system (for example, a pump in a process plant). The aim is to determine what the can happen in the system, both upstream and downstream and what the consequences can be. This method can, of course, also be used for more general processes. For example, the method can be used to determine the effects of non-availability of an energy source, a supplier, storage of intermediate products, a customer, a specific market segment, means of transportation, etc.

In a simplified form, I used this method when working as a technical representative for INA, the Insurance Company of North America between 1968 and 1974. My job was to visit factories to make underwriting reports and part of that was to provide an indication of the potential property and business interruption losses. So my questions to the plant representatives included: What would happen if you would not be able to get your raw materials? What if your power plant would be destroyed? What if you would lose your lab? If this product line would be out of business, how long could you supply your market? Etcetera.

Fault tree

The fault tree starts with a certain undesirable outcome and then looks at what the possible causes of this outcome could be. For a simple tree with "fire" as the undesirable outcome, the causes would be the availability of oxygen, combustible material and an ignition source.

In principle, any unwanted event or situation could be the starting point which is normally the top of the tree with the possible causes underneath. The top event could be loss of a specific warehouse or production unit or be more general such as loss of market. The more general, the larger the tree will be, going all the way down to root causes which may very well be in the management system or even beyond that. In principle the system is simple: the underlying events or causes must lead to the event or situation above it, either in combination with each other or on their own. In the example shown in the picture below, the event "fire" can only evolve from the causes or aspects below it: oxygen, combustible materials and an ignition source. Take any of those away and you will not have a fire. The necessary combination is shown by the AND-gate indicating that all lower aspects have to be there to produce the top event. The "loss of warehouse" can also be caused by a natural disaster; each on their own could lead to the loss as is indicated by the OR-gate.

The tree will develop downward. In case of the "fire" part of the tree, the sources of ignition could be static electricity or smoking, work with open flame, bearing friction. Static electricity could be caused by lack of proper grounding or earthing which could exist due to be not following procedures, inadequate maintenance/inspection or simply a design "oversight"; all these will bring us to design procedures, control of critical tasks, work procedures, training/instruction, management of change etc., - aspects that one should be looking for in the management system.

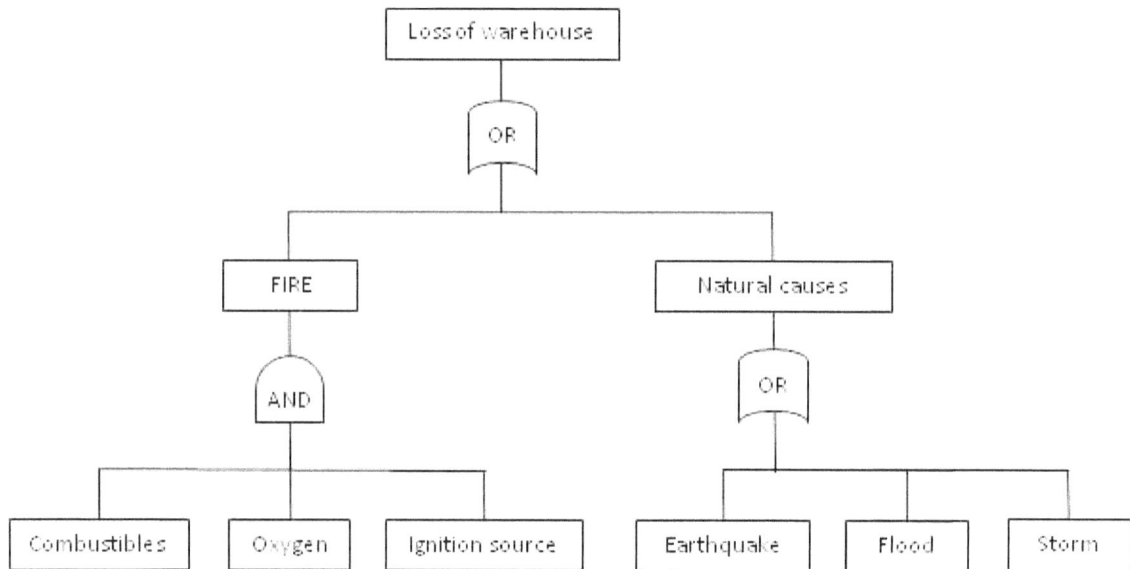

Picture 9.2. FAULT TREE Example "loss of warehouse"

The fault tree can also be used to calculate the failure rate of the unwanted situation or event. This will be done by using the failure rates of the underlying aspects; in case of an AND-gate these will be multiplied, in case of an OR-gate they will be added.

A well-know fault tree is MORT (Management Oversight and Risk Tree) which was developed during the early seventies of the 20th century within the context of the Department of Energy (DOE) in the USA, Atomic Energy Commission (AEC, later ERDA), Systems Safety Development Centre (SSDC). MORT provided a framework for accident investigation in atomic power plants and extended later into the oil- and other industries. The total of MORT looks rather complex but parts of the system can be used on their own as "mini-MORTS" and be applied more generally. Adequate knowledge of MORT is normally not found in a single company but may be available within organizations providing accident investigation services.

MORT may be an "overkill" in most situations but it could be a necessity in complex situations, potentially catastrophic events or media sensitive events requiring a very thorough approach because of possible social concern.

Notice the importance of the management system in the picture below showing the top of the MORT tree. LTA means "Less Than Adequate" which is the key used when considering the aspects that are part of the tree. If an item is considered LTA it is considered a (possible) cause contributing to the event or situation above it. Another term for LTA may be the one that we have been using: substandard, meaning "less than standard", less than what it should be.

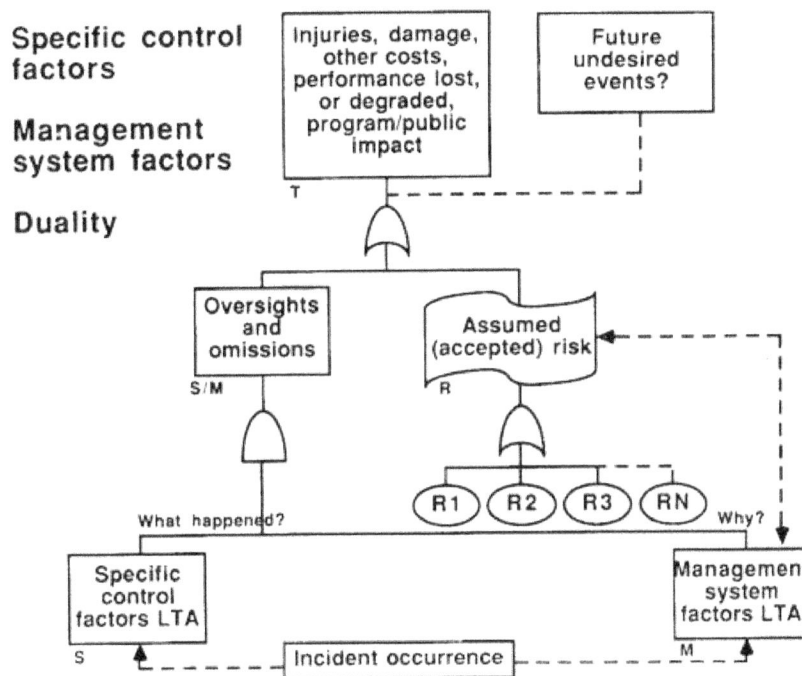

Picture 9.3. MORT (Management Oversight and Risk Tree) the top

MORT has been the "mother" of many MORT-like products; one of those being the Operational Readiness Tree, mentioned below.

Event tree

Purpose of the event tree is to find out what the consequences of an event were or could be and why.

For example, in case of the Moerdijk fire (The Netherlands, winter 2011), the starting event was the defrosting of a flammable liquid pump with an open flame; the final consequence was bankruptcy of the plant. Consequences in between were ignition of the flammable liquid, spreading of fire to nearby storage of combustibles, etc.

When looking at the construction, the event tree is similar to the fault tree. The difference is that the fault tree starts with an unwanted event with the aim to uncover causes while the event tree starts with an event and then leads to its consequences. So, if you want, they are complementary and in combination form what is known as the "bow-tie".

In the picture below, the event tree is from the event going to the right to find out about the consequences. The fault tree is to the left of the event to find its causes. In essence, our cause-consequence model covers both trees - going from the causes on the left to the consequences on the right - but concentrates on the causes.

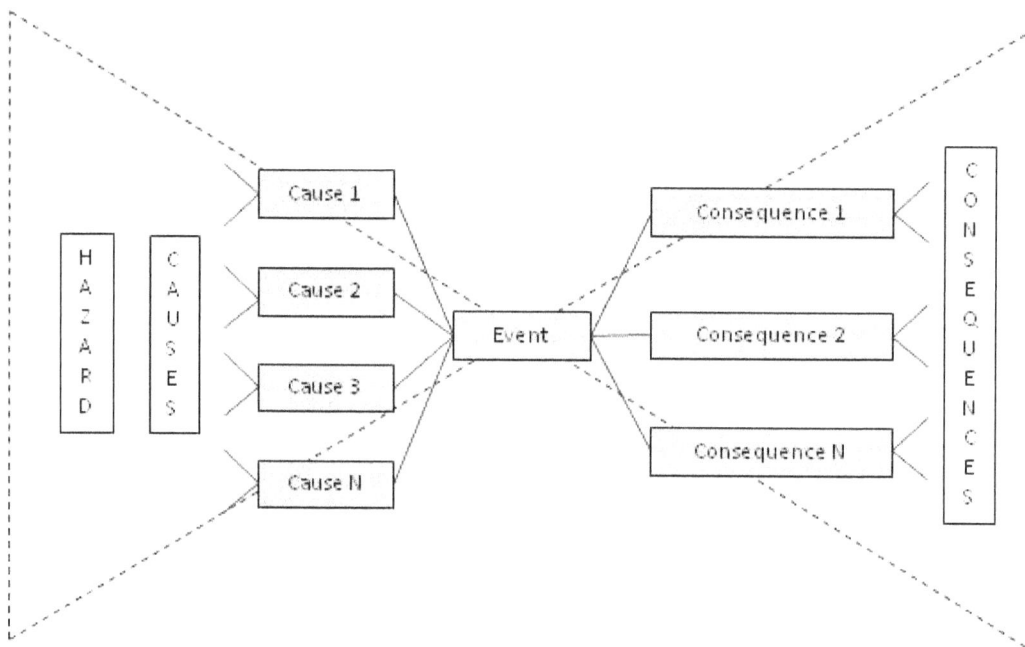

Picture 9.4 – Bow-tie, combination of fault tree and event tree

Operational Readiness Tree

The Operational Readiness Tree – also referred to as "Occupancy-Use Readiness" is a tree like the fault tree but the top event is a desired situation; in this case "operational readiness" or "ready to operate" or, expressed in a term I used before: "safe-to-operate". The process basically is to obtain the "green light" status of the system or process by assuring that all the underlying aspects of the tree are adequate in contrary to the LTA of the MORT tree where the top event is an unwanted occurrence or consequence. Or, if you wish to relate to the cause-consequence model, all causal aspects – management system, basic and direct causes - have to be "standard".

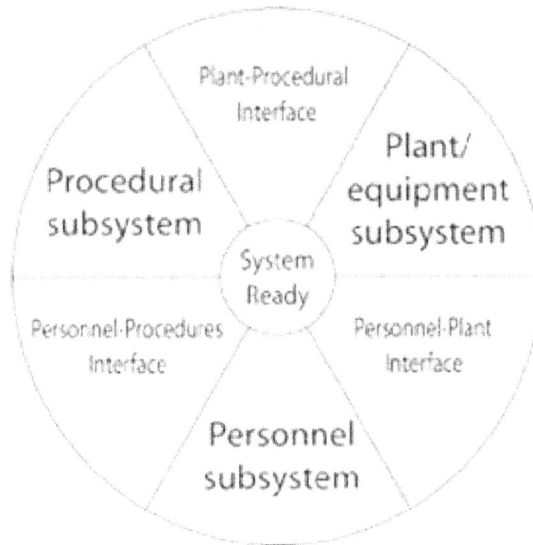

Picture 9.5 - Main elements of operational readiness

The Operational Readiness Tree can be used when designing new installations, plants, organizations and parts thereof. It is not really a risk identification method as such but it can help to uncover important aspects that may otherwise be overlooked when designing a new activity, process or organization.

The MORT tree can be used to determine operational readiness. If used for that purpose, all applicable items have to get the "adequate" status and none should be LTA, resulting in no injuries, damage, etc. at the top of the tree.

Like design methods, operational readiness aspects should also be considered when making changes to existing procedures, installations, products etc. and be part of the Management of Change (MOC) procedure.

9.1.2. Selection and placement of personnel

While goods and equipment are being purchased or designed, people enter the organization through recruiting and placement. Like goods and services purchased and installations and products designed, people may also bring a certain risk aspect with them when brought into the organization. People, the work they do and the working environment should be brought in balance with each other so work can be carried out as intended without undue risk and unwanted events. This is true for operational personnel but certainly also for those who are hired into management and support staff positions.

It is not just technical and physical capability criteria that are important while selecting people. At least as important are the mental capabilities including attitude in relation to risk taking. I remember that I once gave a presentation about risk management to a group of people from an organization in The Netherlands involved in road transport of the hazardous goods. Their concern was that the (Dutch) government would stimulate hazardous good transport by rail rather than over the road. At the end of the presentation we had a discussion during which one of the people around the table was complaining about the truck drivers taking unnecessary risks. My response to that was that they hired those people themselves and not using adequate selection criteria may very well have been the reason for his concerns. On top of that, the companies also have an important say in "on the road behavior" by selecting and arranging transportation equipment, routes and schedule.

Taking risks by people in management and support staff positions adds another dimension as they may accept risks, or even create them, whereas others may be suffering from the consequences of their decision-making or work results.

As necessary you may want or need to include attitude or behavior aspects as criteria in your selection process to prevent getting risk takers at crucial positions. Training/instruction and retraining may help preventing people getting off-track one way or another. A great help would be setting up a management system providing margins within which management and operational work should take place. Doing this properly and involving the people that should be doing the work will not only benefit from their input but also allows the emotional ownership that is so important to get the job done properly without undue loss. In organizational change processes, such as middle management downsizing and employee empowerment, a properly designed management system is an absolute must as decision making will be delegated to lower organizational/operational levels. Such management system will need to take into consideration the knowledge and expertise levels at the sharp end of the organization.

The principle of shared responsibilities

More often than not are accidents and other unwanted events the result of work done by many people at different levels in the organization and at different times. They all share responsibility for the consequences.

In addition to establishing education and experience requirements, it is important to examine the safety/health aspects someone will be exposed to during the execution of the work he or she is supposed to be doing after being hired. Those occupational aspects may be identified and evaluated through a relatively simple investigation related to the work to be done and the normal and abnormal work environment/-conditions. This should include both physical as well as mental aspects. This information may be used during the selection process and may serve as a basis for carrying out medical examinations prior to and during employment. Don't get me wrong though, it is not my intention to simply say that the actual operating conditions are the only or main determining factor to find people fitting the working conditions. As necessary, the working conditions should be adapted to the capabilities of the people concerned; requirements by government in relation to ergonomics and employment of people with reduced physical and mental capabilities should be taken into account. See appendix D (page 253) for an example of a simple form that may be used for this purpose. Bringing work conditions and human capabilities/limitations in balance which each other would create a win-win situation for the organization and for the people it hires.

The scope of the evaluation process depends very much on the type of work and the work environment in normal as well as in other situations. Think about fire fighters, pilots, train drivers, police, the military and so on.

9.1.3. Purchasing

Organizations may design their own (future) problems or have them designed by third parties. Not necessarily because they do that on purpose but because risks may not be adequately considered when designing installations, product or procedures. Risk- and safety criteria may be insufficiently included in the different design phases. Another reason could be having insufficient (financial) resources available to reach the "safe-to-operate" status.

The same applies to the purchasing function: not seldom do companies purchase the problems of tomorrow when not sufficiently considering the risk related aspects of materials goods, tools, equipment or services that they buy. Possibly due to lacking guidelines to include relevant safety and risk criteria when buying. Or inadequate control and coordination of what is being bought allowing people in the organization to bypass the purchasing department. Or primarily considering the technical aspects possibly resulting in buying the less expensive stuff which could be a reason for purchasing unsafe equipment. The same applies to services and buying at the lowest price may mean insufficient attention to quality of supplier or contractor which may result in damage during the execution of the contract, causing unwanted delays, or worse.

What is true for design is also true here: use proper criteria to keep risks outside the organization whenever possible. Don't buy your future problems! Prevent that and use the same or similar methods as discussed under design to assess risks. Set up a system to safeguard the purchasing process to include:

- A policy plus guidelines and criteria making clear who is allowed to buy and how to include risk/safety aspects.
- Safety expertise in the procurement process. What was said under design also applies here: identifying and assessing risks requires expertise and a certain "state of mind" that buyers may not normally possess when used to buy at the lowest price.
- Regular evaluation of procurement activities to determine whether the function is working properly and criteria are being used as intended. This could be on the basis of

purchase orders, but also by visiting warehouses or storage areas to check whether purchased goods and equipment match the specifications set. The functioning of purchasing activities and procedures can also be evaluated when carrying out inspections, task observations/-discussions and accident analyses; the latter not being the preferred way to find out that the purchasing function allowed risk to enter the organization.

Purchase of goods and services can be broadly divided into two categories:

- Goods and services that are purchased regularly. This can be through preparation of standard specifications (in cooperation with the safety function and end-users) that will set the margins within which the purchaser is allowed to operate. Particular specifications are made and will be used as long as the product or service is being purchased. Other similar products or services, for which the specifications do not apply, may not be obtained. In this case, it would not be unusual to also specify the supplier or suppliers from which to buy the product or service.
- Goods and services that are not regularly purchased. These fall outside the standard procedure and should require specific approval including that of the safety function

The safety or risk management function meant here could be within the organization but could also be hired from outside. It should be obvious that the final decision what to buy and where would include the consent of other functions in the organization, not in the least that of the end-user.

Of special concern is the purchase of goods and chemicals with known or suspected hazards. It is important that you know what the potential problems can be that are associated with the products (to be) purchased. This information can normally be obtained from the suppliers through "Material Safety Data Sheets" (MSDS). This information should include the instruction to employees and supervisors regarding how to deal with the products concerned, what precautions to take and what the emergency actions should be in case something goes wrong. This may include any specific medication to be distributed to people that have been exposed to the product. This information should also be made available to senior management levels so that they know what risks are being introduced into the organization. Of course this information should be part of training/instruction and related documents should be readily available at places where the products are being used. They should also be available to people expected to provide help in case of an emergency.

Special attention is also required when purchasing services of third parties, including contractors. Bringing third parties into your organization means bringing in certain risks and you should work with these parties to prevent any damage to your organization and installations; it is in your interest as well theirs. Normally a contractor will do a job the way he is used to and that may not necessarily mean working in line with your safety expectations. Having contractors sign an agreement including to follow available or legally required safety precautions may not be sufficient. Showing the well known safety presentation at the gate and having people sign for having attended the show may not bring people to do the work differently from what they used to.

In practice there are only two possibilities (often in combination), if you want to assure that contractors will execute their work safely, without unwanted events, damage to your facilities and interruption of your processes. These are:

- Have a close look at the contractor's safety efforts and management system. Take a good look at the contractor's safety policy, the management attitude, how he selects temporary employees and subcontractors that are going to work for you, his training/instruction program in particular where it concerns control of critical tasks, how risks are being assessed, accidents are reported and investigated and what the contractor's safety record is. In short: carry out an audit of the contractor's safety efforts and performance to establish how he normally does his (safety related) work. Obviously, you have to use a good safety auditing tool and know how to carry out an audit. Asking questions when doing an audit is one thing – you also have to know what the right answers should be. In a number of countries contractor safety certification systems exist which would indicate a certain minimum safety performance level.
- Have people – yours or hired externally – supervise the work done by contractor personnel. In this case, supervising people need to know how the work must be correctly done, safely, without unwanted events and unnecessary interruption.

You may want to rely on certification, accredited or otherwise, to select companies to work on your premises and take advantage of the fact that certification is normally shared between principals all having the same concern: having work done without loss. Obviously that shifts the focus from doing the assessment yourselves – which is time consuming and not really be you core business – to having another party, a certification institute, doing the work for you. This sounds good but be aware of the fact that the certification market is often commercial and competitive. Competition between certification institutes may actually be detrimental to the objective of certification which is to guarantee an acceptable performance level. (See my comments regarding certification on page 29.)

If you cannot rely on available certification systems - which you should do not unless your experience with the contractor(s) involved proves otherwise - the best approach would probably be a combination of the two possibilities.

9.1.4. Work methods/-procedures/task analysis

The type of business – products, services and the processes to deliver those – is a main source of information when looking at risk and taking control measures. Using the production process as the sole source, however, may not be sufficient as the focus in this case will often be on the technical side of the process and not, or to a lesser extent, on the way that people carry out their tasks in relation to the processes. The tasks carried out by people are another important source to categorize and classify potential problems. Both "access points" should be followed to achieve proper control of (potential) problems, risks, unwanted events and losses.

Task Risk Analysis (TRA) is a good starting point to identify risks as it focuses on the work that needs to be done and, by doing so, related aspects should be considered such as: products involved, tools and installations, human capabilities/limitations and conditions under which tasks are to be carried out, normally as well as in abnormal situations. TRA should not be limited to (production) process related functions only but should be part of all functions in the organization, including management functions and related decision-making.

All functions include some risk and all tasks could produce some loss if not properly done. There are no functions where nothing can go wrong. So all functions should be part of the TRA exercise. There is also another reason to include all functions: excluding certain functions is like saying: "In your job nothing can go wrong". Does that not sound like: "Your job is not really important"?

Preparation of work or task procedures, often the end result of the TRA process, is extremely important. These procedures serve as a basis for training and instruction of employees, play a role in accident investigation, when observing or discussing how task are to be carried out, when updating/improving work procedures and work environment and as subjects in operational meetings. Task- or work procedures, and related rules, guide behavior and, by doing so, relate to culture.

The first three steps when making task-or work procedures are:

- Make a list of all functions in the organization
- Determine all tasks that will be performed in each of those functions
- Establish which of those tasks have an increased risk potential

A task – sometimes also called a job – represents a sequence of acts or operations to perform a specific assignment. A "critical" task is a task that may generate unwanted events when not carried out properly. Such adverse events may produce quality problems, injury, occupational diseases, damage, pollution, etc.

To determine the degree of risk, an often used method is the one developed by Fine and Kinney; see appendix B, page 241. Making a critical tasks list can best be done using a form designed for that purpose – a simple example is shown in appendix E, page 254.

After the (potential) critical tasks have been identified and a risk rating or classification has been assigned, the tasks can be further analyzed in order of their risk class, to identify the task elements or -steps in which problems may occur. After that, determine what control measures should be taken to bring potential problems to an acceptable level. During the process further optimization of the work can be obtained by eliminating or reducing potential problems.

After a list has been prepared to include the chronological steps of the task to be performed and after control measures have been established, preparation of a task-/work procedure, to control residual risks, should not be all that complicated. The work procedure or -instruction should include: (i) steps for the "standard" (= safe) execution of the task, (ii) materials and tools to be used, (iii) the environment in which the work is to be done, (iv) problems that may arise, (v) measures that should be taken to control them and, (vi) what to do if the problems occur when control measures fail to work.

The entire process of risk elimination/control should, whenever possible, include participation of the people who will carry out the work. This allows making use of their expertise and knowledge and - at the same time – helps to implant the emotional ownership that is so important to make work procedures/instructions that will be complied with. See appendix K (page 275) concerning "How to make rules with a high degree of success" which largely also applies to the preparation of task procedures/-instructions.

The work procedures thus established form the basis for training and instruction of people to carry out the work without the occurrence of unwanted events.

The TRA process forms an important part of safety and risk control. It leads directly to the identification of potential problems in the execution of work and is directed at controlling those problems and thus at improving an organization in many aspects. The process forms the basis to establish the need for work rules and regulations, permit systems, personal protection, handling of hazardous substances etc.

Control of critical tasks is not new and has been known for decades as Job Safety Analysis (JSA) which used to be largely focused on injury type accidents in operational work. It should be clear that the method can be used more generically to control any type of unwanted event associated with the work done and it certainly does not have to be limited to operational personal. It can be used in administrative functions and management decision making in any type of industry or activity.

While the process is often referred to as Task Risk Analysis (TRA), it includes more than analysis alone:

- Listing of all functions in the organization
- Determination of tasks per function
- Identification of risks involved when executing tasks – use risk classification
- Determination of main steps of "critical" tasks identified to consider:
  - Elimination of risk
  - Risk reduction measures
  - Measures to control remaining risks, often leading to work procedures, instructions or rules to be followed
- Training/instruction of people using established work procedures, including performance observation
- Periodic observation or discussion of the execution of critical tasks to see if tasks can still be carried out following the work procedures established
- Feedback from accidents, incidents and other unwanted events

The last two points are important to improve existing procedures because of introduction of new tools, changes in the working environment, etc. and to also add any tasks to the critical task list for further processing. You probably heard the saying "practice makes perfect". That may be true but only when those two points are properly taken care of. If not, practice may just create wrong habits that may cause losses.

```
Practice makes perfect?
OR
Practice makes habit?
```

9.1.5. Rules, instructions and procedures

Rules and instructions prescribe desired behavior and can help to control (potential) problems that may occur when work is carried out. Rules, regulations and task procedures are to be followed to obtain desired results. In order to facilitate compliance to rules and procedures, their preparation should take into account:

- No rules etc. if they are not needed
- Keep them as simple as possible
- Involve end users during preparation of rules
- Ensure proper instruction/re-instruction
- Provide good example
- Respond positively to compliance
- Make clear what the consequences will be if rules are not followed

- Periodically measure compliance and provide feedback
- Adjust rules when necessary based on experience, changed circumstances

Unwanted events may occur due to not having proper rules, instructions or procedures or because of noncompliance. Reasons for noncompliance can often be found in relation to one or more of the above mentioned points.

See also appendix K (page 275) "How to make rules with a high degree of success" for additional detail.

The principle of deviation from normal behavior

The more a rule or procedure deviates from normal behavior, the more effort is required to reach compliance

---

Procedures

We use that term – procedures - a lot but sometimes I get the impression that we may not realize what procedures really are or should be. Procedures normally are there to guide work such that there will not be any unwanted events. A procedure describes how work shall be done, when, by whom and why. Procedures can be very detailed such as those that guide design processes. If we cannot eliminate risks or engineer them out of our systems, we make work procedures to handle the risks that remain.

Procedures should follow a certain structure, to include:

- Management statement to underline importance and reasons – why the procedure is there
- Objective(s) – what is the expected result
- Procedure owner – sponsor/coordinator
- Work/activities to be carried, when, by whom, how
- Training/instruction of relevant people
- Approval, signatures
- Publication date and identification (ID)
- Periodic review – including relevant people
- Periodic assessment to verify compliance
- Feedback from unwanted events

Up-to-date procedures should be readily available at the place where they are supposed to be used, at the "point of control", and should be considered for inclusion in the document control system of the organization. If they are not considered important (enough) to be included, the conclusion may very well be that they are not important at all and should possibly be terminated.

9.1.6. Training/orientation of managers and supervision

How work is being performed in an organization will largely depend on people in management and supervisory positions. What they do or don't do and the way they deal with risks issues in their organization and departments will influence organizational as well as individual behavior reflecting company "culture". I have already mentioned several times that most accidents, damages and other unwanted events and their losses are ultimately caused by the improper functioning of the management system. The management system that, from the top of the organization through the various hierarchical levels, has its effect on the work done at the shop floor, operational, level.

Training gives people in a management position information and knowledge regarding risks, losses and how to deal with them. Training of management and supervision - from the top of the organization down - is essential for proper risk management and the basis for effective control of unwanted events and their loss consequences. Training outs the noses in the same – right (?) – direction.

Training of management personnel must be adapted to the level at which people operate. Training of senior management will emphasize the leadership roles that those people have, to allow effective and efficient implementation of management system activities. Training provided to middle management and supervision will concentrate on coaching people at lower levels, and assist and support those doing the work required by the management system.

Training/instruction of management is part of the 17-steps process for improvement, in particular steps 2, 3, 9, 11 and 14.

One of the main tasks of the management function is to control loss

To close the gap between "practice" and "theory"

Between "how it is (done)" and "how it should be (done)"

Mishaps, errors, accidents etc. occur in the gap
between "what is (done)" and "what should be (done)"

They drain away your profits

Training of management and supervisors may include the following subjects:

- Why should we control risks, damages, accidents, losses?
- How do we do that?
- Where do we stand on this?
- Some basic definitions – talk about unwanted events rather than "accidents"
- What are the underlying causes of unwanted events and their losses?
- Basic cause – consequence model
- Basic improvement model: Plan-Train-Do-Leadership
- Role of a management system - its place in the causation model
- How to build a management system that works?
- Problem solving/risk management process
- Risk assessment
- Control of critical tasks
- How to obtain a desired safety culture?
- Measuring safety
- Keeping risk outside the company: design, purchasing, recruitment of personnel
- Training of employees
- How to make rules that work
- Planned inspections
- Taking care of the unexpected: emergency preparation
- Learning from unwanted events

This training could and should be provided within the context of the company where these people are working and should, if possible, be specific to the management system of their organization. A good start of such training would be to use the safety & loss control maturity profile in appendix G (page 258); this could help to start discussing present and desired situation seeking answers to the questions: "Where are we and where do we want to be?

My own practice during the eighties of last century did not indicate that safety training was commonly provided to managerial personnel. This is also shown in picture 8.16 (page 174), where the average score is 26% for safety management training of managers. These figures are based on about 50 ISRS audits carried out. This 26% included the training of the safety officer, representing 20% and thus leaving only 6% for training of managers. These were relative figures but they did indicate that safety management, in-company, training of managers was not a hot topic in the 1980's.

Safety and risk management training should also be included in the formal (college/university) education of those people who will fill management or supervisory positions in industry. So what is the situation there?

I managed to get two BSc degrees during the sixties of last century, in Chemical and Industrial

Engineering in The Netherlands. Safety was only a very limited part of either program and focused mainly on issues such as the legislation and occupational safety subjects such as ladders and personal protection. Process safety was not really addressed. Neither was management. Both programs, however, were preparing students for management positions in industry.

I recall that, during the 1980's, a U.S. study was conducted under graduates of Business Schools (the "schools of managers") to find that less than 1 percent of those people had some exposure to "safety management" during their study.

So is it better now? In 2010, the European Agency for Security and Health at Work published the report: "Mainstreaming occupational safety and health into university education". Quote from the report:

"It is important to integrate OSH into university-level education as promoting a safety culture in the workplace is not just about ensuring that shop floor workers learn how to act safely. Modern OSH legislation is goal-setting and follows a non-prescriptive risk-based approach – risks must be assessed and appropriate measures put in place. All parts and all levels of industry and business need to understand how risk assessment and risk management are essential to good business management.

Future designers, architects, engineers, finance officers, doctors and other health professionals and managers and supervisors at all levels, right up to the director level, are among those who need relevant education about their future OSH roles and responsibilities. Future teachers and trainers also need OSH education in order to deliver OSH education themselves effectively."

To me this indicates that there is still plenty of room for improvement at the level of formal educations. As a result, quite a bit of the safety management training may still have to be provided after these people have finished their studies and en route to hopefully a successful career. In practice this means that these people have to be instructed/trained after being hired and – hopefully – before they are given any (important) management responsibilities.

Note that the 2010 quote above starts with reference to safety and then goes on mentioning "risk based approach", "risk assessment" and "risk management". With that in mind, remember ISO 31000 mentioned on page 74 as well as the title of this book.

The meaning and importance of safety-/loss control- and risk management may actually be taught during practice, not during formal education. And practice shows that safety is often a legislative issue and therefore mandatory and refers to injuries, to blood and victims. Victims who usually can be found in the workplace. Therefore the incorrect understanding may be that, safety is something that relates to the workplace and has to do with glasses, helmets, shoes, regulations, machine protection etc. Safety actions therefore may often be aimed at employees and their behavior. This is not in line with what quality guru Deming said at his seminars that top management—not the work force— is directly responsible for 85% of all problems.

It became clear during the last decades – but certainly not to everybody - that safety (and loss control and risk management) is mainly an issue of management and organization and in particular of management systems. Training of executives and management, top down, is therefore essential for obtaining good risk management, good control of unwanted events and their consequences, loss control management and safety.

In addition to the training of line management and supervision, necessary training should also be provided to support staff personnel in safety, quality, cost control, to people working in design and procurement and, not to forget: to operational personnel. I hope this book will contribute to understanding how safety, risk management and loss control can help people to improve their organizations by controlling actual and potential problems.

Not to be forgotten is the training of health and safety committees. These committees could make an important contribution to an effective risk- and safety management system. Unfortunately, practice learns that the training of these committees is often limited to their legislative context. They learn what their rights and duties are but not how an effective safety and risk management system or program should be set up. Combined with possible limited or lack of training of management this may lead to a situation in which communications between management and committees will often be limited to operational detail, not directed at deployment of policy and management system. Attention going to the wrong level!

9.1.7. Training/instruction of employees

After pre-hiring educational-/experience-, physical- and mental requirements have been determined, it should be established what additional training/instruction people need to get. So that they will get to the level of knowledge, skills and experience that will allow them to carry out the work they are supposed to do after hiring and before placement in the function they are to fulfill. This training – in-company or external as needed – shall include the risks that the job entails, and how work can be carried out without problems, accidents, damage, injury and other unwanted events. The risk aspects of the work to be carried out shall be the basis for setting up proper information and training program for newly hired.

In relation to their work, employee training should focus on tasks with increased risks. The basis for setting up a good training program is the identification of the work (tasks) to be performed, identifying so-called "critical" tasks and the preparation of work procedures such that these tasks can be carried out without unwanted events. See section 9.1.4 and 9.1.5 on pages 188 and 190 respectively.

Please note that managers and supervisors also need to have a good knowledge of the operational work to be done so they can properly execute their roles in controlling unwanted events in the workplace and helping people in their department whenever there is an opportunity to do better. Providing this knowledge should be included in step 14 – "management briefing" – of the 17-step process.

9.2. Maintaining the organization

9.2.1. Policy and policy statement

After the organization has been build "safe to operate", it needs to be maintained in that condition. In practice, this would mean that it needs to be upgraded continuously as the level of "safe-to-operate" will change over time needing increased efforts. An organization is subject to change - machines wear out, new equipment and processes are introduced, new staff is recruited and external circumstances such as legislation, market conditions and others will not remain the same. The structure of the organization should take this into account and processes should be designed and executed in a way to prevent new risks from entering the organization.

If the organization originally was not 100% safe-to-operate to start off with - which would be a likely situation – then unwanted events, accidents, losses, etc. will probably occur from the start. Activities - including auditing, inspections and learning from what goes wrong - that are related to preventing or limiting unwanted events and their consequences form a necessary part of improving the organization to bring it up to the safe-to-operate status. And once that has been achieved, you need to maintain it.

To facilitate the above, a policy should be established; a policy tailored to the needs of the organization clearly indicating how this policy should be put into action. The objective of this policy should be to ensure prevention of unwanted events and their consequences that may, and will, reduce the efficiency of the organization.

Implementation of the policy should include clear guidelines concerning the execution of activities that are part of the elements - such as indicated in appendix N (page 285) - of a management system. Practice, however, shows that clear guidelines may often not be available so people may not know what it is that is expected of them. Or proper guidelines are available but are not updated or not complied, with possibly due to lack of supervision and/or motivation. Or simply because the management system has not been set up including all people in the organization so the system is not really embedded in the organization – lack of emotional ownership throughout!

Next to a clear policy statement concerning safety, risk management and control of loss (see example policy statement - appendix A on page 240) the active visible involvement of (top) management is required to provide the necessary leadership and support when executing the activities that are contained in the management system.

This leadership and support can be provided by:

- Have a management system built, maintained and improved with the involvement of "all" to bring responsibility, involvement and emotional ownership into the organization
- Providing clear guidelines to (management) people involved in executing system activities
- Making sure that necessary training is given to both management and operational personnel
- Visible participation by (senior) management in activities such as: inspections, accident analysis, safety meetings, conducting internal audits
- Periodic review of the more critical management system activities and providing feedback to stakeholders including "principle of control" personnel
- Initiate actions when necessary to reach and/or maintain the safe-to-operate status
- Showing interest in activities aimed at managing risks, safety, control of loss based on knowledge of "what should be (done)"
- Motivating people by engaging them in decision-making and execution of activities
- Positive response to reported incidents and unsafe situations and rapid feedback about actions taken or to be taken

Is a policy statement important? Yes and maybe not so much. More important is what is actually being done. Remember the case that I mentioned of the towage and salvage company when I was asked to review their safety efforts. The policy statement was one of the best I ever saw but after that there were just the "do's and don'ts" for operating personnel. No guidelines for management personnel activity to make sure that the system was working. Actually, looking back at it, this system was not a management system and – by my definition – not even a system.

So if you have to evaluate a management system, look for the involvement of all in the organization to make sure that the system does what it is supposed to do and it can only do that when people do that. When they feel that it is their system because they have been involved in making it and are involved in maintaining and improving it. Look for these three things:

- Was the system built with the involvement of many, if not all? Was there a well identified process to make it?
- Is the content adequate to reach the objectives of the system? Does it have a sufficient number of relevant elements?
- Does it have the structure in each of its elements to make sure that activities are carried out and objectives reached? Are people throughout the organization made responsible for this?

9.2.2. Maintenance/inspections

Maintenance plays an important role when keeping installations, tools, equipment and the work environment in a safe-to-operate condition.

As part of "maintenance" I mention:

- Breakdown maintenance
- Preventive/predictive maintenance
- Planned inspections or "inspective" maintenance

These types of maintenance activities will be briefly discussed below. In practice, they may overlap. All three are necessary for proper control, to maintain conditions in a safe-to–operate status, or bring them to that level, and prevent deviations that may lead to unwanted events/consequences.

Break-down maintenance

Something breaks down and will be repaired or replaced. The unwanted event – failure of a component - has occurred and the situation is corrected. Breakdown maintenance is re-active.

Repair/replacement of equipment and components after breakdown may not be considered maintenance as such as we let the item run till it breaks down. This "maintenance" would only be acceptable after it has been established that the (potential) consequences of the breakdown are limited and acceptable and that repair/replacement can be done within a limited time period and without considerable effort and expense. The advantage of breakdown maintenance may be that inspection of the related equipment can be eliminated or reduced: the equipment runs until it fails.

When replacing what is broken, consider the management of change (MOC) procedure to make sure that the replacement item is the same or better from a risk control point of view. This is true in any situation where a certain component is being replaced, broken or not. If the original component was not meeting "safe-to-operate" criteria the MOC procedure provides opportunities to correct this.

Preventive/predictive maintenance

Preventive maintenance of equipment/components occurs in accordance with an established time schedule or frequency, running hours, etc. Purpose is to check the condition of the component and maintain, repair or replace the item when and if necessary.

Predictive maintenance is similar to preventive maintenance and is based on known failure data of a particular piece of equipment, machinery or component. So we let the machine run to close to the known failure time and then replace it.

This type of maintenance is intended to prevent the unwanted consequences of component failure. Think about changing the oil filter of your car after a certain number of kilometers or miles. Or servicing your car once per year or after 20.000 kilometers, whatever comes first.

Inspective maintenance /planned inspections

"Inspective maintenance" really boils down to inspection of a piece of equipment, tool, component or work environment. This activity does not necessarily lead to maintenance; only when a substandard condition (= deviation from "standard") is found, action will be taken.

Planned inspections are formal activities aimed at detecting substandard conditions. Planned inspections take place at predetermined intervals: once per shift, per day, per month etc. They are carried out by people assumed to have knowledge of the equipment or work environment. The use of checklists guiding the inspections is normal and often a necessity.

Planned inspections help people to be more aware of (possible) substandard situations between inspection intervals; they help people in their day-to-day observations. We sometimes call those observations "informal inspections" but don't underestimate their value; it is very important that people are aware of non-normal situations when going about their normal work. This would be a tremendous help to prevent unwanted events as part of an "abnormal situation management" (ASM) approach.

For the purpose of our discussion, I mention the following types of planned inspections:

- General inspections. These are mainly focused on housekeeping, order and cleanliness. In principle, these inspections shall be carried out by the people of the department concerned: a small team of people with or without the department head, supervisor or manager. See appendix J (page 274) for a sample inspection form. While they are called "general inspections" the checklists used should be made specific to relate to the department or situation they are intended for.

ORDER

An area or department is in order if there are no unnecessary things about and all necessary things are in their proper places.

- Management tours are regular, planned visits by senior and middle level managers of the departments that fall under their responsibility. These tours are not detailed inspections but intended to support department inspection efforts. In addition, they also allow higher management levels to become acquainted with the (safety/risk) situation in the workplace. These tours should demonstrate the importance that senior management attaches to safety and risk management and allows a good opportunity for communication and with operational personnel.

- Inspections by staff functions/specialists. Such inspections have a dual purpose:
  - o To evaluate activities such as purchasing, design, maintenance, departmental inspections, training as well as any deviations that may indicate decreasing attention to risk control by the department, its supervision or management.
  - o To determine the condition of specific items such as firefighting and electrical equipment. These inspections can be performed either by own specialists or by external organizations and the latter may be required by law in some cases; think of pressure vessels, elevators, hoists etc.
- "Critical" parts inspections. These inspections focus on identified parts or components of equipment. In principle, these components will be identified through a risk assessment similar to the assessment the "critical" tasks. Per department or organizational unit the critical components are identified (from the viewpoint of quality, safety, production, etc.) and determined what the possible consequences may be in case of improper functioning, failure, or absence. The critical components indentified that way may become part of an inspection program. Critical parts inspections include the "before use" check of tools, machinery or transportation equipment such as cranes, forklifts, hoisting gear etc.

The principle of point of control

The greatest potential for control tends to exist at the point where the action takes place

---

In principle, inspection activities would include the following criteria:

- Determination of inspection objective and items to be inspected:
  - o What should be inspected, why and how? Using tools such as inspection checklists.
  - o Determination of frequency: when or how often should the inspection be conducted?
- Establishment of responsibility: who should do the inspection to be performed?

- Classification of deviations observed: What can happen if the situation persists, what and how large could the consequences be?
- Reporting and follow-up: ensuring that actions are taken and the substandard conditions are corrected.
- Investigation of deviations noted to uncover causes and take preventive actions including follow-up.
- Periodic evaluation of inspection activities with communication of results to stakeholders.

A risk classification system – such as Fine/Kinney - should be used when preparing the inspection checklist and when reporting substandard situations. The risk level is important to obtain management attention, to make resources available for remedial action and follow-up.

One last word about inspections. Often the result of an inspection is that deviations are corrected. While that, of course, is a proper thing to do, looking for what caused the deviation may get less attention. The result may be that the causes are not removed and the deviation can – and probably will – happen again, possibly with more serious consequences. In order to prevent this and depending on the (potential) risk level a deviation observed may, or rather: should be, treated as an accident. In that case, the same routine should be followed including (root) cause analysis and taking actions in order to prevent recurrence. Assignment of responsibilities, to make sure that proper attention is given to substandard deviations, is important to include two levels:

- An "event owner" – person with overall responsibility for the inspection carried out, possibly the department head
- One or more "action owners" – people with responsibility for the execution of one or more actions or to make sure that others, possibly outside the company, do the necessary.

Normal/abnormal maintenance

In terms of risk management and control of loss it is important to differentiate between normal and abnormal or non-normal maintenance or repair. Normal maintenance is expected and accepted maintenance while abnormal maintenance is not. Abnormal maintenance means unexpected, possibly resulting in unwanted loss/risk, and requires special attention.

Abnormal maintenance can be identified through work order forms. The form basically will ask the question: "Is this repair/maintenance expected or not?" Collecting and processing that information can be facilitated using a computerized recording system to uncover the what, how many and the related cost, possibly leading to further actions to control the unnecessary cost and risk.

Abnormal maintenance cases should be considered as unwanted events and be treated as such including cause analysis and estimation of potential loss. As a matter of fact abnormal maintenance could be included in the unwanted event protocol (appendix T, page 306) and in a software program directed at reporting, registering and processing unwanted events.

9.2.3. Planned observations

Planned observations are formal activities directed at behavior of people and the way work is being carried out. While inspections normally are directed at uncovering substandard conditions, observations are directed at the other category of direct causes: the substandard act.

I will briefly discuss two different planned observations: (i) the planned task observation and (2) planned behavior observation.

As in the case of inspections, the planned observations help to improve the quality of the informal observations as part of the daily routine. The formal observations help to increase the awareness during the daily work to look for deviations that could lead to injury or other loss.

The planned task observation

This observation focuses on the execution of "critical" tasks or parts thereof; the reference is the task- or work procedure established. "Critical" meaning with increased risk.

The planned task observation is actually an important part of (initial) training to make sure people are able to carry out the job according to the standard task procedure or – instruction. The observation also provides feedback on the quality of the training/instruction and is an important means to maintain work procedures at the desired "safe-to-operate" level.

The planned task observation is carried out according to a schedule depending on the risk involved, the environment in which the task will be done and the skill level of the person doing the work.

Planned task observation should include all people, including the experienced that may develop ways to do the work better than the procedure or they may take shortcuts which may cause unwanted events and loss.

The planned task observation not only aims to determine whether the person knows the right way to do the job but also whether he/she can actually carry out the work as it should be done. As such, the task observation is also a tool to see if there are changes in the work environment (through design and/or purchasing) that would prevent work to be done in accordance with the existing procedure. That would provide feedback to purchasing and design and could also necessitate review of the existing procedure.

Existing work procedures may have to be adapted whenever the work environment is different from normal, such as may be the case when contractors work for different principles. In this case adaptation should take place as soon as the specifics of the work environment are known and prior to the start of the job or task; this requires proper communication between principle and contractor.

Practice makes perfect?

Practice makes habit?

PRACTICE MAKES PERMANENT

Periodic review of existing procedures should form an integral part of the observation process. This review should be done with the people using the procedure to carry out their work. Review could be done through: (i) on location observation and, (ii) discussion. The latter method will allow more people to take part in the exercise while observations are normally focused on individuals. Discussion combine with on-location visits may be the preferred way of doing these reviews.

Planned behavior observations

Instead of being focused on the execution of a specific task, these observations are directed at general behavior of people in the work environment. For example in relation to rules and regulations such as no-smoking, use of personal protective equipment, proper bending/lifting, etc. Specific task aspects, however, may also be involved depending on the knowledge and expertise of the person or persons carrying out the observation.

Formal, planned, behavior observations are carried out following to a predetermined schedule and, like inspections, they may involve the use of a checklist highlighting the behavior aspects to be considered. Planned observations help to improve the quality of observations that done informally during the daily routine.

Some types of behavior observations, based on who does the observation are:

- By staff people. These observations are intended to establish compliance with rules and regulations and will often be combined with an inspection of the conditions/situations. This is why these observations do not normally include contact/communication with people observed, unless it is absolutely necessary. These observations may also be used to determine the extent to which direct supervision and management perform their roles with regard to rule compliance and maintenance of standard (= safe) behavior in their department.

- By a (management) team. These observations are carried out by small groups of people including the department supervisor. Team members may include higher management personnel and representatives of support departments such as human resources, finance, insurance, risk management etc. These observations are expected to include contact/communication with people showing substandard behavior. Therefore these observations should be handled carefully, in particular because they focus on behavior of operational personnel. Please consider that it makes little sense to address people in the workplace regarding their behavior when that behavior is allowed due to lack of supervision, lack of training or lack of proper rules/procedures. Observing "substandard" behavior and taking appropriate action should first of all be a responsibility of the departmental manager or supervisor during the daily work situation. It is my opinion that observations by teams should only be temporarily and/or periodically to support managers/supervisors who may be so used to substandard behavior that they do not recognize it when they see it. When periodically done, these observations should be carried out no more than once every six months or less.
- By operational personnel. These observations are done by the employees in communication with their peers. Like all observation programs, thorough preparation and training/instruction is required, coaching by supervision and the consent and cooperation of the parties involved, not in the least the employees themselves.

The ultimate objective of planned observations and planned inspections is to improve the awareness to observe and register deviations from the normal (safe) situation that could result in undesired events and loss. This awareness is the basis of abnormal situation management (ASM) as well as the more down to earth routine involved in last minute risk assessment (LMRA) answering the question: "Can the job be done safely, without undue risks?"

9.2.4. Management of change (MOC)

Although often seen as part of maintenance activities I like to mention modifications - any deviation from the original design of the original production processes, product, procedures and other related aspects - separately because of their importance.

Assuming a safe-to-operate status at the start of operations, modifications can introduce new risks. To avoid this, a clear procedure should be established (and complied with) to guide modifications to process and systems including risk considerations prior to making those changes.

If the original risk assessment has not been 100%, activities such as inspections, observations and investigation of unwanted events will help to fill the gap between "what is" and "what should be" by generating actions to improve risk- and loss control.

As applicable, the management of change (MOC) procedure should include the safety and risk management functions in addition to the involvement of end users. Such involvement should, as in the original design, be at the earliest possible stage. Risk assessment methods such as HAZOP (see Section 9.1.1.1, page 177) may also be applied here.

9.2.5. Preparation for Emergencies

Control activities will (almost) never be 100% effective so prepare for the unwanted and, possibly, unexpected: take measures to cope with unwanted events and their consequences.

Within the context of emergency preparedness, consider the availability and deployability of:

- People - trained, skilled, experienced
- Resources/equipment to cope with problems expected to control the emergency itself as well as the consequences
- The emergency plan combining people and resources to act promptly and effectively
- Post emergency plan – what to do when the emergency is over

Consider in-house facilities and those that are provided by outside sources such as public fire brigade, police, hospital/ambulance service and others such as recovery and salvage services.

The basis for establishing the need and extent of emergency procedures and actions is to identify what emergency situations that can be expected and what the response shall be. These situations can vary from "limited" (wounded, cardiac arrest, etc.) to catastrophic (major fire, multiple deaths, environmental disaster, etc.).

Some of the sources leading to emergency situations may include:

- Injury to employees, visitors
- Fire/explosion
- Flood, water damage, leakage
- Earthquake
- Landslide
- Storm
- Machinery breakdown
- Loss of suppliers
- Loss of customers
- Loss of transportation
- Environmental pollution
- Bomb alert
- Kidnapping
- Terrorist activity

- Loss of "key" personnel
- Loss of information, industrial espionage
- Theft, mysterious disappearance
- Product damage/liability claims
- Liability claims due to other reasons
- Building collapse
- War, riots
- Vandalism
- Computer loss

Steps to take in case of emergency include:

- Determine that an emergency is there or on its way to occur. The alarm system is important here, the sooner you are aware of the (potential) emergency the better
- Activate and implement the emergency plan
- End the emergency situation
- Take measures to limit losses

The emergency plan may include the following aspects:

- Evacuation of people to a safe place
- Involvement of internal and external emergency services
- Emergency procedures
- Management of hazardous substances and energy sources
- Removal/protection of vital data, machines etc.
- Prevention of secondary damage, losses
- Rescue activities
- Re-entry procedure.

Of great importance is the proficiency of services (internal and external) that will respond to an emergency situation. Familiarity with the specific risks and (expected) emergencies is essential.

In addition to making sure that the expertise of the emergency services is available, it is necessary to exercise the emergency plan periodically so everyone knows what to do when the 'unexpected" happens. In addition to knowing how to cope with the emergency, exercising the emergency plan will help people to be prepared and able to do what is necessary.

Actions to take to limit the consequences – injuries, damage and other losses - include:

- Taking care of victims and support of family members
- Coping with the emergency to bring the situation back to normal
- Conservation and recovery of vital data, equipment, machines, energy supplies etc.
- Taking actions to assure continuing supply of product/service to the market
- Rebuilding

9.2.6. Communication en promotion

To maintain the desired level of risk management and safety activities, it is almost mandatory to work towards a certain mentality/culture that allows all personnel to contribute, obtain and maintain a safe-to-operate status.

In addition to the information and training programs, regular communication plays an important role. A number of communication possibilities are mentioned below.

Safety meetings

Safety meetings, sometimes called "toolbox meetings", are regular meetings with operational personnel addressing specific safety related topics. The topic presentation will normally be done by the immediate supervisor or the department head. A good possibility is also to have employees of the department present safety topics that are of interest to their peers and can reach across departmental boundaries as needed or desired.

The objective of these meetings is to maintain meeting subject knowledge and awareness at the desired level. They also allow discussion concerning the subject, the purpose, practical application and suggestions for improvement. Preferably, these safety meetings should include other important work related issues such as quality, cost control etc. which will underline that these seemingly different aspects are all interrelated.

People who lead these meetings may need training/guidance in giving presentations as it may be assumed that first line supervision or operational personnel are not equipped to provide effective presentations. The consequence of that may be that the presentations are less effective or not kept. Or they may be provided by a higher level manager or the safety officer, bypassing the "point of control" people who should have the best knowledge about the work, the work conditions and the risks involved.

> **The principle of point of control**
>
> The greatest potential for control tends to exist at the point where the action takes place

A proper setup of a meeting "program" should consider:

- Establishing the frequency*) of meetings, for example presented by:
    - Direct supervisors/operational personnel - monthly
    - Their (department) managers - once per quarter
    - Higher management - once every six months
- Instruction/guidance of people on "how to give an effective presentation"
- Planning of subjects, possibly one year in advance so meetings can be properly prepared
- Support and guidance of people to prepare presentation material, use of audio visual equipment, handouts etc.
- Discussion time – planning of any actions after meeting
- Meeting evaluation by attendants
- Periodic evaluation of meeting activities, quality as well as quantity

    *) the frequency of meetings will depend on the number of "critical" subjects requiring periodic attention.

Operational meetings

These meetings and the safety meetings mentioned above can be combined if and when practical. The difference between these two is that safety meetings center around a specific (safety) subject that is planned in advance while current issues are discussed during the regular operational or work meetings.

The advantage of combining the two may be that it underlines that safety is part of regular work and not a separate issue.

Committee meetings

In particular, this concerns meetings of committees that are required by law.

Although these committees could positively contribute to setting up and implementing a proper risk management/safety system, their actual involvement may be limited. Reasons for this, in addition to possible political backgrounds, may include the lack of understanding of how an effective safety- or risk management system can be established and maintained in harmony with other objectives of the organization.

Meetings of line management and support staff

As far as safety and risk management is concerned, these meetings are mainly about deployment of the policy of the organization and providing resources and support for effective implementation of management system activities. These meetings could be organized top-down according to the "linking pin" principle in order to carry messages further into the organization; preferably down and up – two way communication.

These meetings could be combined with the committee meetings mentioned above.

Other communication and promotion possibilities

In addition to the above mentioned meetings, further promotion of risk management, loss control and safety is possible through:

- Campaigns related to a specific subject. Depending on established needs, such campaigns may be directed at the entire organization, a large part of the organization or a specific department. Preferably these campaigns should be headed by a manager with vested interest and include a combination of activities: posters, meetings, hand-outs and quizzes.
- Regular poster program, focusing on the specific needs in certain departments.
- Recognition of individual and group performance regarding safety and risk control. Recognition should not only be based on having "no accidents". For a major part, recognition should include knowledge and behavior aspects regarding safety and control of unwanted events. A combination of input efforts and output results is a good choice.

While these activities focus on in-company matters, they can also be used to address relevant subjects outside the company ("off-the-job "). My experience when doing ISRS audits – including a chapter on off-the-job safety - showed that most people like to have this information even though the formal (company) point of view always was that this is a private matter and the company should have no dealings there. When introducing off-the-job activities - related to safety, health and security at home, on the road, at school etc. - care should be taken to prevent patronizing. If properly done and in a mature way, this could be very good, positive, publicity to include employee family members, friends and the neighborhood.

Many in-company safety and loss control subjects would also be applicable and valuable outside the work environment. To mention a few: lifting, preparing for emergencies, inspections, handling hazardous materials, working at heights, with ladders etc. A good idea, when having an internal safety communication, would be to make the link to off-the-job and at home situations.

Or have an in-company communication specifically addressing an off-work subject, for example how to work with the BBQ, precautions to take when on vacation, etc.

9.2.7. Periodic evaluation of activities

One of the best methods to keep risk management/loss control/safety activities at the desired level, and improve as necessary, is through conducting periodic evaluations/assessments.

These evaluations or "audits" basically include a reference or checklist and knowledgeable people deciding whether criteria are met or not. Their purpose is to assure a desired performance level and to take remedial actions in case of deviations.

Audits of the total (risk - or safety management) system.

These audits include all elements and activities that are part of the management system and will be carried out by people who have received special training. These could be experts from outside the organization or location being audited in order to reduce any possible bias. If external people are being used – such as in case of certification audits - it is important to make sure they have the necessary knowledge, including experience in your type of industry.

In-company audit frequencies may vary from once every 3 to 6 month for systems in development to once every 1 to 3 years for mature systems. Frequencies significantly less than once every three years are not considered very useful.

I consider three different types of total system audits as indicated in the table below.

Type of audit	Reference	Main purpose/objective
Internal	Company reference or ISO, OHSAS or other in case of certification	Meeting own requirements, maintaining self-established level or certification level prior to external audit
External – certificate	ISO, OHSAS, other	Certificate – meeting external requirements for certification level
External – other	Commercial (ISRS, etc.)	Improvement of own system

Internal audits are related to requirements set by the company and as such they are not intended to improve unless the application of the system is still in process. Extension of the company system could take place when end-of-pipe results – accidents, unwanted events - are less than expected or following management reviews uncovering deviations from external requirements such as legislation or customer demands.

Internal audits are often mandatory as part of the process to obtain or maintain a certification level. In that case the audits are done prior to the audit by the certification institute and the internal audit report may be reviewed by the external auditor in preparation of the certification audit.

External audits for certification are carried by auditors working for certification institutes. The objective is to verify the certification level. External references are used such as ISO, OHSAS or other standards. Certificates are often required by external parties such as customers or the legislator.

Commercially available references – such as the ISRS - can be used to carry out a base-line audit to prepare for the development of the in-company management system. Normally these audits will be carried out by auditors trained by the organization making the reference available. These audits can also be used to improvement opportunities for the in-company system in case objectives are not being obtained. These external systems may provide a recognition level that can be used for system improvement as well as for communication to third parties.

Frequent (departmental) evaluations of risk management or safety activities

While the audits mentioned above cover the entire management system and the whole organization or location, it may be useful to carry out more frequent evaluations covering critical elements of the management system, such as:

- Inspections
- Task analysis/task observations
- Accident/incident investigation

These more critical evaluations may be performed by an unbiased staff person, such as a safety officer or someone from the human resource department, but also by individual supervisors or managers or a multidisciplinary team including operational personnel.

In principle these evaluations will be conducted on the basis of documents such as checklists, registrations, etc. They are limited in size and may be executed with a relatively high frequency, for example once per month or quarter. These evaluations may be done per individual department on an at random basis while covering all departments within a period of one year.

Please look at appendix S (page 305) for an example questionnaire concerning accident/incident investigation.

Audits done by middle or senior management involving a number selected parts of the risk management or safety program/system.

These evaluations need to be structured such that every middle and senior will participate in such activity at least once a year. Audits mentioned above (example, appendix R on page 302) are recommended for this purpose and could allow a good interaction between higher management and operational personnel concerning matters important to all.

Periodic evaluations of the general workplace situation

These hardware oriented evaluations may be executed using pre-established checklists. These can be designed to include value factors to allow numerical evaluation regarding the general safety situation of a department. The numerical evaluations can be used as feedback regarding departmental inspections and could be the basis to reward departments for the quality of work done. See appendix I (page 271) for an example of a possible evaluation reference.

These evaluations may be done once per year, every 6 months or more frequent. They should be done by unbiased people and preferably should be preceded by similar evaluations by department personnel to prepare themselves for the "official" evaluation.

Periodic evaluations of processes

These, technically oriented, evaluations should be performed periodically in order to determine if the technical status of the process still meets the actual state of the art requirements. These "process reviews" are to be done by people with specialist knowledge regarding the process and related technical developments. As a rule, these evaluations should be done using a multidisciplinary approach. They may be done less frequent, say every 3 to 5 years.

9.3. Improving the organization – learning from unwanted events

In chapter 9 (section 9.1, page 175) my assumption was that an organization would be created "safe-to-operate". If you have that status from the start then basically "all" you have to do is to maintain it (section 9.2, page 196) and you should be OK. In theory that is so but, in practice, you will almost never obtain the safe-to-operate status from the beginning. So you will have to learn from deviations and unwanted events that will take place not only to maintain the desired status but also to improve it. Remember also that safe today may not be safe tomorrow due to (external) developments and expectations.

Most of the aspects/activities mentioned in section 9.2 will also provide improvement opportunities bringing the organization from "what is (done)" to "what should be (done)".

Improving the organization includes two main routes:

- Auditing, assessing what is and what is done
- Learning from events that do or could lead to loss

Auditing is already mentioned in sections 8.2 and 9.2 so I will not repeat this here and in this section will direct attention to learning from what does or could go wrong: unwanted events and their (potential) consequences.

Accidents, incidents and other type of unwanted events and their losses are "excellent" sources to improve the management system and further the control of risk and loss. Behind this is the reasoning that – in principle – all unwanted events can be prevented and, eventually, they all originate from the management system.

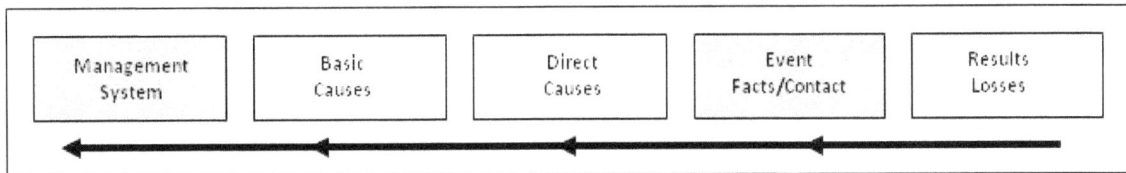

"Excellent" sources to improve but maybe not the preferred sources as results of unwanted events may be serious or catastrophic and you really do not want to learn from those.

9.3.1. Learning from events that are reported

Learning from unwanted events requires that events are reported and information is gathered to allow proper cause analysis all the way back to the management system.

To learn from unwanted events you need to have a process described in an accident investigation protocol (see appendix T, page 306 for a limited example of protocol content).

Learning from unwanted events with serious consequences is a must but not the preferred way to learn as you may be learning from event consequences that are irreversible.

Learning from unwanted events with relatively minor consequences, or no consequences at all, is the better way. You need to use a risk classification system (see appendix B, page 241) to select the important ones. So that those receive proper attention and resources will be made available to investigate, to analyze causes and take remedial actions all the way back to the management system.

Cause analysis - uncovering causes for remedial actions

When analyzing accidents, consider two routes:

- From the event going "upstream" to uncover why the event took place – cause analysis
- From the event going "downstream" to find out why losses are what they are and what they could have been – (potential) extent of loss analysis and evaluation of the effectiveness of the after event (emergency) actions.

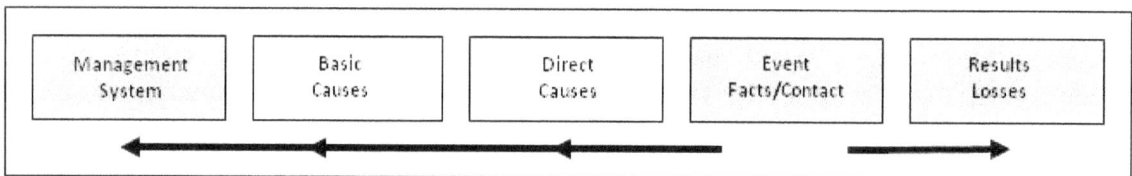

Management System	Basic Causes	Direct Causes	Event Facts/Contact	Results Losses

Event Cause Analysis – "upstream analysis"

Upstream analysis of unwanted events is directed at finding the causes that have lead to the event and its consequences.

Cause analysis should normally be directed at three levels:

- Direct causes
- Basic causes
- Management system aspects

Basis causes and management system aspects can be considered the "root causes" of unwanted events. Root causes are at the practical end of causes analysis; "practical" meaning that the causes can (still) be controlled through efforts and resources that are in proportion to the expected or desired results.

Preferably these cause analyses should be done using a team approach under the guidance of a "facilitator" with sufficient knowledge and expertise of the analysis method(s) used. The role of this person is of particular importance if the analysis data will be put in a database for future use and retrieval of information.

Extent of Loss Analysis - "downstream analysis"

The downstream extent of loss analysis should consider:

- Presence and effectiveness of barriers between the event and the resulting loss
- The availability, quality and effectiveness of private and public emergency means
- The presence and effectiveness of a post event or post emergency plan (PEP) to also limit commercial losses and bring the organization back to normal as soon as possible

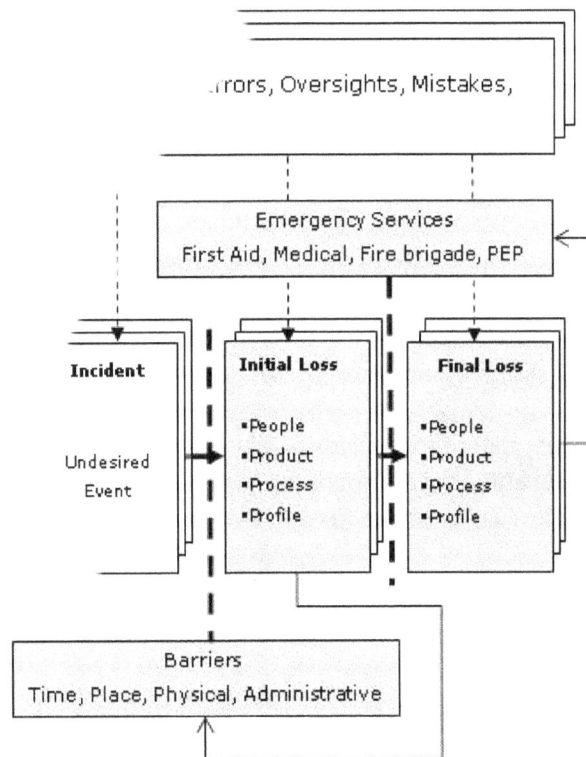

Picture 9.6 - Downstream analysis to determine why the loss is what it is

Remedial actions

Remedial actions – following either upstream or downstream analysis - should preferably be developed through a team approach. The following people may be included as team participants:

- Managers and supervisors with vested interests in the event
- People of the department where the event took place
- People that carried out the activities that took place prior to or during the event
- Staff people from maintenance, human resources and other relevant departments

- People involved in emergency actions including external sources as appropriate
- Facilitator to guide the process of investigation, cause analysis and remedial action development

To make sure that remedial actions will be carried out properly and within the established period, consider the following functions:

- Event owner - person responsible for everything that is related to the event, including the actions to be taken. Probably the head of the department where the event took place. Or higher up the organization depending on the (potential) impact of the unwanted event.
- Action owner - person responsible to assure that a particular action, or a set of actions, will be carried out. This could be the person who actually carries out the action or who makes sure that somebody else, possibly outside the company or organization, carries out the work.

An event would normally have one event owner and several action owners, depending on the number of actions.

9.3.2. Learning from events that are not reported

Accident ratio studies suggest that many incidents may not be reported for one reason or another. These include the events that do not result in visible loss or they may not be reported because in-company procedures may not require that. Other reasons may include:

- Fear of discipline
- Concern about the record
- Concern about reputation
- Fear of medical treatment
- Dislike of medical personnel
- Desire to avoid work interruption
- Desire to keep personal record clear
- Desire to keep the company record clear
- "No-accident" award, bonus of recognition
- Avoidance of red tap
- Concern about the attitude of others
- Poor understanding of the importance

In order to learn from those events they need to be known. There are several ways to find out about them:

Inspections

During inspections substandard or unsafe conditions may be noticed. These conditions did not occur by themselves - they were caused, most likely because someone did something or because someone did not do something (right). Unfortunately, deviations noted during inspections are normally not analyzed for their causes. Risk classification on deviations noted during inspections may not normally be done.

Observations

Behavior observations are like inspections. Only now they are directed at what people do and how they do it. These observations are to uncover behavior deviations that may result in unwanted consequences.

These observations tend to consider more general behavior such as rule compliance, often because the background of the people does not include the detail to carry out observations of specific tasks.

Critical task observations are directed at how critical (risk sensitive) tasks are being carried out. They are a good way to see if these tasks are, and can be, properly carried out in accordance with procedures or work instructions, the "standard (= safe) way of doing the work". Critical task observations form an excellent source to find deviations that could lead to unwanted events.

Incident Recall

Incident Recall is a structured process of communication/interviewing to uncover events that could have resulted in unwanted consequences; events that may be used for learning before they are forgotten.

The interviewing could be done by a supervisor/manager with vested interest or by a staff person more experienced in interviewing techniques and possibly with less bias. The interviewer should have a good knowledge of the work involved and the conditions under which this work is done.

9.3.3. Learn from events that COULD happen - accident imaging

Basically "accident imaging" is: imagine what could happen. When you do that, look at the broad picture and include all possible unwanted events, all scenarios and all consequences.

Accident imaging is answering questions such as: "What if?", "What could happen if the situation was different from what it is now?" Imagination is the only limiting factor.

Accident imaging could provide important information to secure continued operation of your company or organization and improve the management system.

Accident imaging can take place during design of installations, work environment and procedures. But also during inspections, observations, safety meetings, exit interviews, etc. The basic question is: "WHAT IF?"

One example of "What if?" from my own experience:

This happened in 1970 when I was working as a technical representative for INA, the US insurance company. My job was to look at factories and give my opinion about the insurability of the operation concerned. Central to this was the question: "What if". In relation to property damage and business interruption (consequential loss).

The cardboard manufacturer had cardboard rolls stored end on end, close to the ceiling, no sprinklers and smoke detectors no longer connected to the local fire brigade due to previous frequent "false" alarms caused by diesel fueled forklifts. After I visited the plant, my advice was simple and straightforward: not recommended for insurance with an estimated maximum property loss of 90% of sum insured. Two months after my visit the plant burned down killing six people and with an almost total property loss, saving only the space separated power plant representing 10% of sum insured.

The quality of the management team is determined by:

1. Knowing in advance what problems could occur in their organization or unit
2. Knowing the number and size of those problems
3. Knowing what the causes of those problems could be
4. Knowing the actions that should be taken to minimize the negative consequences

A quality management team should only have known problems with limited consequences

---

Accident Imaging - remember Murphy's Law: "What can happen, will happen". A matter of chance. Not doing anything is like Russian roulette.

Think about the train derailment in Spain (see page 12). The problem was known. The obvious question was or should have been: "What can go wrong?" Was the question asked? If so, what was the answer? In any case, the situation was not corrected and the answer came with about 80 people dead – Santiago de Compostela, July 24, 2013.

9.3.4. Processing of selected events

When known, all unwanted events, independent of their source, should be risk classified and - if above a certain level – investigated and cause analyzed to include aspects to also improve the management system whenever possible and applicable.

Learning from unwanted events accumulates in the management system giving direction to procedures and instructions and determining how work environments and installations are to be designed and equipment is to be purchased. How work procedures are to be set up and people are to be trained to properly, safely and without undue loss, carry out their work. This way the management system, by creating a better working environment, better communications and influencing the behavior of people, helps to mold the culture of the organization while at the same time obtaining better cost control and sustainable profitability.

This is why it is it important that the organization should be clear about the following topics:

- What unwanted events and losses shall be reported and investigated?
- What shall be reported?
- How shall these events/losses be investigated and by whom?
- How shall cause analysis be done and by whom?
- Which people shall be included for suggesting actions to remedy the situation?
- How shall the follow-up take place and by whom to make sure that suggested measures are implemented effectively?

My own practice as a safety/loss control management consultant shows that the way incidents and accidents are investigated and analyzed could be less than what it could be in many companies. The focus may be limited to lost time injuries only. There is no clear procedure or protocol including a structured method to carry out cause analysis. There is no proper risk classification system or the system is not used correctly. Or people responsible to carry out the analysis are not properly trained/instructed. That way much valuable information is lost and nothing, or little, learned from what has happened. The result? It can happen again!

To carry out investigation and cause analysis these are some of the methods available:

Traditional method using an accident/incident investigation form

The quality of this type of investigation depends largely on the quality of the form that is being used serving as an information carrier and as a guide for investigation and cause analysis.

Lack of methodology and structure could compromise the objectivity of investigations causing this method to be limited to only find out "who did it", often the victim. As we have seen when discussing the cause-consequence model we can often not even think of THE culprit or THE cause as there are normally several causes and more people involved in creating the undesired event. The traditional method often stopped at the direct causes (the "unsafe" acts and conditions) and did not go beyond that to find the basic, underlying or root causes. The result of that was that the underlying causes were often not removed; they remained allowing the same event from happening again ….. possibly with more serious consequences.

An example of a good form including all necessary elements for proper investigation, cause analysis and remedial action management is shown as appendix U (page 308).

A well-designed form and a proper protocol would be a great help to improve this traditional method. (Elements to be included in an accident or unwanted event protocol can be found in appendix T on page 306.)

Systematic Cause Analysis Technique (SCAT)

This method is consistent with the traditional method mentioned above and includes the elements as mentioned on the form in appendix U. It adds value to the traditional method by focusing on the basic causes of accidents and losses: the personal and job factors (see picture 5.4, page 88) and the management system behind those. The technique allows a structure helping the investigator(s) to identify the aspects that may have led to the unwanted event/loss.

The SCAT method was first developed by Frank E. Bird, Jr. and described in the book "Practical Loss Control Leadership". Cause analysis is facilitated by using SCAT charts that can be obtained from DNV-GL (www.dnv-gl.com).

A technique that is very similar to SCAT is RCAT – Root Cause Analysis Technique – which has been developed by IRCA – International Risk Control America. RCAT charts can be obtained from IRCA (www.ircamerica.com).

Cause analysis, using the SCAT or RCAT charts, is systematically shown in picture 9.7 below. After collecting the necessary factual information the analysis goes from direct causes to the management system. At all levels actions can be generated to prevent future unwanted events. You will note the phases of the Bird cause-consequence model with the consequences at the top and the management system at the bottom. The similarity between the two approaches – SCAT and RCAT – is given by the fact that the related DNV-GL activities come from the 1991 acquisition by DNV of ILCI which was set up by Frank E. Bird, Jr. while IRCA was founded later by Frank's son David.

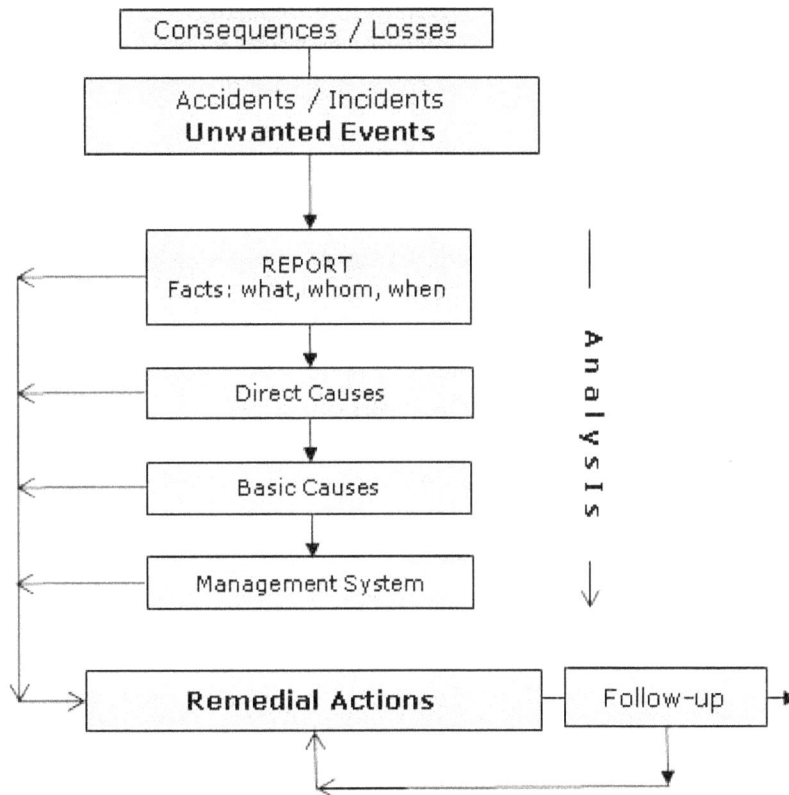

Picture 9.7 – Flow sheet showing cause analysis process using SCAT or RCAT charts

Working with those charts is relatively easy. Going down the chart from the top, questions should be asked when considering relevant aspects listed under each of the phase headings. The questions should lead to three possible outcomes:

- The aspect considered is not involved in causing the unwanted event
- The aspect is involved in causing the unwanted event
- More information is needed to decide about this aspect

In principle both SCAT and RCAT are fault trees like MORT with the undesired event and consequences at the top and the different cause levels underneath.

MORT (Management Oversight and Risk Tree)

This method is an application of the fault tree which has been constructed for the purpose of accident cause analysis in the high hazard industry. The method is relatively complex and should preferably be used by people who specialize in investigating and analyzing accidents.

The methodology was developed by Bill Johnson for the Department of Energy in the U.S. for use in nuclear power generation industry. Gradually, however, the method also became used in other industries.

Starting with the unwanted event, the tree divides into two main topics: "technical" and "management" (see picture 9.3, page 181). The total tree includes about 1500 aspects.

Characteristic for the application of the tree is asking questions – included in the MORT user manual – leading to the following conclusions:

- The aspect considered is "less than adequate" (LTA) and possibly one of the causes of the aspect above it, ultimately leading to the top event
- The aspect in question was adequate and therefore not a likely cause
- Information is insufficient to decide on LTA or not and additional information should be obtained, as necessary
- The aspect is not considered relevant

Causal Tree Method

Originally called "Arbre des Causes" (Tree of causes), the Causal Tree Method (CTM), also referred to as the "fact tree method", was developed within French industry during the 1970's. It differs from other methods as it is exclusively intended to be used in groups, including staff functions, line management and operational personnel.

As in MORT, this method is also based on the principles of the fault tree. CTM only considers facts (hence "fact tree") and not possibilities. This is why the tree only shows AND gates and no OR gates. All facts mentioned in the tree are required to produce the resulting fact at the higher level and are targets for improvement. Elimination of any of these facts would have prevented the resulting fact from occurring and thus also the end result of the tree.

All aspects that could be involved in contributing to the accident or unwanted event are subject to the following questions:

1. Was this aspect necessary to deliver the consequence considered?
2. Was this aspect essential to deliver the consequence?
3. Was this aspect sufficient to produce the fact above it? If "no", other aspects must have contributed to produce the consequence - so look further.

Application of the analysis process is guided by facilitators ("Guarantors"), people who are specially trained in the used of the method and who make sure that the method will be used correctly.

Use of computer

The use of the computer in the recording and analysis of accidents has really taken off since early the 1980's. One of the first publications that I remember regarding the use of computers was: "In case of accident, call the computer" by Bill Pope (1912 – 2011), founder of the National Safety Management Society (US).

The use of software – sometimes available free of charge - ranges from simply recording incident facts to the interactive software to analyze causes and generate and follow-up remedial actions. While earlier software had to be installed on mainframe computers and later on individual PC's or in-company networks, the use of web-based ("cloud computing") applications have become more available in recent years. The latter applications are normally made available for an annual or monthly fee as SaaS – Software as a Service - meaning that you buy the right to use the software but not the software itself.

Some unwanted event related management principles

To close this section on "improving the organization", remember the management principles below.

1.   The principle of multiple causes

The principle of multiple causes
Accidents and other loss producing events are seldom, if ever, the result of a single cause

I am not sure where it originates from but I know that it was used by Frank E. Bird, Jr. in his 1974 book: "Management Guide to Loss Control".

The principle means that an unwanted event rarely has only one cause and the message is that you should not stop at "person did not follow rules". Look beyond that to find the reasons why he or she did not follow the proper rules or procedures for doing the work. Refer to picture 7.6 on page 129 showing the cause-consequences matrix; relating a particular consequence (loss) to root causes ("business areas") will most likely underline the above principle.

2.   The principle of shared responsibility

The principle of shared responsibility

More often than not are accidents and other unwanted events the result of work done by many people at different levels in the organization and at different times. They all share responsibility for the consequences.

This principle follows the first one and highlights the fact that there are almost always more people involved when it comes to finding out what caused an unwanted event to occur. Think about the phases of the cause-consequence model left of the unwanted event; from the person directly involved in the operational activity to those responsible for making the management system work as it should.

3.   The principle of multiple consequences

The principle of multiple consequences

More often than not will a single cause result in multiple consequences

---

This principle is the reverse of the principle of multiple causes. Refer to picture 7.6. on page 129 and visualize the relation between a single cause and its possible consequences.

4.   The principle of definition

The principle of definition

A logical and proper decision can be made only when the basic or real problems are first defined

---

Louis A. Allen, management consultant and writer. Founder of Louis Allen Worldwide

The principle of definition highlights the fact that you need to go back to the root causes of unwanted events to really solve problems; the real root causes can be found in the management system or rather, in the failure of that system.

More management principles can be found on www.topves.nl; go there and search the website using "management principles".

10.   SOME SPECIFIC LOSS CONTROL MANAGEMENT AREAS

In addition to the general aspects and instruments of loss control management outlined so far, I briefly mention some specialty areas:

- Product safety/-liability
- Fire safety
- Security
- Environment

I will not discuss these in much detail which, I feel, is outside the scope of this book: an introduction to risk management, safety and control of loss.

General principles

The same methods and principles mentioned so far can be used in any specific area – those mentioned above or any other. The basics include:

- Identification of (potential) problems/losses – what can happen?
- Evaluation of consequences – how large can they be?
- Take actions if the (potential) problems appear bigger than acceptable

Apart from the possible elimination of potential problems, the actions to reduce future problems or losses (= risks) include:

- Reducing the frequency of causes that can lead to unwanted events
- Limiting the consequences of those events should they occur anyway by using barriers and emergency plans
- Making sure to have proper financing available to absorb the financial loss
- Learning from what goes wrong so unwanted events will not happen again in the future

10.1   Product safety/-liability

Product safety is usually considered together with the liability aspect. These two aspects are almost always related but the extent of that may, however, vary greatly. Product safety is mainly concerned with the prevention and mitigation of injury accidents or damage that may result from the use of the product or service delivered by the organization.

Actual losses can be much larger than the liability; negative publicity involving use of product or service may cause loss of market and customers while the liability loss could be relatively small. Or the liability is limited while millions of dollars could be lost that went into creating a brand name. On the other hand, liability losses could be catastrophic and could bring a company to bankruptcy. Much depends on the specific situation.

While all aspects relevant to a general loss control or risk management system or program are applicable here, some specific aspects of product safety to consider are:

- Product safety policy – commitment from the top down
- Product design specifications to meet market conditions taking into account the use of the product, operating conditions/-environment, storage conditions etc.; in general and with regard to specific application of products by customers; in normal and abnormal use situations
- Thorough research into possible undesirable effects of product application or use; consider normal and abnormal use, conditions and environment
- Use of test equipment and procedures to meet product specifications
- Special attention to production, storage and transportation and related quality issues to assure meeting product specifications
- Caution concerning promises regarding product capabilities in brochures, advertisements or made verbally during sales and marketing activities
- Training/instruction of personnel covering all product or service related aspects including product/service limitations, tests, marketing and sales
- Storage of manufacturing, test and sales data throughout and beyond the lifetime of the product
- Recall possibilities of product from the market in case of defects
- Field modification procedures where recall is not possible or practical
- A system for notification and reporting product complaints and other incidents, investigation and analyzing reported incidents and taking appropriate action
- Ensure proper functioning of product safety activities by establishing coordination of all relevant activities using a (product safety) team including senior management involvement

Product safety aspects are also involved when supplying services as well as in areas such as professional liability and directors and officers liability.

A product safety/loss control risk management system can be build using a practice similar to the 17 –step process (appendix L, page 280).

10.2 Fire safety

The unwanted event in this case is the occurrence of fire.

There are three main areas that need attention:

1. Actions to prevent of fire
2. Limitation of fire area
3. Actions to extinguish the fire

As I mentioned earlier, when I worked for INA, my job was to prepare underwriting reports for decision making by the underwriters concerning fire and allied perils property damage and business interruption insurance.

The acronym to collect information when visiting industrial sites and for preparing the underwriting report was COPE:

- Construction
- Occupancy
- Protection
- Exposure

Under "construction" we would in consider height of structures/building, materials that were used in buildings and installations as well as the separation between those in terms of distance and fire walls. Important items were the combustibility of constructions and the possible spread of fire between them. We would consider construction classes: frame, all metal, brick, non-combustible and fire resistive. We would look at exterior and interior walls, floors and roofs and fire spread between floors and along ceilings etc.

"Occupancy" was the key word to consider what the company was doing inside the buildings and installations. Processes, fire load, flammable and combustible materials, height of storage, etc. We looked at separation of combustibles inside buildings, housekeeping etc. Occupancy would also include outside storage, in particular storage of combustible materials (such as pallets) close to building walls. Occupancy would be divided into "common hazards" and "special hazards" in relation to the type of occupancy class. Common hazards would cover such issues as heating, electricity, air conditioning, hot work and smoking. Special hazards would include cleaning using flammable liquids, paint spraying, storage heights, etc.

"Protection" directed attention to private protection as well as public protection. What did the company install to fight fires and what facilities could be offered from outside the company, including help from neighboring facilities and the public fire brigade.

"Exposure" had two sides: exposure from the surroundings to the company as well as exposure from the company to the surroundings. Surroundings such as other buildings, factories, storage facilities, roads, open water, woods and bushes, railroads, nearby airfields, housing areas and the (quality of the) neighborhood in general.

The underwriting report would include a description of all the aspects covered by COPE and would highlight any aspect that could influence the underwriter's decisions, positively or negatively. And of course, my opinion of the status of these aspects, in particularly concerning those that would negatively affect the insurability of the company concerned. The end conclusion would be an indication of the company "in its class" in terms of Poor, Fair, Good or Excellent. "In its class" meaning how the insurability of the company concerned compared to other companies in the same occupancy group. If a company rated less than "poor" then it was not recommended for insurance. I used that term only once in connection with a cardboard paper manufacturer in Belgium which burned down two months after I saw it, also killing six people.

Actions to prevent fire

Fire is a combination of combustibles, oxygen and an ignition source. If any of those three is not present, there will be no fire.

Combustibles can be anything that can burn: wood, paper, gas, flammable liquids, textiles, natural materials (trees, grass), plastics, etc. Their behavior should be considered when considering type and distance of ignition sources. Flammable liquids, vapors and gasses can travel quite a distance from their source of origin so take that into account when looking for potential ignition sources.

Under normal conditions, combustibles and oxygen (in the air) are always there, so if you do not want the fire to start you need to take care that no ignition source is available where the flammables, combustibles are. Ignition sources such as smoking, welding, open flames, electrical systems, friction, static electricity, chemical reaction, self-ignition of certain materials, etc. Also consider rioting, vandalism and other willful actions that may introduce ignition sources.

After a fire, you probably have heard people say that the cause was not yet known. Put that in perspective and you will consider two aspects:

1. It is very likely that there is not just one cause but, more likely, there are multiple causes as we have seen during our discussions. There are causes of causes. Remember the principle of multiple causes.
2. The "trigger" cause would most likely have been an ignition source given the fact that oxygen and combustibles are almost always there. What may not be known is the actual source of ignition.

So the more proper reaction to the question should have been: "We do not yet know what the ignition source was and what have been its causes." The ignition source is a direct cause and you and I know that preceding that are the basic causes and those that are part of the management system.

Limiting of fire area

Basically: how far can the fire spread if it would happen?

Consider open space (distance) between combustibles, fire walls, dikes around storage tanks containing combustible liquids, bushes and trees around buildings.

Also consider protection systems that may be needed but remember that those systems can be subject to failure or maybe out of service for maintenance or other reasons. Sprinkler systems are good means to limit spread of fire but they have proven to fail or been made inadequate by changing the occupancy for which they were designed.

Smoke alarm systems are only as good as the follow-up. In case of the Belgian cardboard manufacturer (mentioned on page 218), the smoke alarm system was disconnected from the fire brigade due to the many false alarms that were caused by the forklifts being used to transport rolls of cardboard paper that were stored end-on-end.

Actions to extinguish the fire

Detectors (smoke, fire or otherwise) are intended to provide early signals that something is going on and the sooner people become aware of a fire happening, the more effective the actions to extinguish the fire can be.

When looking at actions to extinguish fire, consider fire extinguishers, fire hydrants, standpipe and hose, water supply, pumps, water pressure, sprinklers, CO_2 and other extinguishing systems, need and availability of foam, fire engines and their capacity, fire brigade training and equipment, watchman and alarm services, etc.

When working for the insurance company we separated the fire protection into:

- Private protection – anything that the company would provide to fight fires
- Public (exterior) protection – provided by the municipal fire brigade

When working for INA in Europe, we missed a public fire brigade classification system that existed in the USA. This classification was needed as part of the underwriter's decision making process. So, to grade public protection in Europe, my boss Ernie, an American Fire Protection Engineer, designed a system late 1960's to be used internally based on:

- Available water supply – hydrants (number and size of water pipes, flow and pressure), open water
- Accessibility – distance between water supply and insured values (buildings etc.)
- Fire brigade – type (professional, volunteer, combination), alarm system, distance to location, obstructions such as bridges, railroad crossings, etc.
- Fire alarm systems – automatic/manual from central station to public telephone
- Construction of buildings/installations – from frame to fire resistive
- Occupancy – from extra hazard to light or incombustible

The exterior protection grading resulted in Good, Fair or Poor and was used by the underwriters for insurance acceptance.

The grading of public protection developed in the USA since the early 1900's and is presently (2014) maintained by the Insurance Services Organization (ISO) as the PPC (Public Protection Classification) system. A community's PPC depends on:

- Fire alarm and communication systems, including telephone systems, telephone lines, staffing, and dispatching systems – accounting for 10% of the classification
- The fire department, including equipment, staffing, training, and geographic distribution of fire companies – accounting for 50 % of the classification
- The water-supply system, including the condition and maintenance of hydrants, and a careful evaluation of the amount of available water compared with the amount needed to suppress fires – accounting for 40% of the classification

Looking back at the system that Ernie set up – more than 40 years ago – and after having done some comparison calculations, I can only conclude that he did a pretty good job. He was also the nicest boss I ever had.

A fire safety/loss control management system can be build using a practice similar to the 17 – step process (appendix L, page 280).

10.3 Security

Security includes special risk aspects and is different from safety in the sense that normally or often there is an opponent, an "enemy" taking action. Even though that is true, the "general principles" of loss control management – mentioned on page 225 - still apply.

Security and safety sometimes have conflicting interests. For example: for security reasons it may be desirable to keep people inside the building while safety may want them out. Or the other way around.

Although there are exceptions, it is often not practical or desirable to install 100% security protection. After all, buildings, systems etc. have to remain accessible to the people who have to make use of them. Customers have to make use of shops and banks and of payment systems and employees should be able to continue to carry out their work.

Some of the risks threatening organizations and requiring attention within the context of security include:

- Accidental risks caused by lack of discipline, lack of concern for property
- Disorderliness or vandalism by personnel or third parties
- Theft or embezzlement of goods or money by own personnel or third parties
- Theft of company information, recipes, drawings
- Espionage for and by third parties
- Fraud by own staff through the misuse of trust placed in them
- Corruption due to bribing of staff by third parties
- Conducting "working by the book" actions by own personnel, strikes
- Company occupation by own personnel or third parties, picket lines
- Riots by own personnel or third parties
- Sabotage, intentional disruption of the normal processes
- Blackmail
- Kidnapping, hostage, hijacking of persons or goods
- Bomb threats

Depending on the nature of the risk and its extent, measures should be taken which would often involve the creation of "barriers" that will make it more difficult or less attractive for the "enemy" to act.

A particular aspect of security relates to the use of computers and the loss of information critical to the organization. The use of computers can often lead to increased vulnerability of the company or organization. Not only due to the combination a large amounts of information and the vulnerability thereof, for example in case of fire, but also the possibility of fraud that this may provide. Attention should be given to the possibilities of fraud by own staff and by third parties. This issue is almost daily in the media and does not need any further explanation or attention within the context of this book.

A security management system can be build using a practice similar to the 17 –step process (appendix L, page 280).

10.4.   Environment

Basically, environmental pollution can come from three "sources":

- Environmental impact below the maximum level set by the regulatory agency. The pollution is allowed, at least during the period for which those levels are set. It is expected that the lower levels will develop in the future requiring the search for processes, technologies and practices that will have lesser environmental impact.
- (Temporary) impact above accepted levels as the result of an unwanted event. This relates to deviations from normal situation, an "accident".
- Deliberate pollution of the environment beyond the allowed maximum levels. This involves violation of the regulations: environmental crime.

The first source really takes place within the context of the regulations. Progressive insight into environmental situations is a reason for lowering the upper margins and may eventually lead to environmental sustainability.

Decreasing societal acceptance of environmental pollution will produce lower maximum levels of allowed pollution and increasingly force companies to upgrade their performance in this area. More and more, companies do not want their reputation damaged by suppliers not following the principles of sustainable development. As such this should be considered within the context of risk management, looking at future opportunities that present themselves today. Not taking this development into account means creating the business losses of tomorrow.

Even though the pollution maybe within the regulatory context, problems may arrive due to continued pollution over a longer period of time. Or improper use of waste dumps of which Love Canal is an example, making headlines during the second half of the 1970's.

The third source relates to criminal activity and I do not think that there is a need to discuss this here.

The second source of pollution refers to an accident causing pollution of the environment and is the result of an unwanted event. Environmental pollution that we know under names such as Bhopal, Sandoz, Seveso etc. are the results of accidents showing the relation between internal and external "safety". The approach to this accidental pollution is to follow the general loss control/safety methodologies described throughout this book.

Basis for determining potential risks is to find out which substances are being processed, transported and stored, the amounts thereof, etc. And, of course, if there is a change that these substances can be accidently released, what can cause this to happen? As applicable, computer models may be used to calculate the spread of pollution that could develop.

Determining potential risks should include questions such as:

- What products are processed, stored, traded?
- How are products processed, stored, transported on and off premises?
- How vulnerable are the surroundings?
- How is processing of waste, including packaging, organized?
- What intermediate or byproducts are being produced?
- What substances can be produced in case process conditions deviate from normal?
- What products can be formed by mixing substances other than those desired?
- What products can be created during emergencies (e.g. fire)?
- How are products, including those used to fight the emergency, contained or removed during emergency actions (air, water and soil pollution)?

An environmental management system can be build using a practice similar to the 17 –step process (appendix L, page 280).

11.   THINGS TO REMEMBER

1. Risk management, safety and control of loss follow the same principles. The same tools and methods are being used to control unwanted events. For all practical purposes, these three areas are the same.

2. The management system is the heart of controlling unwanted events, risks and losses and contains the management activity areas or elements that are necessary to reach objectives.

3. The management system is a "tool of management" to reach objectives and to control unwanted events that are in the way of getting desired results.

4. The management function is present at every level and in each function in the organization.

5. To build, maintain and improve a successful management system requires the involvement of all in the organization.

6. The basic model for improvement, change and success is the Platform model including the essential ingredients for success: Plan-Train-Do and Management Leadership.

7. The 17-step process is based on the Platform model and is the pathway to build a management system that will work and bring the success that you are looking for. Plan, Content and Structure and the main keywords here.

The three most important pictures to remember whenever you wish to move your organization in a desired direction:

1.   The Platform model:

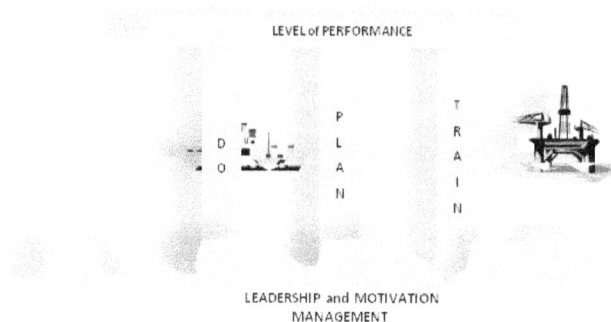

2.	The management system or PLAN:

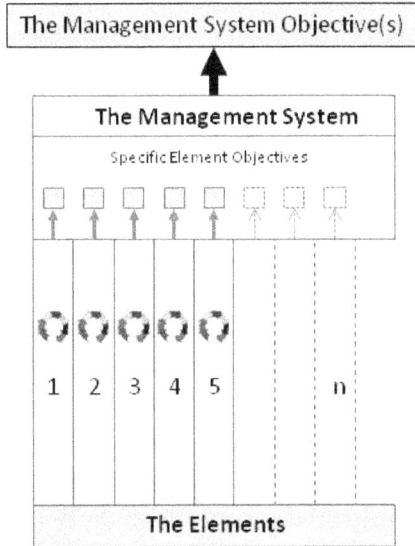

The Management System Objective(s)

The Management System

Specific Element Objectives

1 2 3 4 5   n

The Elements

3.	The process of 17 steps:

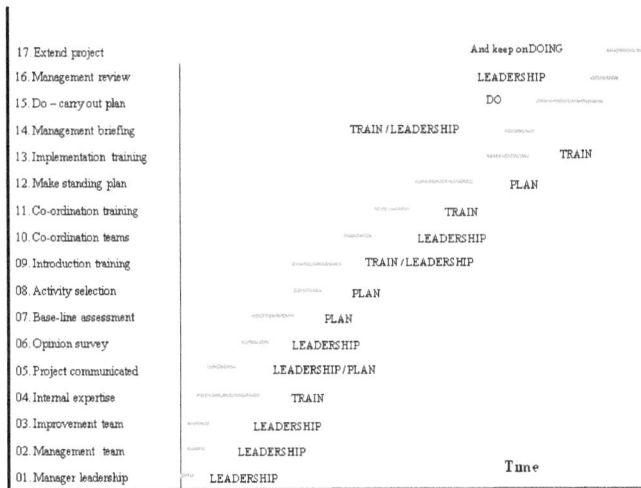

17. Extend project		And keep on DOING
16. Management review		LEADERSHIP
15. Do – carry out plan		DO
14. Management briefing		TRAIN / LEADERSHIP
13. Implementation training		TRAIN
12. Make standing plan		PLAN
11. Co-ordination training		TRAIN
10. Co-ordination teams		LEADERSHIP
09. Introduction training		TRAIN / LEADERSHIP
08. Activity selection		PLAN
07. Base-line assessment		PLAN
06. Opinion survey		LEADERSHIP
05. Project communicated		LEADERSHIP / PLAN
04. Internal expertise		TRAIN
03. Improvement team		LEADERSHIP
02. Management team		LEADERSHIP
01. Manager leadership		LEADERSHIP

Time

LOOKING BACK

I apologize for not being complete, for repeating certain items (which, by the way, I did on purpose but you may feel that I did too much of it), for typing errors and for possibly incorrect use of the English language which is not my native tongue.

Hopefully I have been somewhat consistent using the terminology throughout the book although you will have noticed that I sometimes use terminology rather freely as I do not wish to be too limited by definitions. Examples are the use of terms such as: risk management, loss control and safety, management system, management activity area, element and words like accident, incident and unwanted event.

If I have infringed on copyrights or any other rights, I also apologize; it is not my intention as I like to give credit to those who deserve it.

I hope that you will be able to use some of the ideas presented when communicating with others on the subjects of risk management, safety and control of loss. I hope that I have showed you the importance of risk management and loss control for any organization or business. I hope too that I succeeded in showing that safety really is no different from control of risk and loss, any loss. All you have to do is look at safety the way it deserves to be looked at.

Other than that, I am solely responsible for what I wrote in this book while making an honest attempt to share some of my ideas and experience with you. Should you have any comments and suggestions in relation to the content of this book, I would gratefully receive them at my email address: willem@topves.nl.

Breda, The Netherlands

Willem Top

ABOUT THE AUTHOR

Willem Top was born in 1940 and lives in The Netherlands. After getting BSc degrees in Chemical Engineering and Industrial Engineering he has been working in the area of safety and risk management since 1968, related to industrial insurance as well as certification, and has worked for Dutch, English, American and Norwegian companies.

Willem's safety education included many contacts with Frank E. Bird, Jr. from 1969 until Mr. Bird passed away in 2007. Willem met Mr. Bird for the first time after he joined INA in 1968; at that time Mr. Bird was the INA Director of Engineering Services.

In 1984, Willem set up his own (safety) management consulting firm, Loss Control Centre (LCC), involved in management system auditing, consulting and management training. LCC was based on cooperation with Mr. Bird founder and owner of ILCI (International Loss Control Institute), world safety leader during the second halve of last century and originator of the ISRS. Following the acquisition of ILCI by DNV (Det Norske Veritas, now DNV-GL) in 1989, Willem sold his firm to DNV in 1991.

Willem Top was instrumental introducing the International Safety Rating System (ISRS) into Europe and took the initiative that led to the creation of the contractor safety certification system (SCC/VCA) that received accreditation in 1994. The SCC/VCA system is used in The Netherlands, Belgium, Germany, Austria and Switzerland.

For more information concerning Willem and his ideas, please visit www.topves.nl.

Besides articles in Dutch and English, Willem Top wrote two books:

- Risk Management, Safety and Control of Loss – Protecting Your Organization, an Introduction (2014, ISBN 978-90-820411-3-2)

- Making Your Future – in Business and Other Parts of Life (2015, ISBN 978-90-820411-4-9).

Note from the author about his books:

I like to think that my books form a unity when it comes to improvement, reaching objectives while, at the same time, controlling unwanted events.

Although each these books stands on its own, they actually belong together and include the same ideas, principles, tools etc. and a necessary overlap between them.

APPENDICES

In the remaining part of this book I am providing several appendices to illustrate issues that I have mentioned in this book.

PLEASE NOTE: The information contained in the appendices is provided as example only. If you want to use these in your organization, you need to adapt the contents to your specific needs and situation.

The appendices are:

A. Safety & loss control policy statement
B. Risk classification – matrix and Fine/Kinney method
C. Risk inventory checklist
D. Job physical requirements checklist
E. Task risk analysis (TRA) worksheet
F. Installation lifecycle phases
G. Safety & loss control management maturity profile
H. Safety and loss control opinion survey - management personnel
I. Physical conditions evaluation
J. Inspection report form
K. How to make rules
L. 17-step process to build a management system
M. 17-step process rating
N. Content of a (safety) management system
O. Management system element structure
P. Management system – some questions and answers
Q. Safety & loss prevention manual
R. Safety management system audit questionnaire
S. Safety management questions for departmental evaluation
T. Accident investigation protocol elements
U. Accident Investigation form
V. List of English language books I used to have

Further information can be found on the Internet to also include my own website www.topves.nl. When visiting my website, you may want to use the website search function provided.

APPENDIX A – Safety & loss control policy statement

SAFETY & LOSS CONTROL POLICY

We, the management of (COMPANY), are fully committed to the protection from accidental loss of our employees, property, customers, third party employees, visitors and the environment.

In fulfilling this commitment, we will provide and maintain a safe and healthful work environment as indicated by acceptable business practices and compliance with regulatory requirements. We will strive to eliminate any foreseeable hazards which may result in fires, security losses, damage to property, loss to the environment, injuries/illnesses and deterioration of our company's image.

Unwanted events resulting in accidental loss can only be controlled through management in combination with active employee involvement. Loss prevention is the direct responsibility of all line and staff managers and employees alike. The quality of the management function at all levels in the organization - managerial, specialist staff and operational – plays a vital role in the ongoing success that we all share in reaching our objectives and controlling unwanted events.

All management personnel including business, line and associated management will comply with (COMPANY) loss prevention requirements as they apply to the design, operation and maintenance of facilities and equipment. All employees at all levels will perform their jobs properly in accordance with established procedures and operating philosophy as described in our Safety and Loss Prevention Management System and related documents.

We expect and trust that all of you will join us in a personal commitment to the prevention of unwanted events and loss as a way of life – as "the way we work here".

_____   _____

(Company) Director   (Others, as applicable)

APPENDIX B – Risk classification – matrix and Fine/Kinney method

Classification combines the two main aspects to quantify risk:

- Frequency of occurrence of the event
- Potential (maximum) consequences in areas such as safety, environment, property damage, quality, loss of market, etc. or any combination of those.

Two methods are mentioned:

- Matrix
- Fine/Kinney

Please note: all risk classifications should be considered with great care. In particular be very careful when accepting situations with a very high loss potential (consequence) and a very low failure rate, even if the resulting risk classification may seem to indicate that the risk could be in the acceptable range.

Matrix

This risk classification method comes in various shapes and forms. The most simple one is a 3 x 3 matrix combining failure rate: low, average, high with potential consequences: limited, serious, catastrophic.

Below, a possible 5 x 5 matrix is shown

The failure rate is divided into 5 categories 1 to 5, as indicated in the table below. The highest failure rate is at the top of the table, the lowest failure rate at the bottom.

5	Several times a year
4	1 time per year
3	1 time per 2 years
2	1 time per 5 years
1	Less than 1 time per 5 years

Table 1- Failure rate

The possible consequences are also divided into 5 categories ranging from A to E, as indicated in the table below. The most severe consequence is at the top of the table, the lowest at the bottom.

Category	Loss type	Consequence level
E **Very High Risk**	Safety	Multiple deaths
	Environment	Extensive excess of allowed emission levels. Extensive damage to the environment. Major public concerns.
	Material Damage	> € 1,000,000
	Company Image	Extensive company image degradation.
D **High Risk**	Safety	Death of individual. Serious permanent disability. Serious injury of many.
	Environment	Severe excess of allowed emission levels. Damage to environment. Corrective measures required outside company boundaries.
	Material Damage	€ 100,000 to € 1,000,000
	Company Image	Serious company image degradation.
C **Average Risk**	Safety	Non-permanent serious injury to individual. Workdays lost. Restricted work. Minor injury to many.
	Environment	Repeated slight excess of allowed emission limits. Limited damage to environment outside company boundaries.
	Material Damage	€ 10,000 to € 100,000
	Company Image	Average company image degradation.
B **Low Risk**	Safety	Non-permanent light injury to individual. Restricted work. Pain or injury several people.
	Environment	Slight excess of allowed emissions limits. Non-permanent damage to the environment.
	Material Damage	€ 1,000 to € 10,000
	Company Image	Little company image degradation.
A **Minor Risk**	Safety	Pain or injury to individual. First Aid
	Environment	Emissions or pollution below allowable limits. Within company boundaries.
	Material Damage	< € 1,000
	Company Image	No company image degradation.

Table 2 – Possible consequences

Risk is the combination of failure rate and possible consequences (R = F x C) and the risk class is expressed in a number and a letter, such as 3C, 2A, 5B and so on. See matrix below.

Potential Consequence	A	B	C	D	E
	Risk Class				
Failure rate					
5	5A	5B	5C	5D	5E
4	4A	4B	4C	4D	4E
3	3A	3B	3C	3D	3E
2	2A	2B	2C	2D	2E
1	1A	1B	1C	1D	1E

Table 3 - Risk Classification matrix

Fine/Kinney

The method developed by Fine/Kinney includes the following aspects:

- Failure rate, divided in two components:
  - Exposure – the frequency of the activity that could lead to the unwanted event
  - Probability – the change that the unwanted event occurs during the activity
- Consequence - the possible result or loss following the unwanted event

The above aspects are categorized and provided with a value factor after which the risk classification or risk score (R = E x P x C) can be calculated. Different descriptions of categories and value factors may be found when looking for the method on the Internet. The descriptions and value factors shown below are examples only.

Failure rate:

Exposure - E

Category	Value factor
Continuous	10
Frequent	6
Occasional	3
Unusual	2
Rare	1
Very rare	0.5

Probability - P

Category	Value factor
Might be expected	10
Quite possible	6
Unusual but possible	3
Only remotely possible	1
Conceivable but very unlikely	0.5
Practically impossible	0.2
Virtually impossible	0.1

Consequence - C:

Category	Description	Value factor
Catastrophic	Numerous death; damage > $ 10,000,000	100
Disaster	Multiple death; damage > $ 1,000,000	40
Very serious	One death; damage > $ 100,000	15
Serious	Serious injury; damage > $ 10,000	7
Important	Lost time injury; damage > $ 1,000	3
Noticeable	Minor first aid; damage > $ 100	1

Following determination of E, P and C the Risk Score - or Risk Classification – (R) can be calculated as follows: $R = E \times P \times C$

Depending on the outcome the Fine/Kinney method gives the following risk descriptions and suggested actions:

Risk Score	Risk Description
> 400	Very high risk; consider discontinuing operation
200 to 400	High risk; immediate correction required
70 – 200	Substantial risk; correction needed
20 to 70	Possible risk; attention indicated
< 20	Risk; perhaps acceptable

APPENDIX C – Risk inventory checklist

Identified Check the appropriate box when hazard identified. If not sure, use a question mark and find out later.

Evaluated Check box if risk has been evaluated (frequency x consequence).

Risk Class	Indicate risk classification (Description used below is conform Fine/Kinney method.)
	1. Very high risk - consider discontinuing operation
	2. High risk - immediate correction required
	3. Substantial risk - correction needed
	4. Possible risk - attention indicated
	5. Negligible risk - perhaps acceptable as is
Control	Place an A, B, or C to indicate the degree of control over this exposure.
	A. Complete or Substantial
	B. Substantial
	B. Moderate
	C. Low
	D. None
Financing	Check box when adequate financing is available to cover possible financial loss.
DNA	Does Not Apply - check box is risk does not exist.

	IDENTIFIED	EVALUATED	RISK CLASS	CONTROL	FINANCING	DNA
PHYSICAL HARM TO EMPLOYEES						
Compensated Injury on Premises						
Physical Injury						
Occupational Illness						
Compensated Injury Off Premises						
Physical Injury						
Occupational Illness						
Injury or Illness in Other Employment or Activity						
Recreational						
Highway - Non-occupational						
Domestic						
Casual Employment						
Injury Out of State or Country						
Impaired Capacity						
Alcoholism						

	IDENTIFIED	EVALUATED	RISK CLASS	CONTROL	FINANCING	DNA
Drug Abuse						
Absenteeism						
Mental Stress of Other Influence						
Injury While on Leave of Absence						
Other Organization						
Governmental Service						
Civic Events						
Military Service						
Charitable Service						
Injury or Illness While in Custody of Law Enforcement						
Other than listed above (describe)						
PROPERTY LOSS TO ORGANIZATION						
Normal Wear of Equipment						
Abusive Wear and Tear						
Premature Breakdown						
Premature Obsolescence						
Work Process Interruption						
Power Source Failure						
Energy Reduction						
Materials Supply Interruption						
Materials Supply Contamination						
Natural Phenomenon or Disaster						
Fire - External						
Windstorm						
Pollution						
Flood						
Landslide						
Work Process Fire						
Chemical Action						
Pressure Vessel Leakage or Rupture						

	IDENTIFIED	EVALUATED	RISK CLASS	CONTROL	FINANCING	DNA
Civil Disobedience						
War						
Riot						
Vandalism						
Industrial Sabotage						
Structural Integrity Failure (Buildings)						
Glass Breakage						
Overload Collapse						
Pressure Change						
On Impact From						
Object						
Vehicle						
Aircraft						
Ship						
Due to Natural Deterioration						
Explosion						
Process Materials						
Transient Materials						
Perils of the Land						
Perils of the Sea						
Perils of the Air						
Contamination						
From Foreign Substance						
From Loss of Temperature or Pressure Control						
From Radiation From Corrosive Process Materials						
Work Process Waste						
Repairable Equipment Salvaged						
Scrap Materials Discarded						
Scrap Material Disposal						
Increased Reconstruction Costs						

	IDENTIFIED	EVALUATED	RISK CLASS	CONTROL	FINANCING	DNA
Increased Replacement Costs						
Increased Repair Costs						
Loss of Know-how, Blueprints, Records or Other Process Documents						
Other than listed above (describe)						
PHYSICAL HARM TO PUBLIC						
Product Consumption						
Normal						
Abusive						
Injury or Illness to Guests on Premises						
Physical						
Toxic Substances						
Radiation						
Noise, Temperature, etc.						
Due to Uncontrolled Process						
Due to Motor Vehicle Operation						
Due to Watercraft Operation						
Due to Aircraft Operation						
Due to Acts of Employees						
Due to Acts of Animals						
Due to fire and/or Explosion						
Due to Construction						
Due to Alteration						
Due to Demolition						
Due to Disposal						
Due to Existence of Facilities or Equipment (Interference)						
Due to Malpractice						
Second Party						
Third Party						
Due to Sponsorship of						
Recreation Events						

	IDENTIFIED	EVALUATED	RISK CLASS	CONTROL	FINANCING	DNA
Training Programs						
Libel and Slander						
Third Party Liability in Certification						
Other than listed above (describe)						
PROPERTY DAMAGE TO PUBLIC						
Negligent Custody						
Collision or Impact						
Due to Acts of Employees						
Due to Equipment on Lease or Loan						
Due to Process Equipment						
Due to Motor Vehicle Operation						
Due to Watercraft Operation						
Due to Aircraft Operation						
Due to Acts of Animals						
Fire and Explosion						
Contaminated Waste Disposal						
Environmental Pollution						
Assumed Liabilities of Others						
Product Consumption						
Normal						
Abusive						
Use of Dangerous Materials						
Process Use						
Disposal						
Pilfered Materials						
Acts of Contractor on Premises						
Acts of Subrogation						
Assumed Responsibilities						
Relinquished Responsibilities						
Acts of Sponsored Parties						

	IDENTIFIED	EVALUATED	RISK CLASS	CONTROL	FINANCING	DNA
Civic						
Recreational						
Other than listed above (describe)						
HARM TO THE ENVIRONMENT						
Potential Impacts due to Raw Materials/Feedstock, on and off location Storage and						
Emissions or discharges which could impact:						
Air						
Surface Water						
Ground Water						
Soil						
Flora						
Fauna						
People						
Potential Impacts due to Product:						
Storage						
Use						
Disposal						
Transport						
Potential Impact due to Process Deviations from Normal						
Potential Impact during Emergency Situations						
Potential Impacts due to hazardous waste:						
Process						
Storage						
Transportation						
LOSS OF CAPITAL AND INCOME						
Business Interruption Due to Accident						
Process Materials and Equipment						
Labor, Contractual or Opportune						
Failure of Materials Supplier						
Failure of Process Power Supply						

	IDENTIFIED	EVALUATED	RISK CLASS	CONTROL	FINANCING	DNA
Energy Restrictions						
Patent Infringements						
Domestic						
Foreign						
Loss of Records						
Financial						
Work Process						
Employee						
Failure to Realize Anticipated Market						
Acts of Omission						
Executives						
Managers						
Employees						
Death or Incapacity of Essential Personnel						
Loss of Essential Personnel						
Calls on Indebtedness						
Other than listed above (describe)						
CONTRACTUAL LOSSES AND LIABILITIES						
Due to Inadequate Planning, Organizing, Implementing, Controlling						
Due to Acts of Contractors						
Due to Acts of Trustees						
Due to Acts of Licensees						
Due to Acts of Suppliers						
Due to Acts of Purchasers						
Due to Acts of Employees						
Due to Natural Causes						
Due to Acts of Debtors						
Due to Acts of Lessees						
Other than listed above (describe)						
COSTS OF BENEFITS						

	IDENTIFIED	EVALUATED	RISK CLASS	CONTROL	FINANCING	DNA
Compensation or Illness or Disability						
Compensation for Death or Dismemberment						
Medical Retirement						
Service Retirement						
Insurance of Key Personnel						
Other than listed above (describe)						
SECURITY LOSSES						
Due to Acts of Employees						
Theft of Monies or Securities						
Theft of Materials						
Theft of Equipment						
Theft of Processes and Methods						
Forgery of Documents						
Acceptance of Invalid Financial Instruments						
Negligent Acts						
Acts of Sabotage						
Due to Acts of Other Parties						
Theft of Monies or Securities						
Theft of Finished Goods						
Theft of Materials						
Theft of Equipment						
Patent Infringement						
Copyright Infringement						
Acts of Vandalism						
Acts of Arson						
Acts of Sabotage						
Kidnap of Key Personnel						
Threats of Personnel						
Other than listed above (describe detail)						
OTHER THAN LISTED (describe)						

APPENDIX D – Job physical requirements checklist

JOB PHYSICAL REQUIREMENTS CHECKLIST

NOTE: this checklist is illustrative only and not intended for use in any specific situation.

Department:	Position/job:
EXPERIENCE/SPECIAL REQUIREMENTS	**EDUCATION REQUIREMENTS**

Use the following checklist to indicate potential job related physical requirements needing attention. Use following coding: A – minor exposure; B – moderate exposure; C – major exposure; N/A – not applicable

PHYSICAL DEMANDS				WORKING CONDITIONS			
				CHEMICAL		**PHYSICAL**	
Item	Code	Item	Code	Item	Code	Item	Code
Balancing		Color vision				Inside	
Bending at waist		Depth perception		Dusts		Outside	
Carrying		Field of vision		Gases, vapors		Burns	
Climbing		Turning/Twisting		Liquids		Constant cold	
Crawling		Throwing		Mists, fumes		Constant heat	
Communication		Use right hand		Odors		Changing temps	
Coordination		Use left hand		Oils, grease		Elevation, heights	
Crouching		Use both hands		**BIOLOGICAL**		Pressure extreme	
Handling		Walking		Aerosols		Noise	
Feeling		Working fast		Animals		Humidity	
Hearing		Working slow		Bacteria		Lighting	
Kneeling				Fungi		Moving objects	
Lifting				Food		Radiation	
Pushing				People		Ventilation	
Pulling				Water		Vibration	
Reaching				**BIOMECHANICAL**			
Standing				Monotonous			
Sitting				Fatigue			
Seeing				Repetitiveness			

COMMENTS

APPENDIX E – Task risk analysis (TRA) Worksheet

TASK RISK ANALYSIS worksheet				
Division			Task Analyzed	Approved
Department			Date Completed	Approved
Occupation/function			Coordinated by	Approved

SEQUENCE OF TASK STEPS	POTENTIAL DOWNGRADING EVENTS	RS	RECOMMEMDED CONTROLS

RS = Risk Score (for example: Fine/ Kinney)

APPENDIX F - Installation lifecycle phases (chemical operation)

(Safety) management considerations should be included in all life cycle phases of an installation.

The following phases are suggested:

- Feasibility phase
- Conceptual design phase
- Detailed design phase
- Construction and startup phase
- Operational phase
- Demolition phase

Feasibility phase

In this phase, fundamental decisions will be made concerning design and construction of the installation or plant and the projects that need to be executed. At least the following subjects should be considered in this phase:

- Risks associated with the intended activity
- Willingness to accept the inherent hazards and potential risks
- Suitability of the location being considered for the activity
- Familiarity with the processes and related chemicals and other materials
- Design philosophy

Conceptual design phase

The following subjects should be included when considering the conceptual design aspects:

- Process reactions
- Process hazards
- Security-/safety philosophy
- Process flow diagrams
- Departmentalization of the installation
- Location of process units, storage facilities and control rooms
- Structural design
- Management system concepts, contents, structure

Detailed design phase

Considerations during the detailed design phase should include the following aspects:

- Equipment design
- Choice of materials
- Pipes and attachments
- Thermal isolation
- Instrumentation
- Process controls, alarms and shut down
- Ignition sources
- Electrical system hazards
- Pressure release systems
- Ergonomic aspects
- Fire and explosion protection
- Management system details

Construction and start-up phase

The construction and start-up phase should include aspects such as:

- Implementation of recommendations from safety studies carried out
- Checking for accuracy when ordering materials and equipment
- Checking work carried out by contractors
- Inspections and quality checks at supplier premises
- Inspections and checks of construction sites
- Availability and quality of training programs
- Recordkeeping of design drawings, specifications, certificates;
- Design of operational and maintenance instructions

Operational phase

The operational phase should include the following aspects:

- Normal operation of installation
- (Preventive) maintenance
- Repairs and modifications
- Special operation conditions
- Training, communication
- Emergency equipment and - procedures
- Management of change (installation, processes, updating process chemistry, etc.)

- Registration and analysis of accidents and other unwanted events
- Electrical system hazards
- Pressure relieve systems
- Fire and explosion protection
- Management system implementation, maintenance and improvement

Demolition phase

The demolition phase should include aspects such as:

- Shut-down and isolating the installation
- Emptying and cleaning of installation
- Demolition of installation;
- Disposal of products and materials
- Influence of demolition activities on other process units

APPENDIX G - Safety and loss control management maturity profile

Instructions

The profile allows you to give your personal ideas about the Safety and Loss Control Management situation in your company. Eight relevant issues are being considered (left- hand column) and you can evaluate these efforts on 5 different levels going from "Uncertainty" to "Certainty".

> Loss Control is broadly defined as "the control of losses". This definition can and does include injuries as well as property damage, production delays, product losses, environmental incidents, loss of clients, liability claims (including those arising out of product use/misuse), security losses, etc.
>
> The use of the term Loss Control bridges the gap between traditional safety (injury related) and total quality management and business excellence as also intended through the use of the EFQM (European Foundation of Quality management) model.

The best way to do the assessment is to read the text provided in each row and to determine which best describes the situation in your plant. Please put an "X" in the middle of that box.

The end result of your assessment is a profile that can be made visible by connecting the X's that you put in. The profile helps to obtain a picture of how safety is being experienced in your organization.

You may also want to put values on each of the 5 columns, for example a value of 1 on the column "Uncertainty" and a value of 5 on the column "Certainly" – see top of columns. That way you will also be able to put a numerical score on the results obtained, per individual or average per group.

You can also do this exercise with people from various levels in your organization. That will give an impression as to how people at various levels feel about the safety efforts of the organization. That in itself can lead to an interesting communication and may assist in getting a proper perspective when looking to improve your safety efforts.

The profile is a good instrument to use at the start of meetings to get people to discuss the quality of their safety and loss control efforts. This may be the beginning of an improvement process using the 17-step, or similar, approach.

Safety and Loss Control Management Maturity Profile

Level Category	Uncertainty (1)	Awakening (2)	Enlightenment (3)	Wisdom (4)	Certainty (5)
Management understanding of Safety/Loss Control	Comprehension of Safety/Loss Control as an important management tool is lacking.	Monetary losses capture the attention of key managers. Beginning to recognize the role of safety in the management system, but.....	"We cause our own problems." "We can control most losses" "Losses are greater than anticipated."	"The savings are far greater than expected." "We are seeing results of efforts in all areas".	"We will survive and succeed because of our continuing efforts to control losses."
Management Attitude towards Safety/Loss Control	Tendency to blame others for accidents/losses. "That is why we have insurance".	Reluctant to devote time and effort to safety/loss control. Motivated only by (contractual) responsibilities to customers, employees, community, government.	Safety/loss control is essential to effective management and profitability. "We cannot prevent all losses, but we can control them ... tell us what we can do more."	Positive and enthusiastic. Frustration is an emotion of the past and is replaced by confidence. Control of loss is the guiding principle.	Loss control is an absolutely vital part of our management system.
Management behavior in relation to Safety/Loss Control	Management behavior is a re-active, after-the-fact response to accidents and losses. Much finger pointing. Getting tough on offenders (of rules).	Much sincere, concerned discussion, but ... less action. Trying motivational approaches – speeches, slogans, posters, etc. Top management is NOT visible.	Top management is listening and responding with support and action. Visibility (of Top management) is noticed.	Genuine participation and Involvement by management. Top management is recognizing its personal role in continuing emphasis (on safety and loss control).	Continued growth, maintenance and refinement (of the safety/loss control efforts) are key goals.

Safety and Loss Control Management Maturity Profile

Level Category	Uncertainty (1)	Awakening (2)	Enlightenment (3)	Wisdom (4)	Certainty (5)
Management position towards Safety/Loss Control	Accidents and losses are part of doing business. Low priority (of safety) in relation to other business interests.	Questioning…. "Is it necessary to have injuries and losses?" "Are we meeting legislative requirements?"	We are committed to improving our management system through control of losses	Safety/loss control is a part of what we do and is permanently engraved in our philosophy and strategy. Safety/loss control performances are considered in management appraisals and recognition.	We know why we have few problems with control of losses
Safety/Loss Control position in management structure	Safety is a part-time function within other disciplines (personnel, engineering, maintenance).	Strong program coordinator appointed. May still be part of another discipline. Line management is getting involved.	Safety/loss control activities interact with all business functions. The safety/loss control function is visible in the management structure…. Line managers are "doers" and are held accountable.	Safety/Loss Control staff advisement from power base with high reporting relationship (to senior manager). Safety/Loss Control involvement in all major areas of business.	Safety/Loss Control staff advisement for loss control is a senior position. Prevention and control are vital organizational concerns.
Critical Safety/Loss Control problem approach	Problems are dealt with as they occur. The approach is essential after-the- fact. "Quick-fix" is the standard remedy.	Problems are dealt with in meetings with key personnel. The interest is "symptom oriented". Short term solutions to chronic problems.	(Potential) critical problems are identified and are openly confronted. Input is obtained from a variety of levels and resources. Basic causes are being identified to control recurrence.	(Potential) critical problem identification at the lowest possible organizational level. Specific techniques used to identify potential problems. Problem solving teams of capable people being used.	Prevention and control efforts are effective. Potential critical problems are noted and corrected before they occur.

Safety and Loss Control Management Maturity Profile

Level Category	Uncertainty (1)	Awakening (2)	Enlightenment (3)	Wisdom (4)	Certainty (5)
Safety/Loss Control measurement system	No systematic measurement of losses. An injury log is maintained as required by law.	Increasing concerns for frequency and severity rates and trends as well as for compensation and insurance costs.	Property damage costs and rates are part of the measurement system. Incident reporting gets attention.	Accurate measurement, analysis and communication of losses. Various loss types ("output") are being measured. Vital management system criteria ("input") in the measurement system.	Continuing refinement of both output and input data is being used to improve performance.
Safety/Loss Control system Improvement efforts	Improvement is not considered an option.	Safety programs begin to take shape and show results. Standards are being set and responsibilities for results are being assigned.	Continuing to develop and implement the necessary (management system) control elements. Increase of effectiveness is also being obtained through systems assessments.	Utilizing comprehensive assessments of the Safety/Loss Control system to assure effectiveness and to assist in further improvement (of the system).	Improvement of the safety/loss control system is a normal and continuing activity.

APPENDIX H- Safety & loss control opinion survey - management personnel

This (incomplete) questionnaire can be used to obtain an impression about the way people participate in – and feel about – the safety activities of the organization.

PLEASE NOTE: To see the entire opinion survey questionnaire and those for supervisory and operational personnel, please visit www.topves.nl and use the website search facility looking for: "safety opinion survey".

Questions have been developed at three organizational levels: (1) senior and middle management, (2) direct supervision and (3) operational employees. To a large extent questions are the same going from one group to the other.

I have used these questionnaires in conjunction with audits that I did with the International Safety Rating System. The surveys with these questionnaires were done prior to visiting the location to audit and provided me with quite a bit of information before starting the actual audit.

By comparing the responses from the three groups an impression can be obtained about the way the safety program is working in an organization. If all works well then there should only be minor differences between the three levels. If differences are substantial then the conclusion may be that the safety activities are not properly identified, communicated and/or carried out. It may also indicate that the "management system" and its activities is more dictated by management – top down – than a mutual effort of management and employees together.

If differences between organizational groups are substantial, you may wish to carry out a safety audit to further identify strength and weaknesses. You may also want to do an evaluation using the 17-step rating to identify weaknesses in the overall process that was used to build the management system.

The overall results of these opinion surveys may be considered parallel to the results of the safety and loss control management maturity profile (appendix G) evaluation which is better suited for classroom activities. The opinion surveys will provide more detailed information about several safety program activities in the organization.

The example provided is directed at (higher and middle) management. Similar questionnaires are available for direct supervision and operational employees - see www.topves.nl, website search function using "safety opinion survey".

The surveys are included as step 6 of the 17-step process.

1.	How often, in communication with your people, do you refer to the safety policy/program/guidelines of your organization?	a. weekly b. monthly c. annually d. never
2.	Have your safety responsibilities been clearly defined?	a. yes b. no
3.	How often do you participate in safety meetings with operational personnel?	a. weekly b. monthly c. once per quarter d. annually e. never
4.	How often do you participate in planned inspections concerning the part of the organization under your responsibility?	a. weekly b. monthly c. once per quarter d. annually e. never
5.	To what extent are your safety activities part of your (annual) appraisal?	a. none b. 0 – 10 % c. 11 – 20 % d. more than 20 % e. don't know
6.	In which specific safety activities do you participate? (These are activities that are not part of your normal job.)	a. none b. specific activities are: _____ _____
7.	What is your opinion about the way the following people in your organization feel about safety: a. operational employees b. supervision c. middle and senior management	Not important Very important 0 2 4 6 8 10 0 2 4 6 8 10 0 2 4 6 8 10
8.	How do you feel about the quality of the safety program of your organization?	Non existent Excellent 0 2 4 6 8 10

9.a.	Do you know that work can be interrupted or refused in case of hazardous conditions?	a. yes b. no					
9.b.	If "yes", do you know the work interruption/refusal procedure?	a. yes b. no					
10.	What do you feel are the main causes of accidents that have occurred in your department or organization?	Not important					Very important
	a. unsafe acts of operational employees	0	2	4	6	8	10
	b. unsafe conditions of materials, equipment or work environment	0	2	4	6	8	10
	c. inadequate or insufficient training/instruction	0	2	4	6	8	10
	d. improper man – machine relation	0	2	4	6	8	10
	e. fatigue – monotonous work – stress	0	2	4	6	8	10
	f. use of alcohol, drugs, medication	0	2	4	6	8	10
	g. improper design of tools/equipment	0	2	4	6	8	10
	h. inadequate maintenance	0	2	4	6	8	10
	i. purchasing of unsafe tools, equipment etc.	0	2	4	6	8	10
	j. inadequate supervisory quality	0	2	4	6	8	10
	k. lack of management interest	0	2	4	6	8	10
	l. inadequate communication	0	2	4	6	8	10
	m. improper motivation of operational personnel	0	2	4	6	8	10
	n. improper motivation of direct supervision	0	2	4	6	8	10
	o. improper motivation of middle/senior management	0	2	4	6	8	10
	p. insufficient quality of safety department	0	2	4	6	8	10
	q. insufficient/improper safety rules/guidelines	0	2	4	6	8	10
	r. inadequate machine guarding	0	2	4	6	8	10
	s. improper machine controls	0	2	4	6	8	10
11.	How do you rate the safety training that you received when you joined the organization?	Inadequate				Excellent	
		0	2	4	6	8	10
12.b.	How do you rate the quality of that training?	Inadequate				Excellent	
		0	2	4	6	8	10

13.a.	Do you know that you have to report unsafe conditions?	a. yes b. no
13.b.	If "yes" do you know how to do that?	a. yes b. no
13.c.	Who do you think has the first responsibility to correct unsafe conditions at the work floor?	a. senior management b. safety coordinator c. maintenance d. supervisor e. don't know
14.	How often are you informed about the status of the inspection program of your department or unit?	a. monthly b. once per quarter c. semi-annual d. annually e. never
15.	When was the last time you were involved in the investigation/analysis of an injury or damage accident?	a. last quarter b. last year c. don't know d. never been involved
16.	Have you ever had instruction in concerning the investigation of injury or damage accidents?	a. yes b. no
17.	How often are you informed about the status (quality and extent of reporting) of the accident investigation program of your organization or unit?	a. monthly b. once per quarter c. semi-annually d. annually e. never
18.a.	Do you participate in emergency plan exercises?	a. yes b. no
18.b.	If "yes", when was the last time this happened?	a. last month b. last quarter c. last year d. don't know e. does not happen

19.	When was the last time you received accident statistics of your organization, department or unit?	a. last month b. last quarter c. last year d. don't know e. does not happen					
20.	How do you rate the use of personal protective equipment (PPE) by: a. operational personnel? b. supervision? c. middle/senior management? d. contractors?	Inadequate 0 0 0 0	 2 2 2 2	 4 4 4 4	 6 6 6 6	Excellent 8 8 8 8	 10 10 10 10

26.	Did you receive information about the results of your last medical test?	a. yes b. no c. not applicable					
27.a.	Have you received first aid training?	a. yes b. no					
27.b.	Do you have a valid First Aid diploma?	a. yes b. no					
28.	Have you received training/instruction concerning individual communication techniques?	a. yes b. no					
29.	Have you received training/instruction concerning group communication techniques?	a. yes b. no					
30.	What was the subject of the last safety campaign in your organization?	a. no campaigns b. don't know c. the subject was: _____ _____					
31.	Do you regularly receive a newsletter of company magazine containing safety subjects?	a. yes b. no					
32.	Which percentage of "near-miss accidents" do you think are reported in your department or unit?	None 0	 2	 4	 6	 8	All 10

33.	How important do you find it for the following groups to have knowledge about methods to investigate accidents:	Not important					Very important
	a. operational personnel?	0	2	4	6	8	10
	b. supervision?	0	2	4	6	8	10
	c. middle management	0	2	4	6	8	10
	d. senior management	0	2	4	6	8	10
34.a.	How important do you find it for the following groups to know how safety inspections are carried out:	Not important					Very important
	a. operational personnel?	0	2	4	6	8	10
	b. supervision?	0	2	4	6	8	10
	c. middle management	0	2	4	6	8	10
	d. senior management	0	2	4	6	8	10
34.b.	How important do you find it for the following groups to know about the results of safety inspections:	Not important					Very important
	a. operational personnel?	0	2	4	6	8	10
	b. supervision?	0	2	4	6	8	10
	c. middle management	0	2	4	6	8	10
	d. senior management	0	2	4	6	8	10
35.	Should work procedures only relate to safety aspects or should they include all possible problems that may occur during the execution of work?	a. only safety b. all problems					
36.	How much on-the-job training of operational personnel is provided by:	None					All
	a. experienced colleagues?	0	2	4	6	8	10
	b. direct supervision?	0	2	4	6	8	10
	c. training staff personnel?	0	2	4	6	8	10

37.	Concerning experienced colleagues who provide on-the job training, to what extent do they:	None					Best	Don't Know
a.	make use of task procedures/work instructions?	0	2	4	6	8	10	X
b.	make use of effective instruction techniques?	0	2	4	6	8	10	X
c.	motivate people to learn?	0	2	4	6	8	10	X
d.	observe the execution of the work and coach for improvement?	0	2	4	6	8	10	X
e.	Provide tips to do the work safer, better or easier?	0	2	4	6	8	10	X

38.	Concerning direct supervision who provide on-the-job training, to what extent do they:	None					Best	Don't Know
a.	make use of task procedures/work instructions?	0	2	4	6	8	10	X
b.	make use of effective instruction techniques?	0	2	4	6	8	10	X
c.	motivate people to learn?	0	2	4	6	8	10	X
d.	observe the execution of the work and coach for improvement?	0	2	4	6	8	10	X
e.	Provide tips to do the work safer, better or easier?	0	2	4	6	8	10	X

39.	In your department or unit, how is the compliance with:	None				Excellent	
a.	safety rules/guidelines?	0	2	4	6	8	10
b.	personal protective equipment rules?	0	2	4	6	8	10
c.	safe work procedures?	0	2	4	6	8	10

40.	How important, do you think do direct supervisors find the compliance with safety rules and instructions?	Not					Very	Don't Know
		0	2	4	6	8	10	X

41.	How often, do you think, do direct supervisors commend their people for complying with safety rules?	a. daily b. weekly c. monthly d. annually e. never

43.c. been	If "yes" does this include items that have never purchased before?	a. yes b. no	
44.a.	Do you (sometimes) make work procedures?	a. yes b. no	
44.b.	If "yes", do you have these checked by experts regarding safety aspects?	a. yes b. no	
44.c.	Or do you do that yourself?	a. yes b. no	
45.	How useful do you consider the safety meetings that take place in your organization?	Not Very Do not exist 0 2 4 6 8 10 X		
46.a.	Do you regularly receive information about the cost to your organization of off-the-job accidents?	a. yes b. no	
46.b.	Do you receive other information concerning off-the-job accidents?	a. yes b. no	
46.c.	Would you like to receive information concerning off the-job safety?	a. yes b. no	
47.	How well do operational personnel report damages to tools, machines, equipment, buildings, etc.?	None All Don't know 0 2 4 6 8 10 X		

48.   If the answer to question 47 is less than 6, what then are the two most important reasons why the reporting is not better?

_____

_____

49.   What are the three strongest points of the safety program of your organization?

_____

_____

50.   What are the three weakest points of the safety program of your organization?

_____

_____

56.   How do you measure and evaluate the work of your people with regard to safety?

   a.   I do not do this

   _____
   _____

57.   Do you have any further comments to make subject the safety efforts of your organization?

   a.   No further comments

   _____
   _____

PLEASE NOTE: To see the entire opinion survey questionnaire and those for supervisory en operational personnel, please visit www.topves.nl and use the website search facility looking for: "safety opinion survey".

APPENDIX I – Physical condition evaluation

Purpose of this form is to obtain an average impression of the more general "hardware state" of an organization, department or part thereof.

Prior to carrying out an inspection, previous inspection reports should be examined to determine whether categories should be added under heading G "Other", numbers 38 - 40. If three lines are not sufficient to add categories, just add and adapt the total numbering of categories when done. Value factors should be assigned depending on the relative value of the added categories. After that value factors A through G may need to be re-adjusted to arrive at a total of 100.

During the inspection, the evaluator or inspector should indicate the total number of items belonging to the category that is being observed – column "Number Observed" (O). Observed items found to be "less than adequate" should be indicated in column "Number Substandard" (S). All substandard conditions noted are to be listed on a substandard conditions or inspection report (see appendix J, page 274) and processed according to the risk class provided which will determine the level of attention and follow-up that the conditions should receive.

At the end of the inspection, the ratio of standard observations (i.e. the number of good observations - "O" minus "S" – divided by the total number of observations "O") can be calculated for each category on the form. The score then can be obtained by multiplying the ratio by the value factor provided. The total score of the evaluation will be obtained by adding all individual category scores. The calculated scores provide a positive outcome as they represent the relation of the standard conditions to the total observed.

Category H - Personal Protection Equipment (PPE) is not scored using value factors as the observation here is directed at the use of PPE and related to behavior, not part of a physical condition evaluation.

Organization   :   _____

Address   :   _____

Departments evaluated   :   _____

Evaluator (name)   :   _____

Date of evaluation   :   _____

CATEGORY	Number Observed (O)	Number Substandard (S)	Value Factor (VF)
A. General workplace condition			
1. Floors (walking and work surfaces)			
2. Aisles			
3. Work floors/scaffolds			VF = 10
4. Ladders			
5. Stairs			
6. Exits/accesses			
7. Company roads			
A – Total observations and score	O =	S =	$\frac{O-S}{O}$ x VF =
B. Work environment aspects			
8. Ventilation			
9. Lighting			VF = 15
10. Noise			
11. Ergonomics			
B – Total observations and score	O =	S =	$\frac{O-S}{O}$ x VF =
C. Materials			
12.			
13.			VF = 20
14.			
15..			
C – Total observations and score	O =	S =	$\frac{O-S}{O}$ x VF =
D. Equipment			
16. Hand- and portable tools			
17. Machines and protection			
18. Transportation and vehicles			
19. Hoisting and lifting equipment			
20. Transport materials/slings			
21. Conveyors/chains			VF = 25
22. Pressure vessels			
23. Mechanical power equipment			
24. Hydraulic power equipment			
25. Pneumatic power equipment			
26. Electrical power equipment			
27. Valves/mechanical controls			
D – Total observations and score	O =	S =	$\frac{O-S}{O}$ x VF =

E. **Hazard control**			
28. Lockout/plugging systems			VF = 15
29. Signs			
30. Color coding			
31. Labeling			
32. Alarm systems			
E – Total observations and score	O =	S =	$\frac{O-S}{O}$ x VF =
F. **Emergency systems**			
33. Emergency instructions			VF = 10
34. Fire protection equipment			
35. Emergency-/eye showers			
36. First Aid posts/-equipment			
37. Rescue equipment			
F – Total observations and score	O =	S =	$\frac{O-S}{O}$ x VF =
G. **Other**			
38.			VF = 5
39.			
40.			
G – Total observations and score	O =	S =	$\frac{O-S}{O}$ x VF =
			VF MAX = 100
TOTAL PHYSICAL CONDITIONS SCORE	Total O =	Total S =	$\frac{O\ tot - S\ tot}{O\ tot}$ x VF MAX =
H. **Personal protective Equipment**	O =	S =	
41. Eye protection			NO SCORING
42. Breathing protection			
43. Head protection			
44. Hand protection			
45. Feet protection			
46. Body protection			
47. Fall protection			
H – Total observations	O =	S =	$\frac{O-S}{O}$ x 100 = %

APPENDIX J - Inspection report form

INSPECTION REPORT	Area Inspected		Department
Item Number and Hazard Classification	Type of report	Date	Inspected by
	ITEMS NOTED AND ACTIONS TAKEN/SUGGESTED		

* Indicates reported earlier; ○ circle around number indicates intermediate action taken; X over number indicates item corrected

"A" Hazard:	Any condition/practice with potential for permanent disability, loss of life or body part and/or extensive damage to property or the environment
"B" Hazard:	Any condition/practice with potential of serious injury/illness or damage that is disruptive but less severe than Class "A
"C" Hazard:	Any condition/practice with potential for non-disabling injury/illness or non-disruptive damage to property or the environment

APPENDIX K - How to make rules

(Guidelines may also be applicable when making work procedures or instructions)

"How to obtain compliance with rules"
or
"When to apply disciplinary action"

Preparation

1. Rules only when necessary
2. Involve people concerned in rule making
3. Explain why rules are necessary
4. Make rules as simple as possible
5. Rules must be justified and correct
6. Make rules to comply with "normal" human behavior
7. Rules must not contradict each other
8. Make rule compliance attractive, make non-compliance unattractive

Presentation

9. Give worker preview of rules prior to instruction
10. Provide proper instruction
11. Test knowledge of rules
12. Keep rules accessible to users

Application

13. Provide "try-out" period to test rules in practice
14. Be clear in daily application of rules
15. Provide sufficient time for proper rule application
16. Be positive about rule compliance
17. Be negative about non-compliance
18. Proper example by supervision and management
19. Maintain rule knowledge
20. Periodically evaluate rule compliance
21. Periodically evaluate effect of rules
22. Keep rules up-dated
23. Be clear about consequences in case of non-compliance
24. Be consequent in case of non-compliance

Some further explanation

Preparation

The preparation stage is the period in which people are being made aware of the possible need for a new rule. In this stage people are being involved in the making of the rule. Obviously this can only take place when a rule is being developed. Once developed worker participation shifts to maintaining and improvement of the rule.

1. Rules only when necessary
    Keep rules at a minimum. Rules should be prevented if possible. If we can avoid them we also avoid the problem of getting people to comply with them.

2. Involve people concerned in rule making
    Apply principle of participation - give "emotional ownership" whenever possible.

3. Explain why rules are necessary
    Give reasons for rules, it helps when people see the reasons behind them.

4. Make rules as simple as possible
    Apply "KISS" principle. It will be difficult for people to remember long and complicated rules.

5. Rules must be justified and correct
    Contents of rules must be correct and in line with the present situation.

6. Make rules to comply with "normal" human behavior
    Keep rules as practical as possible. Rules deviating from normal human behavior will be difficult to follow and may be the cause of a constant battle to have people comply with something that is far from "being natural". Apply the Principle of deviation from normal behavior.

The principle of deviation from normal behavior

The more a rule or procedure deviates from normal behavior, the more effort is required to reach compliance

---

7. **Rules must not contradict each other**
Various rules must be such that they reinforce each other rather than contradict. Should the latter happen, it would be extremely difficult to people to comply.

8. **Make compliance with rules attractive, make non-compliance unattractive**
Prepare rules such that it will be attractive to follow them. Make it unattractive not to comply with rules.

   Each time a rule is made ask the questions: "Is it rewarding, one way or the other, for people to comply with rules? Or is it possibly attractive for them not to comply?"

Presentation

This stage is the period in which people are introduced to the "rules of the game". The usual instructional techniques can be used: "motivate - tell & show - test - check".

9. **Give worker preview of rules prior to instruction**
"Motivate" is the first step of the instruction process: let people know what they are going to learn and why, what does it mean to them, how does this rule relate to his/her job.

Make rule booklet available to each individual worker.

10. **Provide proper instruction**
Use "Show & Tell", the second step of the instruction process. Whenever possible make rules "visible" by showing "how" and telling "why".

Provide adequate means in line with applicable rules.

11. **Test knowledge of rules**
"Test" initial knowledge of rules. Find out if the message has come across, if the instruction has been successful.

   Have each worker sign for receipt and understanding of rules and keep signed receipt in personal file.

12. **Keep rules easily accessible to workers and supervision**
Provide each worker with his own rule booklet whenever practical. Make more complex rules (such as Material Safety Data Sheets) available per department or area.

Application

This stage is the "normal" working situation: after rules have been set up and people are instructed the only thing left is to apply them.

13.   Provide "try-out" period to test out new rules
Allow a certain time for people to get used to new rules, get feedback, adapt rules when necessary. Use positive behavior reinforcement more heavily during this period.

This period is primarily to get the bugs out of new rules and see how they work without having to apply the disciplinary policy right away.

This period is *only for new rules*, not for new employees learning existing rules, except for the positive behavior reinforcement.

14.   Be clear in daily application of rules
"Check" people frequently in the proper use of rules. Exercise proper supervision including rule compliance maintenance. This daily supervision can be supported or enhanced by periodic formal observations directed at behavior of people (see 20).

15.   Provide sufficient time for proper application of rules
Provide sufficient time for people to carry out work such that rules can be applied as required.

16.   Be positive about rule compliance
Positive attitude of supervision and management towards compliance with rules - make rule compliance possible through proper decision-making - set the "right atmosphere". Use positive behavior reinforcement when applicable.

17.   Be negative about non-compliance
Disapprove of non-compliance by letting people know each time you see it. Every time non-compliance is noted and not acted upon, it is being reinforced.

18.   Proper example by supervision and management
Not your words count but your acts.

19.   Maintain rule knowledge
Retraining, group meetings, personal contacts, task observations, tests, quizzes - test maintenance of rule knowledge.

20. <u>Periodically evaluate rule compliance</u>
With proper feed-back for correction, or commendation/motivation. Behavior observations (such as Unsafe Act Auditing) may be used here. Periodic discussion of applicable rules, with people for whom rules are intended, may be preferred.

21. <u>Periodically evaluate effect of rules</u>
Use information from accident/incident analysis whenever proper application of rules has, or could have, resulted in less injury, etc.

22. <u>Keep rules up-to-date</u>
Regularly review rules. Relate accident investigation to rules. Periodically discuss rules with people use them during their work to assess their current validity and improve whenever desirable.

23. <u>Be clear about consequences in case of non-compliance</u>
Disciplinary policy: oral warning(s), written warning(s), time off without pay, dismissal or immediate discharge, depending on the violation.

24. <u>Be consistent in case of non-compliance</u>
Apply discipline only when needed: after all the above has been properly addressed to and in the proper order. The disciplinary policy in fact is only there to deal with people who knowingly, willfully, and without "legal" reason, violate rules.

Be consistent about application of discipline. Avoid "measuring with two yardsticks". Be objective. If necessary "built your case" by recording violations, dates, actions, etc. Don't forget: the disciplinary policy is there first of all to deal with the willful violators - the end station of discipline is discharge. And this will not be accepted without proper foundation.

APPENDIX L - 17-Step process to build a management system

The process starts at the top of the organization and goes down while providing information and training and asking the cooperation of people at all levels in the organization when developing the management system, implementing and improving it.

1.   Top Manager Leadership

        Leadership by the highest senior manager(s) of the company, unit or department providing support, resources and ongoing attention to assure that objectives will be obtained as intended.

2.   Management Team Leadership

        Information/training of higher management to put all noses in the same direction and to obtain the cooperation and endorsement from the top down. Include worker representation as appropriate.

3.   Management Improvement Team

        High level management team plus relevant staff and worker representation. This team will have the overall responsibility to see that the management system is properly developed and implemented.

4.   Internal Expertise

        Internal expertise available depending on the objective of the management system and its elements. Also include adequate knowledge concerning process, content and structure of the management system to be developed. This expertise could also include external assistance as needed.

5.   Project Communicated

        Communication of the improvement project to include reasons, objectives and process along which the objectives will be realized. Include a time-path. In principle, this communication should be in writing and to all in the organization. The "hazard" here is that, when you say what you are going to do, people can easily hold you accountable and judge you on what you are actually doing. At the same time, such communication is leadership in action – stand up and be counted!

6. Opinion Surveys

   Opinion surveys at all levels to obtain a good impression about how the management system subject is being viewed and experienced by people at various levels to include higher and middle management, supervision and operational personnel.

7. Base-line Assessment

   Use of a good (audit) reference - commercial or otherwise available - to obtain a zero-base impression of the present situation concerning the management system subject as well as determining the possible gap between what is and what should be.

8. Selection of Elements/Activity Areas

   The selection of the first subjects (activity areas or "elements") to be part of the management system. Selection to be based on need, resources and anticipated (visual) results to be obtained within a limited time period.

9. Introduction Training

   Training of all relevant managerial, staff and operational personnel to convey the philosophy, concepts and models on which the management system and its development shall be based. To include the concepts related to process, content and structure of the system. The training preferably to also include the results of steps 6, 7 and 8 as applicable and available.

10. Element Coordination Teams

    Setting up coordination teams for element development. Persons included should preferably be representatives of all relevant levels in the organization, managerial as well as operational and be knowledgeable about the element subject. The coordination teams should provide the "what, by whom, when and how" of the specific activities in order to reach the element objective(s).

11. Element Coordination Team Training

    Training of people selected to take part in a coordination team to develop a specific element of the management system. Training required including all aspects of the element, content as well structural aspects.

12. Element Development – PLAN

Include specific activities to be carried out for the selected elements; by whom, and when. How the activities should be carried out would normally be described in separate documents including tools, forms etc. to be used. Final approval of the element or activity area should be by the Management Improvement Team.

13. Element Implementation Training - TRAIN

Training of people who need to do the work to be carried out. Includes the element activities as well as the periodic assessments of work carried out and the results thereof.

14. Management Briefing

Management/supervision throughout the organization need to know the critical issues concerning the work that needs to be done so they can stimulate the process and motivate the people. Just asking "How are things going?" will not do the trick.

15. Carry out Element Activities - DO

Carry out the activities according to plan by well trained people (step 13) and supported by their managers/supervisors (step 14). During implementation of activities, periodic evaluation should take place of activities and results achieved in comparison with objectives set.

16. Review by the Management Improvement Team

Review of overall management system results as the basis to set up properly resourced action plans for further extension and improvement in step 17.

17. Extend Project, Repeat process

If results are not there: alter or add element activities and/or add management system elements in steps 15 respectively step 16.

You may want to look at my website to see similar processes. Go to www.topves.nl, use the website search function searching for "Crosby" and select the page: "Steps to make your management system".

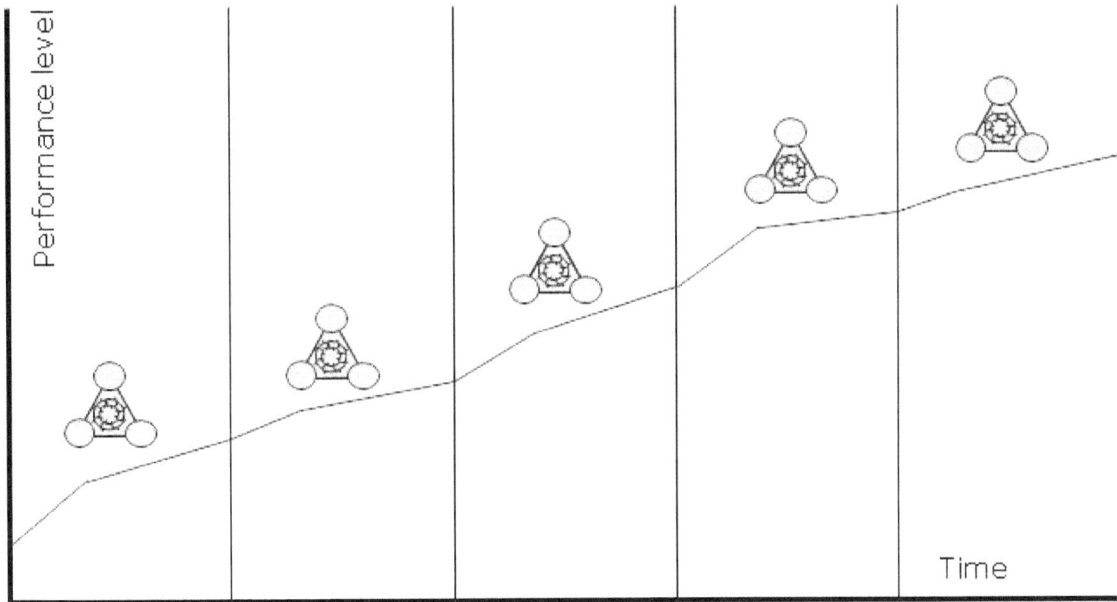

Repeated application of Plan-Train-Do to reach the desired level of success

Reaching desired objectives is pictured above as the ongoing application of the platform model based 17-step process.

APPENDIX M – 17-step process Rating

RATING THIS COMPANY

CALCULATION OF TOTAL ACTUAL SCORE (TAS)

Step	Description	Score Range	Individual Step Score (ISS)
1	Top Manager Leadership – **LEADERSHIP**	0 - 4	
2	Management Team leadership – **LEADERSHIP**	0 - 4	
3	Management Improvement Team – **LEADERSHIP**	0 - 4	
4	Internal Expertise	0 - 5	
5	Project Plan communicated	0 - 5	
6	Opinion Survey	0 - 5	
7	Base-line Assessment	0 - 5	
8	Selection of Activities	0 - 5	
9	Management Introduction Training	0 - 6	
10	Element Coordination Team(s)	0 - 7	
11	Element Coordination Team Training	0 - 6	
12	Element Development - **PLAN**	0 - 7	
13	Element Implementation Training – **TRAIN**	0 - 7	
14	Management Briefing - **LEADERSHIP**	0 - 6	
15	Carrying out Element Activities -**DO**	0 - 10	
16	Review by Management Improvement Team	0 - 6	
17	Extend Project	0 - 8	
	Total maximum score	100	
	TOTAL ACTUAL SCORE (TAS)		

If 15 = 0, then Total Actual Score = 0

Date of assessment: _____

Assessor(s): _____ _____

APPENDIX N – Content of a (safety) management mystem

Oil and chemical company

- Management leadership, commitment and accountability
- Risk assessment and control
- Design and construction of installations
- Information and documentation
- Safety of personnel
- Health
- Training
- Operations and maintenance procedures
- Work permits
- Inspection and maintenance
- Reliability of HSE critical systems
- Environmental care
- Regulatory compliance
- Management of change
- Third party services
- Incident reporting, analysis and follow-up
- Emergency preparedness
- Community awareness
- Operations integrity assessment and improvement

Chemical company

- Safety, health and environmental commitment
- Management and resources
- Communication and consultation
- Training
- Materials hazards
- Acquisitions and divestments
- New plant, equipment and process design
- Modifications and changes
- She assurance
- Systems of work
- Emergency plans
- Contractors and suppliers
- Environmental impact assessments
- Resource conservation
- Waste management

- Soil and groundwater pollution
- Products stewardship
- SHE performance and reporting
- Auditing

Electronic company

- Management commitment and responsibilities
- Safety training
- Safe work practices
- Self assessments
- Government inspections and surveys
- Accident, incident and illness reporting
- Safe environment
- Mechanical safety
- Maintenance safety
- Contractor safety
- Electrical safety
- Fire prevention, fire protection and emergency response
- Chemical control program
- Process hazard reviews
- Materials handling safety
- Ergonomics
- Industrial hygiene exposure assessments
- Asbestos management
- Hearing conservation
- Ionizing and non-ionizing radiation protection
- Laser safety
- Ventilation
- Personal protective equipment
- Motor vehicle safety
- Meetings in non-Company facilities
- Sports safety program

Food company

- Leadership and administration
- Hazards to the environment and identification of critical issues
- Environmental program
- Organizational rules and permits to operate
- Analysis of critical tasks/work activities
- Hiring and placement
- Training
- Communication and motivation
- Engineering controls
- Purchasing controls
- Health control
- Formal inspections
- Environmental performance monitoring and assessment
- Personal protective equipment
- Emergency preparedness
- Reporting/investigation and analysis of undesired events
- EH&S program evaluation

University

- Management leadership, commitment
- Operational risk management
- Communication, participation
- Documents and records
- Purchasing & contractors
- Emergency preparedness
- Incident reporting
- Management system audit
- Monitoring and reporting H&S
- School /service management review
- Legal compliance
- Occupational health
- University management system audit
- University management review

MASTER EVALUATION & DEVELOPMENT GRID

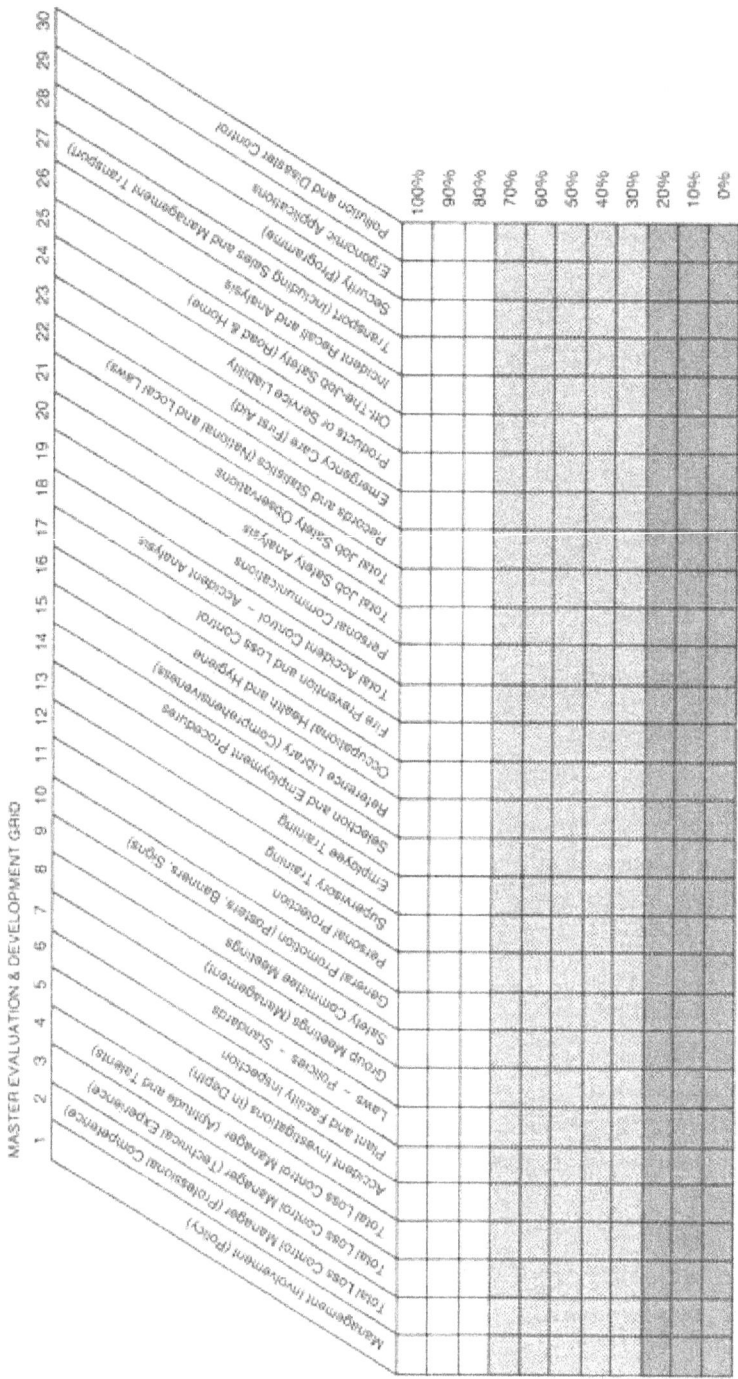

Bron BRITISH SAFETY COUNCIL, London

100% 90% 80% 70% 60% 50% 40% 30% 20% 10% 0%

1 Management Involvement (Policy)
2 Total Loss Control Manager (Professional Competence)
3 Total Loss Control Manager (Technical Experience)
4 Accident Investigations (In Depth)
5 Plant and Facility Inspection
6 Laws – Policies – Standards
7 Group Meetings (Management)
8 Safety Committee Meetings
9 General Promotion (Posters, Banners, Signs)
10 Personal Promotion
11 Supervisory Training
12 Employee Training
13 Selection and Employment Procedures
14 Reference Library (Comprehensiveness)
15 Occupational Health and Hygiene
16 Fire Prevention and Loss Control
17 Total Accident Control – Accident Analysis
18 Personal Communications
19 Total Job Safety Analysis
20 Total Job Safety Observations
21 Records and Statistics (National and Local Laws)
22 Emergency Care (First Aid)
23 Products or Service Liability
24 Off-The-Job Safety (Road & Home)
25 Incident Recall and Analysis
26 Transport (including Sales and Management Transport)
27 Security (Programme)
28 Ergonomic Applications
29 Pollution and Disaster Control

Key to colours

Key Areas which call for PRIORITY ACTION

Key Areas which call for planning

Key Areas where further action is not urgent, but check on Safety Audit

Total Loss Control system – British safety Council (1970)

APPENDIX O - management system element structure

The structure starts with need assessment/management statement and coordination, then goes to the establishment of the standing plan including the specific activities relevant to obtain the element objective, training of people to be involved and ends with assessment of activities, evaluation of results and the periodic review and improvement.

The overview of the element structure shown below is repeated in more detail further on.

1.   Element policy and management statement

        Top management communication regarding the reason(s) why the element is important and what objectives are expected. Each management activity area shall have its own specific objective(s), different from the objective(s) of the management system as a whole.

2.   Coordination of element development

        Assignment of element coordination to a team involving people from various levels, with expertise and vested interests depending on the element subject. To be chaired by a person with sufficient authority. Provision of adequate instruction to perform the work.

3.   Element plan development

        The element plan shall include the specific (element) activities to reach the element objective(s): WHAT must be done, by WHOM and WHEN.

        The element plan should be backed up by (separate) procedures or guidelines describing HOW the activities shall be carried out, including tools and forms to be used.

   3.1.   Review of legislation and standards for minimum requirements

           To establish minimum requirements for element activities set by legislation and applicable industry and certification standards.

   3.2.   Additional element activities as indicated by other sources

           Additional element activities from sources other than mentioned under 3.1.

3.3. Employee participation in development of element activities

Participation of personnel from all levels to develop criteria for execution of the identified element activities. Making use of available expertise and experience and creating "emotional ownership" to facilitate implementation of activities.

The principle of emotional ownership

People tend to be more willing to participate in planned change when they have had an opportunity to participate and influence the process leading to change

---

3.4. Employee training to execute element activities

Include: (i) implementation of element activities, (ii) management of the activities to allow proper stimulation of activity implementation by management/supervision and, (iii) carrying out assessments of activities and results and the preparation of improvement plans.

3.5. Employee participation in executing element activities

Include relevant personnel in the implementation/execution of the specific activities as well as in the possible improvement thereof.

3.6. Communication needs to internal and external parties

Collection and analysis of relevant data for communication to stakeholders and other interest groups.

3.7. Assessments of activities and results

Periodic assessments to establish whether: (i) element activities are being carried out as intended and (ii) element results obtained as desired

4. Review and improvement

Periodic review to assess activities carried out and results obtained against objectives set.

Additional detail about the management system element structure is provided In my book "How to Build a Management System that Works".

APPENDIX P - Management system, some questions and answers

I asked myself some questions which, I think, you may also have. And then I also gave the answers.

<u>Why a management system?</u>

Like it or not but you will always have some kind of a management system in your organization. It may not be written down though which will make it more difficult to communicate to stakeholders, even if your company or organization is small. It may not be very good and it may not produce much or any results. But there are at least some activities there that can form the foundation of a management system that will produce results.

So the question may be: "Why should we have a management system that works?" The answer is very obvious to me: "Why not have a management system that produces results that you want?" You are doing certain things anyway that can be part of a management system, so why not doing them in a way that they work better? And involve people who know what to do, when and how?

You may also want/need a management system because your customers require you to obtain a certain certificate. That is not the type and quality of a management system as I see it. If you are just looking for a certificate, you will be able to find a consultant who will help you to set up a management system to meet minimal certification requirements. And that consultant may also help you to make use a certification institute that will issue a certificate meeting those minimum requirements. That will provide you with a certificate but that may not produce the results you could have and which your customer may expect.

<u>Does the Management System have to be in writing?</u>

No, not necessarily.

But if your organization is a little larger than (very) small it may be difficult to communicate the contents - who shall do what, when, why and how - to others.

And it may also be difficult to close to impossible to communicate to external parties if it is not put on paper.

And if you want a certificate based on your management system it is a requirement to have it on written form.

Does a Management System make the working of your organization rigid?

Could be, depends how complex you make it and sometimes that may be needed depending on the type of industry you are in. If you cannot afford unwanted events, no matter what, then your management system may have to be rather detailed and, if you want to call it that: rigid.

For the average industry if you start small and let your system grow based on results you may just end up with the management system that fits your organization: not to large and not too small, just right for you.

If you develop the management system using the 17-step process detailed in my book, it is very likely that you end up with a system that is supported all the way down in the organization. The detail will depend of the qualifications of the people. That would fit in nicely with a concept such as empowerment.

When is a management system a MANAGEMENT SYSTEM?

A management system includes management activity areas or "elements" which you may also want to call "chapters". The management activity areas - such as purchasing, design, training, management of change - include management activities which indicate WHAT shall be done, WHY, WHEN and by WHOM. The management system would be backed up by more detailed procedures, work instructions, etc. describing HOW the work needs to be done.

A management system is a MANAGEMENT SYSTEM if:

- There is a well defined objective for the overall system
- The system has been developed through a process to allow participation of people from all levels in the organization
- There is enough content - a sufficient number of management activity areas, "chapters" or "elements", each with their own specific objective and their specific activities to reach those
- The specific element activities are embedded in a structure to stimulate activities and to reach results

What to expect of your management system?

Short answer: everything and anything you expect from it. If only certificate, then your management system should deliver that. If you want your management system to comply with legislation, then that should be the results of your management system. If you want more than a certificate or compliance with legislation then it all depends on what you want and you should make your management system to deliver this.

What form or shape should a management system have?

It does not really matter as long as it is clear on what shall be done, why, when and by whom. And if it has the structure to make sure that necessary activities are carried out and desired results obtained.

Many organizations build their management system parallel to the certification requirements. That is OK for getting a certificate and could be the start if you want other results on top of that. However, in that case your management system should have the management activity areas necessary to obtain the results wanted and needs the structure to also get those.

If you build your management system different from the layout of the certification reference, then it may help - for certification purposes - to make a matrix showing where the certification issues can be found in your management system.

What should be in a management system?

The content of your management system will be determined by what you expect it to do. If you want an ISO 9001 certificate, refer to ISO 9001, if you want an OHSAS 18000 certificate, refer to OHSAS 18000, and so on. If you want your management system for other reasons, include the management activity areas or "elements" with their specific activities that you think will bring about the desired results.

In most cases you will include management activity areas that are more or less generic to any objective that you may want to reach. Those include areas like: hiring and placement of people, design of installations and work environment, design of products, training of management, training of operating personnel, purchasing, management of change, etc.

What structure should a management system have?

Any structure that you think is suitable as long as the structure would support implementation of activities and obtaining results. To facilitate execution of management activities that are part of your system, it would certainly help if you build your management system using a process that will facilitate implementation. The 17-step process is a route to management system success.

APPENDIX Q – Safety & loss prevention manual (limited example)

TABLE OF CONTENTS

04 Procedures, Standards and Practices Provisional Contents

04-01 General

04-02 Work Permits

04-021 Cold Work

04-022 Hot Work

04-072

04-073

04-08

……..

……..

04-18

04-19

04-20 Radiation Safety

04-21 Floor and Wall Openings

04-22 Carbon Monoxide Gas

04-23 Hydrogen Sulfide Gas

04-24 Welding and Cutting

04-25 Compressed Gas Cylinders

04-26 Communications

ACCIDENT/INCIDENT REPORTING INVESTIGATION

PURPOSE

The purpose of reporting and investigation of accidents/incidents is the prevention of similar events in the future.

RESPONSIBILITIES

It is the responsibility of all Company management, supervision and personnel to immediately report all accidents and incidents, according to the guidelines provided that result, or could result, in unwanted loss to people, the company or the environment.

NEGATIVE APPROACHES TO THE REPORTING OF INCIDENTS COULD SERIOUSLY HARM THE PURPOSE OF THE INVESTIGATION PROCESS AND OUR SAFETY AND LOSS PREVENTION PROGRAM. VOLUNTARY SHARING OF INFORMATION ABOUT INCIDENTS SHOULD BE APPROACHED IN A POSITIVE WAY. WITHHOLDING VALUABLE INFORMATION ON THE OTHER HAND, SHOULD BE DISCOURAGED.

GUIDELINES

Incident investigation, basically, is problem solving, as related to loss or potential loss. The ultimate purpose, which is prevention of future problems, depends largely on the quality of the investigation, the collection of all related facts and the analysis of immediate and underlying causes. Problem solving is an essential function of management and as such the quality of problem solving - accident investigation and analysis - is a reflection of the control the Manager or supervisor exercises over his area of responsibility.

In principle, the investigation process is directed at all losses and incidents, to find out which do, or could, result in important loss to property, people, the environment, or the business. All such incidents should be thoroughly investigated to discover what caused them and to take proper remedial action.

The investigation process is a problem solving sequence and includes following basic steps: When an accident occurs FIRST:

1. Respond to the site of the accident.
2. First and medical aid to any victims and action to control further damage to equipment, the environment and the business.

THEN, start the investigation process:

3. Preservation and collection of evidence/information, interviews of witnesses.
4. Analysis of information collected, to discover immediate and underlying causes.
5. Preparation of alternative remedial actions, temporarily and permanently, in relation to the risks involved.
6. Choice of best solution to remedy the situation and prevent recurrence of (similar) events.
7. Monitoring remedial actions and results for ongoing control.

PROCEDURES

Training in accident/incident investigation.

- All Managers, Facility Supervisors will receive training in accident investigation, in accordance with the guidelines provided in element 2, "Management Training". This training will be in accordance with the function of the management level concerned, in relation with the investigation process.

- All Managers will review and evaluate the accident/incident investigation reports provided by their subordinate Managers, in order to establish the quality of such reports. If required by the outcome of these reviews, additional training in problem solving will be provided, by the Manager, to his subordinate Manager.

- All Managers, will make clear to all their subordinates the importance of reporting accidents/incidents and encourage them to report accidents/incidents of which they are aware.

Accident/incident Investigation Procedure

A. All accidents/incidents reported to, or otherwise discovered by, the Manager/Facility Supervisor shall receive immediate attention of that Manager.

B. The Manager will immediately evaluate the seriousness, or potential, of the accident/incident and take prompt and appropriate first aid and salvage actions.

C. All of the following are REPORTABLE INCIDENTS and MUST BE REPORTED IMMEDIATELY by the Facility Supervisor involved, using the Incident Investigation Report form:

- Lost Time Accident (LTA)
- Property Damage Accident
- Fire and/or explosion
- Spills
- Infringements of Platform Safety Zones
- Bomb Threat Calls
- High Potential (HIPO) Incidents

D. The following incidents are NOT REPORTABLE but SHOULD BE REGISTERED as indicated on the Summary Forms provided.

- Minor Injuries
- Minor Property Damage Incidents

THERE IS NO RESTRICTION ON THE REPORTING OF INCIDENTS.

ANY PERSON WHO WANTS TO REPORT AN INCIDENT WHICH, IN HIS/HER OPINION, COULD HAVE AN ADVERSE EFFECT ON THE OPERATION AND PERFORMANCE OF XYZOil IS ENCOURAGED TO DO SO.

Reporting of incidents

1. GENERAL

1.1. Anyone involved in, or aware of, a reportable incident will report this immediately to his Facility Supervisor.

1.2 The Facility Supervisor will, without delay, inform his Department Superintendent who will inform the Department Manager and the Safety and Loss Prevention Coordinator about the reportable incident. The Department Manager will inform the Manager of Operations, who will inform the General Manager, about any "A" or "B" incidents that have occurred.

2. OIL SPILLS

All Oil Spills must be reported to the Water Board Directorate and Mine Enforcement Agency. Reporting to these authorities will be done by the Safety and Loss Prevention coordinator (acting as Oil Spill Coordinator). The Production Foreman will notify the Production Superintendent of the spill and complete an Oil Spill Report form (Telex Format Type B) and send this to the Production Superintendent. A copy of the report will be forwarded to the Safety and Loss Prevention/Oil Spill Coordinator).

3. INFRINGEMENTS OF PLATFORM SAFETY ZONES

Infringements of Platform Safety Zones will be reported by the Production Foreman to the Production Superintendent and to the Safety and Loss Prevention Coordinator who will report the incident to the Mine Enforcement Agency.

4. BOMB THREAT CALLS

After having received an Offshore Bomb Threat Call, the Production Foreman will immediately notify the " Police Information Center" (Telephone: 5678 - 54321) and the Production Superintendent or the Onshore Emergency Coordinator (outside office hours).

5. MINOR INJURIES

The medic will evaluate all medical assistance provided by him and inform the Facility Supervisor immediately about any HIPO incidents, for proper action. The Facility Supervisor will fill out an Accident/Incident Investigation Report form for each of those identified HIPO incidents and process it according to guidelines established.

6. MINOR PROPERTY DAMAGE ACCIDENTS

These incidents will be registered on the Minor Property Damage Summary Form by the platform maintenance supervisor and reported to the Facility Supervisor on a weekly basis.

Investigation of Incidents

1. All Incidents will be investigated.

2. All Reportable Incidents will be reported on the proper forms.

3. The Facility Supervisor of the department or unit concerned will, after provision of the required emergency action, conserve the situation on the place of the incident as required for proper investigation. Should an injury occur with an expected absence of 8 weeks or more, the accident situation should be left unchanged until clearance is given by the Mine Enforcement Agency.

4. The Facility Supervisor will carry out the first investigation. For all incidents that can be classified "A" or "B", assistance should be provided by the Department Superintendent and the Safety and Loss Prevention Coordinator. This assistance should also be made available for all "A" or "B" HIPO incidents.

5. If necessary, the Production Superintendent or the Safety and Loss Prevention Coordinator will determine if other Managerial levels will be involved and/or staff assistance will be called in from an ad-hoc "Accident Investigation Committee".

   Notwithstanding the above, any "A" level incident will receive on-site investigation by the Production Superintendent and, if deemed necessary, the Department Manager and the Operations Manager. This includes "A" level HIPO incidents.

6. A review meeting will be conducted, following all "A" classified incidents, to be carried out by the Operations Manager, the Department Manager and his subordinate Managers/supervisors, as deemed necessary, and the Safety and Loss Prevention Coordinator. Purpose of this meeting is to establish the quality of investigation carried out, the effectiveness of remedial actions and to allocate sufficient support for appropriate action.

7. All incidents reported on the Incident Investigation Report form will be reviewed on a monthly basis by the Safety Program Committee. This review will include an evaluation of the effectiveness of the suggested remedial actions.

Remedial Actions

1. It is the responsibility of the Facility Supervisor of the department or unit concerned, to see that remedial actions suggested are carried out promptly and appropriately.

2. Actions on "A" type incidents will be completed within 24 hours, unless there are special reasons why this cannot be accomplished. In such case, the Production Superintendent will inform, in writing, the Production Manager and the General Manager about the reasons why action cannot be taken within 24 hours.

    Actions on "B" type incidents will be completed within 3 calendar days, unless there are special reasons why this cannot be accomplished. In such case, the Production Superintendent will inform, in writing, the Production Manager about the reasons why action cannot be taken within 3 calendar days.

3. The Facility Supervisor of the department or unit concerned will make, at the end of each month, a short status report indicating the status of remedial actions. If necessary explanations will be provided for actions not completed to schedule. This report will be forwarded to the Production Superintendent, with a copy to the Safety and Loss Prevention Coordinator, and be subject of discussion during the next Management Safety Meeting.

4. The Safety and Loss Prevention Coordinator will verify completion of remedial actions suggested and report his findings to the Management Safety Meeting on a monthly basis (Accident/Incident follow-up Status Report).

Near-miss reporting and Investigation

1. Each Facility Supervisor will carry out regular meetings with his employees, to recall important near-miss incidents.

2. The Facility Supervisor concerned will make a plan to make certain that the recalls will take place on a regular basis and record these events in an appropriate manner.

3. The Facility Supervisor will develop checklists, covering potential problem areas, to assist in the proper recall of near-miss incidents.

4. All HIPO (class "A" and "B") near-miss incidents recalled will be reported and investigated using the appropriate form.

5. The interview records will be checked by the Safety and Loss Prevention Coordinator on a monthly basis. He will report his findings to the Management Safety committee.

Information Sharing

1. Information on all "A" and "B" incidents (including HIPO) will be shared with all Managers, supervisors and foremen, to prevent similar incidents to happen in other departments/units.

2. The Safety and Loss Prevention Coordinator will see that the appropriate information is distributed to the Managers concerned.

Evaluation of Program Effectiveness

1. The Safety and Loss Prevention Coordinator will make monthly checks of medical, personnel and maintenance records to identify the number of incidents occurred during the past month for which Incident Investigation Reports should have been received, according to the requirements as provided in this element.

2. The Safety and Loss Prevention Coordinator will evaluate the quality of each Incident Investigation Report received, in accordance with the guidelines provided for that purpose.

FORMS AND PROGRAM AIDS

1. Accident/Incident Investigation Report form.
2. Minor Injury Summary form
3. Minor Property Damage Summary form
4. Incident Recall Interview Register form
5. Incident Investigation Report Quality Evaluation Guidelines
6. Telex Type forms – see: " Notification Diagram, Phone/Telex/Radio" of the "Emergency Procedures Manual".

APPENDIX R – Safety management system audit questionnaire

- Accident/Incident Investigation

5. ACCIDENT/INCIDENT ANALYSIS/STATISTICS (45)

5.1. Procedure for investigating/analyzing accidents/incidents (8)

5.1.1. Is there a procedure for reporting and analysis of accidents/incidents? (2)   yes/no _____

Provide copy of accident/incident reporting/analysis procedures

5.1.2. Does this procedure include:

- reporting of accidents/incidents by employees? (1)   yes/no _____
- system for evaluation of accidents in terms of potential severity and frequency of occurrence? (1)   yes/no _____
- methods to be used for analysis? (1)   yes/no _____

Provide lesson plan and course material subject accident/incident analysis/investigation.

5.1.3. Is this procedure made known to all managers, supervisors and workers? (2)   yes/no _____

5.1.4. Does the procedure include worker involvement in the analyzing/investigation process? (1)   yes/no _____

5.2. Training in accident analysis/investigation (5)

5.2.1. Have all people involved in accident/incident analysis/investigation been trained for this purpose? (5)   yes/no _____

5.3. Reporting/registration of accidents/incidents (8)

5.3.1. Is there a procedure for registration of accidents and incidents? (2)   yes/no _____

Provide procedure for registration of accidents/incidents.

5.3.2. Does this registration include the form or a "log" to register all deviations from normal? (4)　　　　yes/no _____

Provide samples of "logs" filled out.

5.3.3. Is there an adequate form to guide the analysis and reporting of accidents/incidents identified for that purpose? (2)　　　　yes/no _____

Provide form(s) used to report and investigate accidents/incidents.

5.4. Action-plan and Follow-up (6)

5.4.1. Is there a procedure to properly follow-up on actions suggested to remedy the situation? (3)　　　　yes/no _____

Provide description of procedure.

5.4.2. Does this procedure indicate:

- who is responsible for follow-up being carried out? (1)　　　　yes/no _____
- regular reporting on outstanding actions? (1)　　　　yes/no _____
- final check on actions being completed? (1)　　　　yes/no _____

5.5. Central reporting of accidents/incidents (2)

5.5.1. Are accidents/incidents identified for this purpose reported to a central point on corporate level? (2)　　　　yes/no _____

5.6. Injury Type Accidents (4)

5.6.1. Are injury type accidents identified and recorded? (1)　　　　yes/no _____

Provide records identifying injury type accidents.

5.6.2. Are these registrations or records periodically analyzed? (2)　　　　yes/no _____

Provide copies of last analyses.

5.6.3. Are problem solving teams used to cope with identified problems? (1)　　　　yes/no _____

Provide reports of problem solving teams used.

5.7. Damage Type Accidents (4)

5.7.1. Are repair and maintenance jobs other than normal wear and tear identified and recorded? (1)   yes/no _____

Provide records indicating "abnormal" maintenance jobs carried out.

5.7.2. Are these registrations or records periodically analyzed? (2)   yes/no _____

5.7.3. Are problem solving teams used to cope with identified problems? (1)   yes/no _____

Provide reports of problem solving teams used.

5.8. Near-miss incidents (4)

5.8.1. Are near-miss incidents identified and recorded? (1)   yes/no _____

Provide record of near-miss incidents.

5.8.2. Are these registrations or records periodically analyzed? (2)   yes/no _____

5.8.3. Are problem solving teams used to cope with identified problems? (1)   yes/no _____

Provide reports of problem solving teams used.

5.9. Evaluation of accident/incident activities (4)

5.9.1. Is there a regular evaluation of the accident/incident report system? (2)   yes/no _____

Provide last evaluation reports.

5.9.2. Does this include quantitative as well as qualitative criteria? (1)   yes/no _____

5.9.3. Are evaluation results shared with senior management for Proper follow-up? (1)   yes/no _____

APPENDIX S – Safety management questions for departmental evaluation

05   ACCIDENT/INCIDENT REPORTING INVESTIGATION

1. Have all Managers/supervisors/foremen of this department or unit been trained in:
    a.   Problem Solving techniques?   yes/no
    b.   Accident Investigation techniques?   yes/no
    c.   Incident Recall techniques?   yes/no
2. Are the Incident Investigation Reports in this department or unit reviewed for quality, by the next higher level of management?   yes/no
3. Have employees of this department or unit been instructed about the importance of accident/incident reporting and investigation?   yes/no
4. Are the proper accident/incident reporting and investigation forms available in this department or unit?   yes/no
5. Does the Facility Supervisor of this department or unit know the proper procedures for the reporting of accidents/incidents?   yes/no
6. Is the Minor Injury Summary form properly filled out in this department or unit?   yes/no
7. Is the Minor Property Damage Summary form properly filled out in this department or unit?   yes/no
8. Are HIPO incidents properly identified on the Summary forms?   yes/no
9. Is the Facility Supervisor familiar with the Hazard Classification system? yes/no
10. Does the Facility Supervisor of this department or unit get proper support from higher management, concerning remedial actions, following accidents/incidents?   yes/no
11. Are there any outstanding (not completed) remedial actions on accidents/incidents, in this department or unit ?   yes/no
12. Have the reasons for this been communicated to higher management?   yes/no
13. Is there a planning, made by the Facility Supervisor, to carry out Incident Recall Interviews with each of his employees?   yes/no
14. Are monthly Incident Recall interviews carried out, involving all employees and registered on the Incident Recall Interview register?   yes/no

APPENDIX T – Accident investigation protocol elements

Below are just some heading examples with brief explanation that may be part of an accident investigation protocol. Some further detail can be found on my website www.topves.nl; please use the website search facility using "accident investigation protocol" or just "protocol".

1. **Definitions**

    - Unwanted Events:
    - Accident:
    - Incident:
    - (Other, as applicable)

2. **The Model**

    Description of the cause-consequence model used in your organization. Include picture as applicable.

3. **Purpose**

    Describe the purpose of your accident or unwanted event investigation protocol. Why is it important to learn from what goes wrong?

4. **Reporting and Investigation**

    List the accidents, mishaps or unwanted events that need to be reported and investigated.

5. **Risk Classification**

    Explain the risk classification method used in your organization - matrix, Kinney or other.

6. **Cause Analysis**

    Describe when cause analysis shall be carried out – use risk classification values as appropriate. Also refer to the cause analysis method or methods to be used.

7. **Responsibilities for Investigation and Analysis**

List responsibilities for investigation and cause analysis to include such functions as: senior manager, HSE Coordinator, department heads, supervisors, employees, staff specialists. Use facilitator to guide the process. Appoint event owner and action owners as applicable.

8. **Training**

List training requirements of key people involved in the investigation and analysis process including the use of any software program.

9. **Investigation Team**

In case of team investigation/analysis – highly recommended - indicate when teams shall be used – possibly based on risk classification – and which functions/people should be on the team.

10. **Contractor Unwanted events/Incidents**

Describe how to handle accidents involving third parties such as contractors or customers, how these parties shall be involved etc.

11. **Timeliness of the Investigation**

Indicate when accidents etc. shall be reported and investigated.

12. **Investigation Method**

Describe investigation method, use of photographs, drawings, testimonies etc.

13. **Investigation of offsite events**

Describe reporting and investigation of offsite accidents, including vehicle accidents, transportation, offsite servicing, offsite storage, customer use of product, etc.

END

APPENDIX U – Accident investigation form

FRONT		INVESTIGATION REPORT

<table>
<tr><td rowspan="13">IDENTIFYING INFORMATION</td><td colspan="2">1. COMPANY OR DIVISION</td><td colspan="2">2. DEPARTMENT</td><td></td></tr>
<tr><td colspan="2">3. LOCATION OF INCIDENT</td><td>4. DATE OF INCIDENT
/ /</td><td>5. TIME   AM
PM</td><td>6. DATE OF REPORT</td></tr>
<tr><td colspan="2" align="center">INJURY OR ILLNESS</td><td colspan="2" align="center">PROPERTY DAMAGE</td><td colspan="2" align="center">OTHER INCIDENTS</td></tr>
<tr><td colspan="2">7. INSURED'S NAME</td><td colspan="2">14. PROPERTY DAMAGE</td><td colspan="2">18. NATURE OF INCIDENT</td></tr>
<tr><td>8. PART OF BODY</td><td>9. DAYS LOST</td><td colspan="2">15. NATURE OF DAMAGE</td><td colspan="2">19. INCIDENT COST, IF APPLICABLE</td></tr>
<tr><td colspan="2">10. NATURE OF INJURY OR ILLNESS</td><td colspan="2">16. COST   ESTIMATED
ACTUAL</td><td colspan="2">20. PERSON REPORTING INCIDENT</td></tr>
<tr><td colspan="2">11. OBJECT/EQUIPMENT/SUBSTANCE INFLICTING HARM</td><td colspan="2">17. OBJECT/EQUIPMENT/SUBSTANCE INFLICTING DMG.</td><td colspan="2">21. OBJECT/EQUIPMENT/SUBSTANCE RELATED</td></tr>
<tr><td>12. OCCUPATION</td><td>13. EXPERIENCE</td><td colspan="2">22. PERSON WITH MOST CONTROL OF ITEM 17</td><td colspan="2">23. PERSON WITH MOST CONTROL OF ITEM 21</td></tr>
</table>

RISK	EVALUATION OF LOSS POTENTIAL IF NOT CORRECTED	24. LOSS SEVERITY POTENTIAL ☐ MAJOR ☐ SERIOUS ☐ MINOR	25. PROBABILITY OF OCCURRENCE ☐ FREQUENT ☐ OCCASIONAL ☐ SELDOM

DESCRIPTION	26. DESCRIBE HOW THE EVENT OCCURRED

CAUSE ANALYSIS	27. IMMEDIATE CAUSES: WHAT SUBSTANDARD ACTIONS AND CONDITIONS CAUSED OR COULD CAUSE THE EVENT?
	28. BASIC CAUSES: WHAT SPECIFIC PERSONAL OR JOB FACTORS CAUSED OR COULD CAUSE THIS EVENT? CHECK ON BACK, EXPLAIN HERE.

ACTION PLAN	29. REMEDIAL ACTIONS: WHAT HAS AND/OR SHOULD BE DONE TO CONTROL THE CAUSES LISTED?

<table>
<tr><td>30. SIGNATURE OF INVESTIGATOR</td><td>31. DATE</td><td colspan="3">32. FOLLOW-UP: CIRCLE NUMBER FOR TEMPORARY, X OUT FOR FINAL ACTION/DATE</td></tr>
<tr><td rowspan="2">33. SIGNATURE OF REVIEWER</td><td rowspan="2">34 DATE</td><td>1. _____</td><td>3. _____</td><td>5. _____</td></tr>
<tr><td>2. _____</td><td>4. _____</td><td>6. _____</td></tr>
</table>

CAUSE CHECKLIST

27A. CODING OF IMMEDIATE CAUSES - CHECK ALL APPLICABLE

SUBSTANDARD ACTIONS
- ☐ 1. Operating equipment without authority
- ☐ 2. Failure to warn
- ☐ 3. Failure to secure
- ☐ 4. Operating at improper speed
- ☐ 5. Making safety devices inoperable
- ☐ 6. Removing safety devices
- ☐ 7. Using defective equipment
- ☐ 8. Using equipment improperly
- ☐ 9. Failure to use personal protective equipment properly
- ☐ 10. Improper loading
- ☐ 11. Improper placement
- ☐ 12. Improper lifting
- ☐ 13. Improper position for task
- ☐ 14. Servicing equipment in operation
- ☐ 15. Horseplay
- ☐ 16. Under influence of alcohol and/or other drugs

SUBSTANDARD CONDITIONS
- ☐ 1. Inadequate guards or barriers
- ☐ 2. Inadequate or improper protective equipment
- ☐ 3. Defective tools, equipment or materials
- ☐ 4. Congestion or restricted action
- ☐ 5. Inadequate warning system
- ☐ 6. Fire and explosion hazards
- ☐ 7. Poor housekeeping; disorder
- ☐ 8. Hazardous environmental conditions: gases, dusts, smokes, fumes, vapors
- ☐ 9. Noise exposures
- ☐ 10. Radiation exposures
- ☐ 11. High or low temperature exposures
- ☐ 12. Inadequate or excess illumination
- ☐ 13. Inadequate ventilation

28A. CODING OF BASIC CAUSES

PERSONAL FACTORS
- ☐ 1. Inadequate capability
- ☐ 2. Lack of knowledge
- ☐ 3. Lack of skill
- ☐ 4. Stress
- ☐ 5. Improper motivation

JOB FACTORS
- ☐ 1. Inad. leadership/ supervision
- ☐ 2. Inad. engineering
- ☐ 3. Inad. purchasing
- ☐ 4. Inad. maintenance
- ☐ 5. Inad. tools/equipment
- ☐ 6. Inad. work standards
- ☐ 7. Wear and tear
- ☐ 8. Abuse or misuse

CODING FOR INCIDENT ANALYSIS

- 1. LOCATION ☐
- 5. TIME OF DAY ☐
- 8. INJURY TYPE ☐
- 10. SEVERITY ☐
- 11. AGENCY ☐
- 12. OCCUPATION ☐
- 13. EXPERIENCE ☐
- 16. PROPERTY TYPE ☐
- 18. COST ☐
- 19. AGENCY ☐
- 26. SUBST. ACTIONS ☐ ☐
- 26. SUBST. CONDTS. ☐ ☐
- 27. PERSONAL FACTORS ☐ ☐
- 27. JOB FACTORS ☐ ☐
- 34. TYPE OF CONTACT ☐

35. TYPE OF CONTACT
- ☐ 1. Struck against
- ☐ 2. Struck by
- ☐ 3. Caught in
- ☐ 4. Caught on
- ☐ 5. Caught between
- ☐ 6. Slip
- ☐ 7. Fall on same level
- ☐ 8. Fall to below
- ☐ 9. Overexertion

CONTACT WITH
- ☐ 10. Electricity
- ☐ 11. Heat
- ☐ 12. Cold
- ☐ 13. Radiation
- ☐ 14. Caustics
- ☐ 15. Noise
- ☐ 16. Toxic or noxious substances

REVIEW

36. REVIEWER'S REACTIONS TO THE INVESTIGATOR'S ANALYSIS OF THE BASIC CAUSES OF THIS ACCIDENT AND THE REMEDIAL ACTIONS DIRECTED AT POSSIBLE INADEQUACIES IN THE PROGRAM, ITS STANDARDS OR COMPLIANCE TO THE STANDARDS.

37. SIGNATURE   38. TITLE   38. DATE

CONTROL

MANAGEMENT OF CONTROL

PROGRAM ELEMENTS	P	S	C
1. Leadership and Administration	☐	☐	☐
2. Management Training	☐	☐	☐
3. Planned Inspections	☐	☐	☐
4. Task Analysis and Procedures	☐	☐	☐
5. Accident/Incident Investigation	☐	☐	☐
6. Task Observation	☐	☐	☐
7. Emergency Preparedness	☐	☐	☐
8. Organizational Rules	☐	☐	☐
9. Accident/Incident Analysis	☐	☐	☐
10. Employee Training	☐	☐	☐

	P	S	C
11. Personal Protective Equipment	☐	☐	☐
12. Health Control	☐	☐	☐
13. Program Evaluation System	☐	☐	☐
14. Engineering Controls	☐	☐	☐
15. Personal Communications	☐	☐	☐
16. Group Meetings	☐	☐	☐
17. General Promotion	☐	☐	☐
18. Hiring and Placement	☐	☐	☐
19. Purchasing Control	☐	☐	☐
20. Off-the-Job Safety	☐	☐	☐

PROGRAM ELEMENTS   P   S   C

LEGEND: P = Program Element Implementation Need; S = Standards(s) Inadequate; C = Standard(s) Compliance Inadequate

SKETCH OF SITE INVOLVED/CONTINUATION OF EXPLANATION. LIST NUMBER OF REPORT ITEM BEING CONTINUED.

APPENDIX V – List of English language books I used to have

I used to read most of the books listed but often only partly just to find out if there was anything new. As you can see, it is a mixture of safety books, books about risk management, about management and about behavior of people.

In 2004 I gave almost all of these books to younger consultants in Belgium who were starting up their own business.

Title	Author	Publisher	Year
CAP - Common Audit Process	AEI	AEI	1997
The management profession	Allen, A	McGraw Hill	1964
Professional Management	Allen, A	McGraw Hill	1973
Winnie the Pooh on Management	Allen, R.E.	Methuen	1995
Profitable Risk Control	Allison	ASSE	1986
The 59 second employee	Andre and Ward	Houghton Mifflin	1984
Company Insurance Handbook	Association Insurance Managers	Gower	1973
Loss Prevention Controls and Concepts	Astor	Security World	1980
Global Risk Management	Baglini	RIMS	1983
Future Edge	Barker	Morrow	1992
Neanderthals at Work	Bernstein and Craft Rozen	Wiley	1992
The nine master keys of management	Bittel	McGraw Hill	1972
Damage Control	Bird, Germain	ISA	1966
Management Guide to Loss Control	Bird	Institute Press	1974
Loss Control Management	Bird, Loftus	ILCI	1976
Commitment	Bird, Germain	ILCI	1978
Practical Loss Control Leadership	Bird, Germain	ILCI	1986
Profits are in Order	Bird	ILCI	1992
Safety & The Bottom Line	Bird, Davies	FEBCO	1996
The property Damage Accident	Bird, Germain	FEBCO	1997
The managerial grid	Blake & Mouton	Gulf	1964
De one minute manager	Blanchard , Johnson	Veen	1984
Empowerment takes more than a minute	Blanchard, Carlos, Randolph	Berett-Koehler	1996
Putting the one minute manager to work	Blanchard, Lorber	Berkley	1984
The one minute manager meets the monkey	Blanchard, Oncken, Burrows	Morrow	1989
Leadership and the one minute manager	Blanchard, Zigarmi & Zigarmi	Morrow	1985
Industrial Fire Brigades Training Manual	Bond and Kimball	NFPA	1968
Quantitative Methods for managerial decisions	Brown, ReVelle	Addison Wesley	1978
Use your head	Buzan	BBC	1974
Project Risk Management	Chaman and Ward	Wiley	1997
The risk ranking technique in decision making	Chicken and Hayns	Pergamon Press	1989
Avoiding Surprises	Church	Boston Risk Man	1982

Title	Author	Publisher	Year
The winning Performance	Clifford and Cavanagh	Bantam	1985
The art of winning	Conner	St. Martin's Press	1989
System Analysis Techniques	Couger, Knapp	Wiley	1974
The acceptability of Risk	Council for Science and Society	Barry Rose	1977
Hazard Evaluation Procedures	CPS	AIChE	1985
Effective Loss Prevention	Crowe, Douglas	Westprint	1976
Loss Control Management	Davis	Caftsman Press	1976
Modern Safety Practices	DE Reamer	Wiley	1958
Safety Management - improving performance	Denton	McGraw Hill	1982
The Quality Circle Handbook	Donald Dewar	Quality Circle Inst.	1980
Quality Circle Member Manual	Donald Dewar	Quality Circle Inst.	1980
Quality Circle Leader manual	Donald Dewar	Quality Circle Inst.	1980
Effective Management & Behavioral Sciences	Dowling	Amacom	1978
The practice of management	Drucker	Harper & Row	1954
Managing for results	Drucker	Harper & Row	1964
Management	Drucker	Harper & Row	1974
Safety Performance Measurement	EPSC	IChem	1996
Modern Safety Management practice	Everett Marcum	WSI	1978
Safety and the Executive	Findlay	Institute Press	1979
Total Loss Control	Fletcher, Douglas	ABP	1970
Management	Flippo, Munsinger	Allyn and Bacon	1975
Helping the troubled employee	Follmann	Amacom	1978
Coaching for improved work performance	Fournies	Nostrand Reinhold	1978
Apollo Root Cause Analysis	Gano	Dean L. Gano	2003
Safety, Health and Environmental Management)	Germain, Arnold, Rowan, Roane	AEI	1997
Safety, Health, Environment and Quality	Germain, Bird, Labuschagne	IRCA	2011
Human Competence	Gilbert	McGraw Hill	1978
Product Liability	Gray	Amazon	1975
Insurance and Risk management for small business	Greene	SM Association	1963
Safety management	Grimaldi, Simonds	Irwin	1975
Controlling the Controllable	Groeneweg	DSWO	1992
Managing Risk	Grose	Prentice Hall	1987
High Output Management	Grove	Veen	1984
Handbook of system and product safety	Hammer and Champy	Prentice Hall	1972
Reengineering the Corporation	Hammer and Champy	Nicholas Brealey	1993
Industrial Accident Prevention	Heinrich	McGraw Hill	1959
Industrial Accident Prevention	Heinrich, Peterson and Roos	McGraw Hill	1980
Successful Health and Safety Management	Health & Safety Executive (UK)	Crown	1997
The Motivation to Work	Herzberg, Mausner, Snyderman	Wiley	1959
Investigating Accidents with STEP	Hendrick, Benner	Marcel Dekker	1987
The analysis of Behavior	Holland and Skinner	McGraw Hill	1961
Iacocca	Iacocca	Bantam	1984

Title	Author	Publisher	Year
Quality Circles Master Guide	Ingle	Prentice Hall	1982
The Management Oversight & Risk Tree - MORT	Johnson	ERDA AEC	1973
MORT Safety Assurance Systems	Johnson	Marcel Dekker	1980
One minute for myself	Johnson and Wilson	Avon Books	1985
Managerial breakthrough	Juran	McGraw Hill	1964
Balanced Scorecard	Kaplan and Norton	HBS Press	1996
The guidebook for Performance Improvement	Kaufmann etc.	Pfeiffer	1997
The Rational manager	Kepner, Tregoe	Kepner Tregoe Inc	1965
Beyond the Quick Fix	Kilmann	Jossey-Bass	1984
MORT USR's Manual	Knox, Eicher	EG&G	1984
The Behavior Based Safety Process	Krause, Hidley, Hodson	Nostrand Reinhold	1990
Corporate uncertainty and risk management	Lattey	RIMS	1982
New Patterns of Management	Likert	McGraw Hill	1961
Optimizing human resources	Lippitt, This, Bidwell	Addison Wesley	1971
The challenge	Lundrigan, Borchert	North River Press	1988
Swim with the sharks	Mackay	Sphere	1988
Safety & Health in Purchasing	Mackie and Kuhlman	Institute Press	1981
Mind Skills for Managers	Malone	Gower	1996
Loss Control Safety Guidebook	Matwes & Matwes	Nostrand Reinhold	1973
Guide for safety in the chemical laboratory	MCA	Nostrand Reinhold	1972
Handbook of ventilation for contamination control	Mcdermott	Ann Arbor	1977
The Human Side of the Enterprise	McGregor	McGraw Hill	1960
Self Insurance and Captive Subsidiary Concepts	McRell	Twin Coast	1973
Risk management	Mehr and Hedges	Irwin	1974
Behavior Management	Miller	Wiley	1978
The strategy process	Minzberg, Quinn, Ghoshal	Prentice Hall	1995
Are you Listening?	Nichols / Stevens	McGraw Hill	1957
People, Evaluation & Achievement	Nixon	Gulf	1973
Parkinson's Law	Northcote Parkinson	Ballantine Books	1957
Accident Prevention Manual	NSC	NSC	1974
White Collar waste	Olson	Prentice Hall	1983
The Peter Principle	Peter and Hull	Pan books	1969
Product Liability and Safety	Peters	Coiner	1971
Benchmarking Customer Service	Peters	Pitman	1994
In search of excellence	Peters & Waterman	Harper & Row	1982
A passion for Excellence	Peters, Austin	Fontana/Collins	1985
Techniques of Safety Management	Petersen	McGraw Hill	1971
Safety Management - a human approach	Petersen	Aloray	1975
Safety Supervision	Petersen	Amacom	1976
Safety by Objectives	Petersen	Aloray	1978
Techniques of Safety Management	Petersen	McGraw Hill	1978
Analyzing Safety Performance	Petersen	Garland	1980

Title	Author	Publisher	Year
Human-error reduction and Safety management	Petersen	Garland	1982
Safe Behavior Reinforcement	Petersen	Aloray	1989
Managing Employee Stress	Peterson	Aloray	1990
Quality is Free	Philip Crosby	McGraw Hill	1979
The art of getting your own sweet way	Philip Crosby	McGraw Hill	1981
Quality without tears	Philip Crosby	Plume	1984
Let's talk Quality (2X)	Philip Crosby	Plume	1989
Leading	Philip Crosby	McGraw Hill	1990
Inspection of chemical plant	Pilborough	Leonard Hill	1971
Trends in Management Thinking	Pollard	Gulf	1978
Planagement	Randolph	Amacom	1975
The Winner Within	Riley	Putnam	1993
Up the organization	Robert Townsend	Fawcett Crest	1970
Leadership secrets of Attila the Hun	Roberts	Warner Books	1985
Introduction to system safety engineering	Rodgers	Wiley	1971
A case study in Risk Management	Rosenbloom	Prentice Hall	1972
An anatomy of Risk	Rowe	Wiley	1977
The Knowledge Value Revolution	Sakaiya	Kodansha	1991
Office Building Security	San Luis	Security World	1973
In Pursuit of Quality, The case against ISO 9000	Seddon	Oak Tree Press	1997
The Fifth Discipline	Senge	Century	1992
The Fifth Discipline Field book	Senge	Nicholas Brealey	1994
Increasing employee productivity	Sibson	Amazon	1976
MORT Accident Investigation Manual	SSDC	DOE/SSDC	1985
The Measurement of Safety Performance	Tarrants	Garland	1980
Is this your day?	Thommen	Crown	1973
Biorhythms and industrial safety	Thumann	Fairmont Press	1977
What went wrong?	Trevor Kletz	Gulf	1985
Management introduction to total loss control	Tye	British Safety Council	1970
The management guide to product liability	Tye and Egan	New Commercial	1978
Business Systems Engineering	Watson	Wiley	1994
Selected readings in safety	Widner	Academy Press	1973
Risk management & insurance	Williams & Heins	McGraw Hill	1971
Practical Benchmarking	Zairi and Leonard	Chapman & Hall	1994

www.ingramcontent.com/pod-product-compliance
Lightning Source LLC
Chambersburg PA
CBHW051205200326
41519CB00025B/7015